DRAWING

ON

TYPE

I have no idea why you wanted a self-portrait! Hm!

DRAWING DRAWING DRAWING
DRAWING DRAWING DRAWING
DRAWING DRAWING DRAWING
DRAWING DRAWING DRAWING
DRAWING DRAWING DRAWING
DRAWING DRAWING DRAWING
DRAWING DRAWING DRAWING
DRAWING DRAWING DRAWING
DRAWING DRAWING DRAWING
DRAWING DRAWING DRAWING
DRAWING DRAWING DRAWING
DRAWING DRAWING DRAWING
DRAWING DRAWING DRAWING
DRAWING DRAWING DRAWING
DRAWING DRAWING DRAWING
DRAWING DRAWING DRAWING
DRAWING DRAWING DRAWING
DRAWING DRAWING DRAWING
DRAWING DRAWING DRAWING
DRAWING DRAWING DRAWING
DRAWING DRAWING DRAWING
DRAWING DRAWING DRAWING
DRAWING DRAWING DRAWING

ON

TYPE

FRANK NEWFELD

The Porcupine's Quill

Library and Archives Canada Cataloguing in Publication

Newfeld, Frank, 1928–
    Drawing on type / Frank Newfeld.

Includes bibliographical references.
ISBN 978-0-88984-304-2

    1. Newfeld, Frank, 1928–. 2. Book industries and trade – Canada – History.
3. Publishers and publishing – Canada – History. 4. Book designers – Canada –
Biography. 5. Illustrators – Canada – Biography. 6. Graphic artists – Canada –
Biography. 7. McClelland and Stewart Limitied – Biography. 8. Society of
Graphic Designers of Canada – Biography.
    I. Title.

Z116.A44.N49 2008   741.6092   C2008-900343-8

1 2 3 4 • 11 10 09 08

Published by The Porcupine's Quill, P.O. Box 160, 68 Main Street,
Erin, Ontario NOB 1TO. http://www.sentex.net/~pql

Readied for the Press by Amanda Jernigan.
Cover design by Frank Newfeld. Interior design by Tim Inkster.

Represented in Canada by the Literary Press Group.
Trade orders are available from University of Toronto Press.

We acknowledge the support of the Ontario Arts Council and the
Canada Council for the Arts for our publishing program. The financial support
of the Government of Canada through the Book Publishing Industry
Development Program is also gratefully acknowledged. Thanks, also, to the
Government of Ontario through the Ontario Media Development
Corporation's OMDC Book Fund.

ONTARIO ARTS COUNCIL
CONSEIL DES ARTS DE L'ONTARIO

Canada Council   Conseil des Arts
for the Arts   du Canada

TABLE OF CONTENTS

My mother and I in Collingwood.

PREFACE

I was born in Czechoslovakia in 1928, just nine years after the birth of that newly minted nation. We lived in Brno, the second biggest city in the country. Brno was a fifty-minute drive from Vienna, Austria, and a four-hour drive from Prague. Naturally, we were bilingual: Czech and German. My father and my uncle Leo were partners in a rather large bicycle and sewing-machine company, which afforded us a comfortable lifestyle. My mother, who came from a family of doctors, lawyers and politicians, was an amateur skier. She took me and my sister Dorrit to endless winter ski meets across Western Europe. I hated skiing.

And I was nine years of age when my mother decided that Europe was doomed. In spite of my father's assurances that we were quite safe – and the guarantee of one of his best friends (who some months later would become Heydrich's Gauleiter of Brno) that Herr Hitler had no ambitions regarding Austria, let alone Czechoslovakia – my mother insisted on leaving. And leave she did, with Dorrit and me, well before the nightmare of German aggression began.

The three of us left for England, and settled in Hove, Sussex, where we lived until 1946. I first attended Claremont, a private school. The headmaster and his wife, Mr and Mrs O'Byrne, two wonderful human beings, did as much as they could to ease the transition to foreign custom and language for a rather small and confused young boy. Nothing was the same, starting with breakfast. I was used to coffee and croissants; the sight of morning porridge, kippers, tea and toast was daunting. Still, I got used to it, and even learnt to play cricket well enough to join the Second Eleven cricket team: quite an honour, in spite of the fact that Claremont only had one First Eleven and one Second Eleven, when using all available players.

The British custom of caning I never did enjoy too much.

Then it was off to Bradfield College in Berkshire, where I was introduced to the fierce xenophobia of Britain's public schools' finest aristocratic bullies. Luckily (I thought) both money and scholarship

Dorrit (as a young man) and me (as the girl) at a fancy-dress party
in Czechoslovakia, circa 1936.

ran out, and my mother was forced to rescue me. I escaped back to
Hove, where I finished my basic education at the Hove County School
for Boys. I passed my Oxford School Certificate with enough credits to
be granted a Matriculation Exemption – a wartime expedient to get
young 'men' into the forces as soon as possible – when I was barely sixteen.

After eight months of being attached to a British army unit, and
aided by a Sussex County Scholarship, I enrolled at the Brighton College of Art. I had decided on a career in stage design. But to tell the
truth, I missed the military. The transition from the safety of strict
regulation to total independence was confusing.

In 1947, my stepfather – Alexander D. Macpherson (Mike, for
short) – and my mother announced that they had decided to move to
Canada. Security won out over independence: I happily agreed to join
them. We arrived in Toronto in the late fall of 1947.

This new transformation in scenery, dialect and values was distracting, to say the least. Toronto seemed to be on another planet.
Everybody in England had long been aware of the horrors unleashed in
occupied Europe during the war. Canadians at that time seemed either

unaware or disbelieving of any tales of monsters: 'The war was over two long years ago, and should now be just a bad dream.' But the people in Toronto were kind and made us most welcome.

Still, my stay was short. Seven months after coming to Canada, I left for the Middle East. War was about to break out, and well over thirty of my relatives, predominantly Jewish, who had perished in Nazi camps, enjoined me to go. I knew next to nothing about Palestine or Israel. I had never heard of a kibbutz. My idea of a sheik was Rudolph Valentino. The only thing I knew was that the new Israel could not be allowed to fail, nor a second holocaust to happen.

Strangely enough, I took a sketchbook with me, and, surprisingly, my Israeli superior, who had been a poet and editor in civilian life, arranged to have some of my drawings published. It was in war-weary Israel, then, that I illustrated my first book – which was not an easy task, since I could neither read nor write Hebrew and, even after one year, could barely speak the language.

I fell in love with illustration. So much in love that I quickly realized I didn't know what I was doing. I decided I had to go back to art school, and in 1952 I returned to England, where I enrolled in the design department of the Central School of Arts and Crafts in London. There I had my first exposure to typographic design. I soon recognized that although illustration was just an infatuation, in which I cheerfully changed philosophy and style, typography was true love.

Some time later, armed with an NDD (National Design Diploma), as well as a diploma from Central School, I came back to Canada. This time to stay, marry a pretty Toronto lass, have two sons and find fulfilment in love, labour, books and teaching.

My stories start in 1944. A long time ago.

I must confess that I have a terrible memory for names, and frequently have to ask my wife Joan the name of this or that cousin or aunt from one side or the other of the family. Partly because of this shortcoming, and at the odd time to protect the 'innocent', I have occasionally invented names, but never any of the players in these sketches.

1. MY FIRST COMMISSION

lowly but surely, my mother ran out of money.

With the German occupation of Czechoslovakia, both the sporadic visits of my father and the regular transfers of funds ceased. Just before the German invasion my mother sent an honest and sympathetic young Englishman over to bring out a last supply of funds. He returned with just £4,000, saying that was all my father could raise. (After the war, my father told me that he had, in fact, sent over £40,000 plus 20 carats of diamonds.)

There had been negotiations with a well-known British bicycle concern with whom my father had done business for a number of years, to set up a new company to be called 'The Royal Sewing Machine Company'. The cabinets were to have been made in England and the heads in Brno. A rail-shipment of well over a thousand heads was attempted three or four weeks prior to the German invasion. The whole consignment was duly stopped in Germany. The Nazis later forced my father to buy his own machine heads back; however, they were never returned to the company, on the grounds that storage charges had not been met.

In Hove, the erosion of funds became onerous. Where at first the exodus to England had seemed (to me, at least) just a fun adventure, the discomforts of financial rationing, more stringent than the Ration Book, now became oppressive. My mother and sister felt it the most. I was too young at the time to be fully aware of the changes, beyond the sudden, and quite drastic, decrease in my weekly pocket money.

Dorrit had to leave Westcombe, the private girls' school she attended, and I had to leave Claremont. I was sent to the local council school, which was run like a prison. I was abruptly taught my new social status on my first day there. I was in the schoolyard with the rest of the horde when a whistle blew. Every boy in the yard froze. Not knowing what this was all about, I started to amble over to a group of my snotty-nosed and rather dirty fellow inmates – only to be halted in my tracks by a great roaring voice: 'You! Yes, you, you horrible creature. Stand still! Didn't you hear the whistle? How dare you move?'

'I'm a new boy, sir. I was only going over to find out what the whistle meant. I didn't know I wasn't supposed to move.'

The teacher, about nine feet tall, carrying a cane and (of course) a big, black book, strode over to me. 'A new boy!' he hissed. 'And judging from your accent, a bleeding little foreigner. Well, we will just have to make certain that you remember things in the future. Hold out your hand.'

I was compensated for the pain of this encounter, two hours later, by the arrival of Mr O'Byrne. He took one look at my hand and announced that I was forthwith going back to Claremont where I belonged. And rescued me from purgatory.

Our house on Brunswick Place was sold, and 34 Waterloo Street purchased with about half of the proceeds. This provided some badly needed capital to live on.

Waterloo Street was in a slightly humbler part of town. No. 34 was a four-storey building with toilet, kitchen and bathroom on the half-floors in between. The top floor comprised three small rooms, one of which my mother had converted into a sort of a kitchenette. This flat she rented out to two young ladies, called Evelyn and Valerie. Neither lady appeared to have a surname.

Two years later, my mother managed to get a private club licence for No. 34. She planned to convert the main floors into a gaming club, and use the two top storeys for our living space. Which meant that Evelyn and Valerie would have to find other business quarters.

My mother dreaded having to break the news to them. But the girls were philosophical. 'Look, ducks. You really can't have a couple of tarts living here – not when the coppers are sure to visit the premises left, right and centre. In any case, what with the Canadian lads stationed here now, we've been thinking of expanding the business for some time. So it'll all work out for the best. Don't you worry none!'

The evening before the girls were to leave, Val asked me to come upstairs. She and Evelyn offered me their puppy. The pup had been a gift to them three months earlier. He appeared to be a mix of cairn, Welsh terrier, dachshund, corgi and wolf (the last in temperament). Inappropriately, he was called 'Duke'.

In actual fact, Duke and I got on well together. Apart from *les demoiselles*, I seemed to be the only inhabitant of No. 34 who was neither growled at nor bitten. Duke had very few redeeming qualities. He was housebreaking rather than housebroken, and preferred to defecate only in the more public rooms. He ate his own food reluctantly, and then only when he couldn't steal people's rations. He was particularly fond of black-market delicacies. But he kept his plunder for only a short while after each theft. Any rich food made Duke bring up. He usually chose to do so in the middle of the lightest-coloured carpet he could find.

I wasn't too sure how news of this generous legacy would be received downstairs. Still, I thanked the girls for the gift, and told them I hoped I would be permitted to keep it.

At this point, Evelyn asked how things were going at school. I explained that I had been approved to sit for the Oxford School Certificate, and that I hoped to do well enough to qualify for matriculation exemption. If I got that, I would probably be finished with school.

'And what do you want to do then?' she asked.

'I'd been thinking of becoming an artist,' I said. 'I know that sounds silly, but I can draw a bit and prefer to read art books over any others. To tell the truth, I can't think of anything else I really want to do.'

'I suppose that you'll be getting girls to pose for you then,' she said. 'Or have you already done that sort of thing?'

I shook my head.

'I bet you could, though,' Evelyn opined. 'You should try it sometime.'

'Who would pose for me?'

'I might, if you would also do a drawing for me to keep, as payment. Would that interest you?'

'But you're leaving tomorrow.'

'Well, there's no time like the present, I always say. Valerie luv, don't forget that you have to meet that Canadian captain this evening.'

'I almost forgot. Lord, I'd better put my face on and get going.'

I went downstairs in order to get some paper and pencils, as well as something to act as a drawing board. At the same time, I felt it prudent to go to the bathroom and scrub myself down a bit. I wasn't sure what lay ahead. I only had a vague idea of what I was supposed to do if anything actually did lie ahead. Still, hope sprang eternal.

When I got back upstairs, a space had been cleared in the centre of the drawing room. The plush sofa remained where it had been, but now there were two chairs placed two feet apart, across from it. The small table that had stood in the middle of the room had disappeared. As had both Evelyn and Valerie.

The bedroom door was open. Inside the room I could see a large bed with the covers pulled back. To one side of the bed stood a night table with two glasses, a bottle of gin and one of tonic water, as well as a saucer which had a number of small, unmarked packages on it. The night table on the other side of the bed carried a small candelabrum, with three lit candles. Evelyn appeared, wearing a rather tired-looking dressing gown.

'I think I should do your drawing first,' I said, 'just in case you don't like it. Would a portrait do?'

Evelyn agreed that this might be the best way to proceed. She assured me that we had all night, and she didn't want me to rush anything. By going about the art slowly and surely, we could be certain that we would both get 'nuffing but' the best result.

The portrait took about an hour to complete. When it was done I was pleased. She was an attractive woman, and I had rendered her likeness in what I thought were the 'bold yet delicate' strokes I had read about in art books. Evelyn oohed and aahed. She said the drawing was lovely, and she would have it professionally framed at the local art store.

'Well, you've held up your end of the bargain, and then some. Now I'm going to make us both a lovely cup of tea, and then I'd better do my bit. Believe me, you've more than earned it.'

Over tea, she asked me all sorts of questions. How had we come to England? Where was my father? How did I get on with the other kids in school? Was I going to stay in England after the war? The questions were mostly about me; at no time did she inquire into my mother's personal affairs. Finally, she remarked that she was sure I had made love to lots of young ladies.

When I asked her in what way, she smiled and said: 'We'd better get on with your drawing. When's your mum coming home, then?'

'She said not to wait up for her. So I don't expect her till late. Did you want to speak to her?'

'No, I just wondered whether you'd have to hurry up. How would you like me to pose?'

As it happens, I had been giving this matter a lot of thought. Having never drawn a woman – or anyone, for that matter – in the flesh, I wasn't sure how one went about this sort of thing. Then I remembered the Goya book in my modest art-books library. It contained two full-colour reproductions of his *Maja* paintings: 'vestida' and 'desnuda'. That was how I would draw her: *Evelyn Desnuda*. 'If you could lie on the sofa, with arms behind your head, that would be super.'

From *The Grasshopper* by Bernard Suits. U of T Press, 1978.

'I think you'd better pose me.' Seeing the look of alarm on my face, she added, 'Come on, I won't bite. Anyhow, they say that being an artist is like being a doctor when it comes to touching.'

Evelyn was slim, with smallish breasts – and she was, as I discovered, a true blonde. She had a fair complexion and looked almost too young to be in her profession. I judged her to be no more than eighteen.

Posing all her bits and pieces properly was taxing. I could feel the perspiration trickling down my face. When I asked her to cross her ankles, she said she wasn't sure what I meant, and that I had better do it for her. As I bent over to take hold of them, she waved both legs up in the air in a most personal display, and laughed: 'Take your pick, luv.'

Finally, I started to draw. But the work went at a snail's pace. It was much harder than I had imagined. Drawing a head was hard enough. But a head attached to such wondrous masses of distracting nudity made every attempt at setting an artistic course an impossibility. My eye kept straying to the light, reddish-blonde lock of hair, no more than three fingers in length and in shape an inverted isosceles triangle, where her legs met. A charming, mesmerizing distraction!

'I can see where your mind is, you naughty boy. Is this the first time you've seen a lady's privates?'

'Of course not!' This was actually quite true. When I was twelve years of age, my best friend had been a boy called Michael Myers. He was one of the few Jewish boys at Claremont, and came from one of the wealthiest families in Brighton. We were the same age, but where I stood under five feet and weighed seventy pounds at the most, Michael was at least five foot eight, and weighed well over 150 pounds. I used to visit his home on a regular basis, and we were just at an age where the mysteries of sex were vehemently discussed in the school playground, and measured comparisons made in private. One evening Michael and I were joined by his thirteen-year-old cousin, Rebecca. One subject leading to another, she asked if I had ever seen a *nackette maidlach*. After some hems and haws, I finally admitted that I hadn't. Whereupon she confessed that she herself had never seen a man without his clothes on, except in a book. She looked at me thoughtfully for a long while. Then she nodded decisively. 'I'll show you mine, if you'll show me yours.' And I did. And she did. And we both said, 'Yeech!'

Evelyn continued: 'And were any of them prettier than mine?'

'Not one.'

'Aren't you a dear! Well, we'd better get on with the masterpiece. Or should I say mistress-piece?'

We went back to my drawing. Which meant that I had to first put Evelyn back properly into her pose, as she insisted. The work did not progress a lot better than before, but I was at least getting a couple of acceptable lines down on paper. After twenty minutes or so, Evelyn said that this posing business was harder than a full night's work, and that she would have to take a rest.

'In fact, luv, I'm going to lie down on my bed for a few minutes. You be a dear, and fetch me my fags. I'm going to have a quiet smoke, and a nice gin-and-it. I don't suppose you drink, but I do believe you will definitely have one of my fags.'

I fetched her pack of Benson & Hedges – very fancy, I thought; business must be good – and an ashtray. Apart from the big bed and the two night tables, there was no furniture in the room. So I stood awkwardly by the bed, not wanting to get too far away from the ashtray.

'Why don't you sit down? But you'd better take your shoes and trousers off. Neither look clean, and I don't want my good linen to get dirty. Come on, it'll only be for ten minutes or so. Then we can get back to your artwork.'

We finished our cigarettes in silence.

'It's a bit bright in here. Be a dear, and switch off the lamp on my night table.'

In order to manage that, I had to lean over Evelyn. As I brought my hand back, she took hold of it and placed it gently upon her isosceles triangle. Not knowing whether to rejoice or retreat, I simply left my hand where she had placed it, not daring to move, and looked at her, terror-stricken.

'You're allowed to fiddle with it a bit,' she said. And then, 'Don't worry, there's a first time for everything.'

Afterwards, she gave me a piece of advice.

'That wasn't bad at all. But if you're going to be an artist, and thinking of making love to someone you'd like to pose for you, do it before you draw her the first time. I've had a couple of gentlemen callers who were artists, and they see things different to other people. Tiny faults won't matter after you've "done it", but they can be bloody unignorable if you've painted the model first.'

And that, as it turns out, was the most important thing I learnt from my first commission.

2. THE WATERLOO STREET REGULARS

After *les girls* left, in the spring of 1944, I was moved upstairs – well out of the way of the world. Which suited me just fine: I suddenly had a flat of my own. There was no separate entrance, but my personal activities – *les girls* aside – had not yet encompassed the need for private comings and goings!

The club was now enlarged, the two lower floors given over completely to the pursuit of games of chance. Where at first the club had boasted just one poker table, my mother now installed two more gambling tables and a small bar.

Like many of the Brighton or Hove Regency houses, 34 Waterloo Street had a small glass conservatory leading off the second floor. This was newly renovated and locked off. When asked what she intended to do with it, my mother invariably changed the subject, in no uncertain manner.

Another innovation was the introduction of 'Forces Day'. My mother reserved Tuesdays strictly for members of the Armed Forces – commissioned, of course. Refreshments and memberships were free; but the club took a small percentage from each pot for supplying cards, poker chips and high tea.

At the time of the inception of Forces Day, there were two major military outfits in the Brighton Area. The British Columbia Regiment of the Fourth Canadian Division was stationed in Hove. The flamboyant fighting men of No. 6 Commando were also in the Brighton-Hove area, with the unit's commissioned ranks billeted all over the place.

Before long, a number of officers from both these units made 34 Waterloo Street their home away from home. By coincidence, they were all avid poker players. The military habitués from British Columbia included Captains Neary and Bergklint, as well as a Sergeant-Major de Vries. Captain Bernard Neary, later promoted to the rank of Colonel, took on the role of CO – mentor to our 'Waterloo Brigade'. After the war, he became the director of a major Canadian publishing house, where he eventually resumed his role as my personal mentor in mufti.

From No. 6 Commando, the poker enthusiasts included the Leppard brothers, both lieutenants, as well as the Regimental Medical Officer, and the occasional drop-in junior officer. But the main supporter and best friend of my mother's renovated gaming club was the Adjutant of No. 6, Major Ryan H. ('Harry') Price. Major Price preferred to be called Captain Price (which, according to the good Major, had a more melodious sound to it; not only that, it would appear to be a more important rank, once he was demobbed). In civilian life, he was one of England's best racehorse trainers. He was related by marriage to Lord Allenby. But Harry Price was as unpretentious an upper-class Englishman as one could imagine.

Of our civilian regulars, four remain firmly etched in memory. These four appeared every day of the week, excepting Sunday and Tuesday, come rain, storm or the Luftwaffe. They were:

1. Mrs Davies, five foot nothing and a widow. When she was seated, her feet dangled. And any time she stayed in a pot, she left her opponents dangling: uncertain of whether or not she was bluffing. She was seldom known to end a gaming session down. Her only fault was her frequent amnesia, especially in the matter of paying poker debts and dues. My mother hated to remind her – though the other three regulars never missed an opportunity.

2. Miss Boaz, white-faced and frail. Once, when we were acutely short of players, she responded to a desperate phone call from my mother, staggering in some ten minutes later. She apologized, saying that she had been in bed with 'a bit of a temperature': 100 degrees or so. She was very civic minded, even in her poker playing strategy. She simply stayed in every pot, as long as she had a pair of deuces or better.

Miss Boaz never spoke above a whisper. We were all certain that each week would be the last that we would see of her. But somehow she remained a regular to the bitter end. The family had long discussions about the secret of her titanium white face. We finally decided that she poured refined flour into a large bowl, immersed her face in it, and blew.

3. Big Ben, Smokey, for short. We never knew his family name. Ben was over six feet tall, but walked with such a stoop that he never

exceeded five foot eight in actual stature. He was ill-kempt and shabbily dressed. He sported a perpetual yellow cigarette clenched between four yellower teeth. The smoke from his hand-rolled fags caused tears to come down his cheeks without respite. He also had a terrible stutter, made worse by his continuous hacking cough. Strangely enough, he was a bookie, though how he could ever c-c-c-c-call the odds was beyond us. Harry Price maintained that any horse race would be well over by the time Ben finally confirmed a wager.

4. Sam (the Ganeff) completed our Four Riders of the (Poker) Apocalypse. He was the best poker player of the regulars. But he seemed to be a mean man and was certainly a mean player. With an unmistakable winning hand, he would bump mercilessly, especially when his victim was having a run of bad luck. He was foul-mouthed in defeat and humiliating in victory. To none of our surprise, he was intimate with all of Brighton's black-marketeers, and could get you anything, for a price. To all of our surprise (we learnt this quite by accident), he had provided free room and board to at least two families who had been bombed out.

Officially, Sam ran a small factory which made handbags, purses, gas-mask-container covers and so forth, out of some new synthetic material. But what he did officially could not possibly have provided him with anything more than a little poker-money. Yet Sam carried a roll of five-pound notes, held together by an elastic band, which Mike – my mother's new husband – swore could not have contained a penny less than £500.

By 1944, Mike had returned to England from South Africa, where he had been posted as a flight instructor on Spitfires. One evening, he had held forth in the mess on how to safely manage a belly-landing: that is, landing a Spitfire without the use of landing gear. One of the officer cadets said that he didn't understand exactly what Flight Lieutenant Macpherson was attempting to explain. Mike, who was more than a little drunk, took the whole flying school cadre outside for an instant real-life demonstration. Whereupon Air Training Command decided that it was time for Warrant Officer Macpherson to return to England, and be posted to Bomber Command before he demolished any more Spitfires.

The poker club's regulars dealt their own cards. They played five-card draw poker, exclusively. The deal rotated according to the number of card players. If there were seven players, then each player dealt every seventh game. If there were six, then the deal changed accordingly.

The game followed a strict sequence: straight poker for all but the last deal of each player, who could then call his or her own wild game. We allowed three raises, and players could not check and raise, which kept gouging to a minimum. The lowest bet was sixpence and the top bet was one shilling. The game required at least five players and was filled at seven.

In 1944, I was conscripted to make up the table on the few occasions that Miss Boaz was too sick to make it to the game. First, however, I was given strict instructions by my mother: '*Don't* win more than £1; *don't* lose more than £2!'

The Canadian contingent played strictly seven-card stud, with a shilling minimum and a half-crown maximum. The Commando table kept much the same betting levels but, like the regulars, played straight draw poker. Both these tables required the services of a dealer, so my mother was always in attendance on Forces Day. When Mike was home on leave, he would also deal.

Then, one Saturday morning, quite a quantity of furniture, covered by drop-sheets, arrived. This was all moved into the renovated conservatory, which had had velvet curtains installed on the door and the windows that flanked it. My mother sat me down in our dining room, and said that she had something to tell me, in the strictest confidence. 'We are going to play baccarat in the conservatory. Nobody must know about this, not even our oldest members. None of our present players will be admitted to the game – not that they would even want to play. The players will come in after the 11 p.m. regular closing, and I don't want either you or Dorrit around. Understand that this is strictly illegal, and if found out, we could all go to jail.'

Seeing the look of alarm on my face, she added, 'It's perfectly safe. We will have protection.' And then: 'In any case, we have no choice in the matter, since the organizer is the chief of police for Brighton. But for heaven's sake, don't mention it to anybody. Not even to Dorrit. I will be handling the game and will let you know in advance on which nights you are to be invisible. Is that understood? Good.'

★ ★ ★

In April, I sat for my Oxford School Certificate. The exams were interrupted three times by air raids, and we all trooped dutifully down to the bomb shelters. On the way down, divers members of the faculty reminded us that cheating was a poor show. And since there was no way of checking up on us, we were on our honour, as British gentlemen, to play the game. Strangely enough, nobody from the Hove County School for Boys failed that year.

I managed to get 'credit' in three subjects, and 'excellent' in the three others – grades more than sufficient for me to be granted the matriculation exemption. I was the youngest of that year's batch of boys, and by June I had already bid good-bye to most of my (combat-bound) friends. These frequent farewells made me feel like a draft-dodger. This, plus the idea that the chief of police was going to be a habitual gambler twice a week, below my bed, convinced me that I might as well join the army.

I could foresee two major problems: first, given my citizenship, I would have to join the Free Czech Forces – and I really couldn't speak Czech; second, I was barely sixteen, and I wasn't certain I was capable of growing the moustache I'd have needed to look two years older.

Still, I made up an excuse, about wanting to look at some Art Schools in London, and bought a train ticket to town. Once in London, I went directly to the Czech Embassy in Exile, and asked to see the military attaché.

'I don't know if we have a military attaché,' said the receptionist – who spoke English with a Cockney accent and did not look at all Czech. 'But there's a lot of military types running around here and if you wait a minute, I'll get one of them to see you.'

Five minutes later, she returned with an officer in tow, a Kapitan Belsky. By coincidence, he was also from Brno, and by another coincidence his first name was Franta – more or less the Czech version of Frank. When I told him my family name, he asked if I was related to the sewing-machine company, Frank & Neufeld. I nodded, and he said that he knew our Brno store well and that all his bicycles had been bought at our store on the Křenova. When he asked, in Czech, what he could do for me, I replied that my Czech was not very good. 'Like all good industrialists' heirs,' he said. 'But that isn't your fault, so we'll speak English. I doubt either of us really wants to speak German if we don't have to. Right?'

I explained that, while my mother had remarried an Englishman, I was still Czech, as one could not be naturalized until after the war. I wanted to join the army, but thought that I would be of better use in the British army than in the Czech army – purely from a communications point of view. 'I know I have to do something,' I said. 'Most of my relatives are still back home. And I hear dreadful things about what the Nazis are doing.'

He asked what I hoped to do after the war. I told him I'd been offered a county scholarship to go to art school, but had asked to have it deferred.

He considered. 'Well, you and I have three things in common. One: we're both from Brno. Two: we both have the same first name, more or less. Three: I am an artist, and you are hoping to be an artist. So I'd better give you an official letter to take to the British Forces Recruiting people, which will do the trick.'

The Captain returned in less than ten minutes, and handed me two copies of some sort of document of permission, plus a Free Czech Army badge and shoulder flashes with the word 'Czechoslovakia' embroidered on them. 'Perhaps our friends in the British army will let you wear these. And maybe we will meet again in Brno. Good luck!'

When I got back to Hove, I decided that 'Captain' Price would be the best person to sound out about joining the British army. He had become a very good friend, and had brought a goodly number of new members to the club. I also felt that I could trust him to be discreet and to help me tell my mother I intended to join up, only when the time was right.

I showed him the letter from the Czech embassy, which he considered most carefully. Finally, he turned to me and said: 'Look, old chap, you don't want to rush into anything too hastily. You've spent some time with the cadet corps, but that's quite a bit different from the regular army, believe me. In any case, why does the document give your year of birth as 1927? You're barely sixteen.'

'I've got matriculation exemption. I'm the only one from my class not in uniform, and what's worse, I feel guilty about doing nothing, when most of my family is under the bloody Nazis. So I put my age up a bit.'

'Well, that's all very commendable. And I mean that. I have an idea. How would you like to be attached to No. 6 Commando for all training whilst we are in the Hove area? I'm sure I can fix it with the adjutant of my unit.'

'But I thought that you were the adjutant.'

'My God, I think you are right. Well then, that's all fixed. Report to No. 6 Commando Headquarters tomorrow morning at eight, and ask for Major Price.'

The next morning, I duly reported at eight sharp, only to be told that Major Price never got in that early, but I could wait in his office. He finally rolled in around nine thirty, and asked if I had been waiting long. Without waiting for a reply, he told his clerk to get a Staff Sergeant Huddlestone. Ten minutes later, a huge man – he must have been at least six foot six, and weighed well over fifteen stone – marched in.

'This is Cadet Newfeld,' said Captain/Major Price. 'He's going to be attached to us for the next while, and I'm putting him into your No. 3 Troop. Let the MO have a look at him and while he's being checked out, come back, and I'll brief you on what we expect of him. That's all.'

Thus started a time of intensive training and a radical change in my physical state and mental attitude. I jumped up three inches and gained some fifteen pounds, all of it muscle. I became quite sure of myself, both in situations of stress and in relation to people's comportment – friendly or hostile, respectful or patronizing – toward me.

No. 3 Troop was designated the Reconnaissance troop. On my second day, we went to the Sussex Downs for field exercises. By chance, the area chosen was the same that had been requisitioned by the War Department for the local cadet corps – of which I had been a member, not three months earlier – to use as the training and testing ground for its 'A'-Certificate designation.

Once there, we were split into two groups. Each trooper was given a topographical map to study, on which our position was marked. Next, we were shown the enemy's location on the same map. Our task was to reach an offensive position without being detected. Each man was given ten minutes to do this. The distance to be traversed was about 750 yards, across rolling terrain covered by sparse gorse. Still, there were a sufficient number of hillocks to hide one's route, if one knew how to read a map. Or if one knew the place already.

The first man, a corporal, had barely gotten a hundred yards before Staff Sergeant Huddlestone blew his whistle. The next trooper was clearly visible some two hundred yards away. The fourth man finally made it safely across, only to find that he had exceeded the ten-minute time limit. The rest of our group fared a little better: the best time was six minutes. Of the thirteen men who took their turn before me, only nine had made it without being spotted, however.

'All right, Newfeld. Your turn. I'll give *you* fifteen minutes to get to the enemy position. Look sharp.'

The whole thing was very similar to the test we had been given in the cadets; there, we'd all been allotted fifteen minutes to get over this exact same ground. I had managed it cold in just over twelve minutes, then. This time, knowing more or less how to go, I managed it in just under ten.

When we got back to HQ, Staff Sergeant Huddlestone pulled me aside. 'You did pretty well today, and I'll tell Major Price about it. He was a bit worried that we shouldn't expect too much of you. I suppose that I didn't really need to give you any extra time.'

'Well, I don't know if I could have managed it in time if I hadn't done it before – with the cadets.'

'I'm glad you told me. But we won't tell anybody else. Just one piece of advice: try not to try so hard for a while. All right?'

COMMANDO
SERVICE CERTIFICATE

Italy   Crete   Burma   Greece
Norway   France   Sicily   Albania
Holland   Belgium   Germany   Madagascar
North Africa Yugoslavia Western Desert Channel Islands

This Certificate is an Appreciation,
of Loyal Service given to Commandos by

Cdet. F. Newfeld.

October 1944

Chief of Combined Operations

Was attached to No 6 Commando for all training while the unit was in the Herne area. November 1945.

Which taught me an invaluable lesson, one a 'foreigner' should never forget. There are times when it is best not to be best.

The rest of my first week with the Commandos was spent polishing up on a number of skills. First we spent a day on small-arms drills – the U.S. M1 rifle and the good old Sten gun – both of which were now general issue for No. 6. The Sten gun I knew intimately, but I had never seen an M1 rifle.

Then we were given a full day of practice in a particularly nasty form of unarmed combat. Which really wasn't unarmed, since we were taught some rather unsportsmanlike ways of hurting people. With emphasis on the best method – or worst, depending on which way one looked at it – of permanently disabling someone with the standard issue Commando killing knife, or any other handy instrument.

Then we were off on a three-day bicycling spree: No. 6 Commando's version of the Tour de Sussex, from Brighton to Petworth via Lewes, and back again. We bivouacked in farmers' fields, foraging food from the unsuspecting populace. We actually were fed fresh lamb roasted on a spit the first night. When I asked if these were standard army rations, the corporal sitting next to me on my groundsheet said, 'Of course! Nothing but the best for us, lad. Now don't be a silly little bugger, and don't ask stupid fucking questions. And don't mention the bloody roast lamb never no more!' All in all, though, that first week seemed to me rather encouraging. It certainly did nothing to put a damper on my intention of joining up.

The following Monday I reported to the No. 3 Troop office at eight o'clock on the dot, only to be told by the corporal of the groundsheet that I was to report to the adjutant's clerk ASAP. When I got there, I found Staff Sergeant Huddlestone having a cup of tea. I asked him if he wanted to see me, to which he shook his head. At that moment, Lieutenant Leppard and Major Price emerged from the office, accompanied by a very young colonel. This was the Hon. Anthony Lewis, the new CO of No. 6. He looked toward me. 'Does this belong to anyone here?' Lieutenant Leppard replied that he was afraid I probably belonged to him. Whereupon the three officers held a quick, quiet conference, followed by the lieutenant bellowing: 'Sergeant Major Huddlestone! Is this man going to a fancy-dress party?'

'No, sir.'

'Then I think we should get him fitted out properly. Don't you agree?'

'Yes, sir. May I be dismissed in order to do that immediately, sir?' To me he said, 'Look sharp. I haven't got all day. I've got to get my own new uniform and insignia at the quartermaster's, so we'll kill two birds with one stone.'

I was fitted out with everything! Green beret; army shirts (two); uniform (one) with insignia (not attached); cord undershirts (two) and cotton pants (two); gaiters (one pair); webbing-belt and equipment (one); socks (three pair); boots, black (one pair); gas mask and case (one); M1 rifle (one) with ammunition clips (two: empty); groundsheet (one); killing knife (one); rucksack (one). After we left the quartermaster's store, Staff Sergeant Huddlestone pulled me aside. 'I've been promoted to sergeant-major. So you won't see that much of me from now on. But if you really need to talk to me, about something, you come direct to me. You don't need to go through the troop sergeant. Come only if you really need to, mind you. Don't misunderstand: the lads like you, but you may get into the odd scrape with … I don't know what. If you do, you tell whosoever to contact me. Understand?'

I wasn't quite sure what he meant, but I nodded gravely.

The next few weeks passed quickly, in a flurry of lectures on subjects ranging from 'How to Set Up an Enfilade Fire Position' to 'How to Take Protective Measures Against Venereal Diseases'. There were field exercises, route marches and weapon drills.

The first trip to the firing range filled me with trepidation. The targets looked smaller than the ones used by the cadet corps, and they seemed much farther away from the firing position than were the butts I was used to. I was pleasantly surprised, however, to find that the M1 was not only a much more accurate weapon than the Lee-Enfield I had been trained on, it also carried far less of a kick.

The two-inch mortar drill was another story. The first time I fired it, it gave me such a scare that I never lost my repugnance for the weapon. What happened was idiotically negligent on my part. I was 'loading', which meant that I was to drop the mortar shell into the two-inch tube as soon as it had been properly aimed. Only, on the third round of the 'rapid-fire' exercise, I decided not to wait for the proper touch, letting me know that the weapon was aimed and safe to fire.

The mortar shell went vertically up into the air.

'Take cover!'

Commandos scattered in every direction. All, except for me. I was transfixed, watching the projectile ascend. Just as it began to slow, a burly arm caught me around the waist and the two of us nose-dived some twelve feet into a nearby sandbag redoubt. Just in time, as all manner of dirt and shrapnel came raining down.

By some miracle, no one was hurt. Needless to say, there were quite a few dirty looks – and any number of unprintable epithets – thrown in my direction.

'Now look what you've done to my new uniform, you silly little bugger! Don't ever do something so bloody stupid again. Do you hear? Or you'll be up on a charge.' The burly arm and dirty uniform belonged to Sergeant Major Huddlestone, who had chosen this day, of all days, to visit the butts. He picked himself up, dusted himself off, and marched away without another word.

To my surprise, two days later I was told that I had been detailed to the weapon-training staff, and would be sent to Achnacarry for a two-week training course, immediately after Christmas. Since I had expected to be executed, at the very least, I wasn't sure how to interpret this news: was it a slap on the back, or a slap on the behind? Certainly, I had heard all kinds of horror-stories about Achnacarry.

For Christmas, the Waterloo Street Regulars gave me two tickets to the local theatre, which was showing the annual pantomime. I decided to take Clifford Bryant. Clifford was a young cockney – the youngest member of No. 6, next to me – who had the reputation of being the best cadger the regiment had ever had. He and I had been co-conspirators on a 'special field training mission' in November: a cross-country orienteering test that had turned into a pleasant afternoon at the East Grinstead pub, thanks to Clifford's local connections. (Clifford's uncle, a police officer in East Grinstead, had driven us back to Brighton in the Station car so that we could report for duty – back from our cross-country 'trek' in record time – the following day.)

Clifford wanted absolutely no part of my invitation to the theatre. I finally persuaded him, however, when I told him that all British theatres boasted pubs with charming barmaids. And that, if the play turned out to be a dud, we would retire there as soon as the first act was done.

The play was *The Babes in the Woods*. This was the first time

F. N. and Clifford Bryant, No. 6 Commando, 1944.

that Clifford had ever been to the theatre, and he was quite entranced by the whole thing. Once he had accepted the tradition of the 'principal boy' being a girl, he readily accepted the notion of the 'dame' being played by a man. In fact, he laughed so heartily at everything he/she recited that the audience applauded his laughter more than they did the performance of the 'dame'.

When I asked him if he wanted to stay in the pub after the first intermission, he shook his head, and we hurried back to our seats.

After the show, Clifford said he wanted to thank the Regulars personally. The next afternoon, he came to the club looking the cleanest I had ever seen him. I had told my mother and the Regulars that he would be coming by. Miss Boaz, wanting to make him feel at ease, asked him what play we had seen, and had he enjoyed it. 'We saw the *Bloody Babes in the Bloody Woods*,' he said, 'and it was loverly!'

A few weeks later, Ryan Price came by the house and said that No. 6 would be leaving Brighton that evening, and he had come to say goodbye. So I would not be off to Achnacarry in the new year. I asked him if I should turn in my uniform and weapons. 'You can straighten that out with Sergeant Major Huddlestone,' he said. 'He's remaining behind with the holding unit. But I think you might come and see us off at the station. Both the officers and men would like that. We're leaving at ten tonight.'

3. THE GAY HUSSARS

I told my mother and Mike that I had, after all, decided to take the (deferred) Sussex County scholarship, which had been offered me on graduation the previous June. I applied to the Brighton College of Art, and was accepted. To my surprise, this news was met with genuine enthusiasm at home, and all the poker players were told of my embarking, without any doubt, on a path of great artistic fame and fortune.

And so, when the time came for me to make my first foray into the art world, I went laden with more supplies than were carried by the college art store. My mother and Mike had quietly assembled an assortment of pencils, pens and inks, an eraser and a ruler, a complete drafting set, and a wooden box holding oil painting supplies. And my former victims, the Waterloo Street Regulars – the same people who had cheerfully allowed me to beat them at cards on a regular basis – had bought me a lovely set of Rowney watercolours and squirrel-hair brushes, plus a portfolio complete with at least a quire of fine-quality hot-pressed paper.

On arriving at the college, I identified myself as one of the new lot to the porter, who told me to go right up to the fourth floor and report to a Miss Coke. I reached the fourth floor – which was as high as the building went – and found myself facing eight-foot-high, closed double doors, with no more than three feet of landing between the doors and the top stair.

My attempt to open the doors, with all the supplies I was juggling, proved not only futile but noisy. Then the door was opened for me. Never had I been so close to nor seen so clearly the spectacle that now confronted me. Within ten inches of me stood five foot two inches of the plumpest and nakedest lady I had ever seen in dream or reality. My shock was complete. I dropped every last piece of my art supplies and started running down the stairs, three at a time.

'Are you looking for Miss Coke, dear?' the bare lady shouted after me. 'If you are, she's inside the studio. Come back!'

'I have to go back down to the shop, I forgot my paper.'

'Well, you'd better hurry up. I start posing in five minutes, and once I'm set up, you can't come in.'

'I understand. I'll be back in time.' To tell the truth, I didn't understand. What had I not yet seen, that I could be prevented from seeing if I did not get back in time? I shuddered to think.

The whole atmosphere at the art college was a refreshing and new experience – certainly different from both the Hove County School for Boys and No. 6 Commando. My fellow students proved heavenly compared to the Bradfield Bullies. The tolerance and encouragement practised, without affectation, were contagious. Bigots, braggarts and barbarians soon surrendered either college or creed. Another's greater talent was cause for admiration, rather than envy. Another's lesser talent was cause for concern and encouragement, rather than humiliation.

Quietly and effectively the college turned the greater number of us into more aware and caring human beings. By the same token, many of the behavioural taboos of that age were shrugged off at the college as being bourgeois and tawdry. These were not for artists!

We learnt to perceive our environment with a fresh eye and our prejudices with a critical eye. I even, before long, waxed impervious to the daily presence of masses of nude flesh – the days of holding on tightly to the drawing board in my lap now far behind me.

In my second term at the College, a second-year student by name of Paul Edler asked if I would consider working with him on a project. The Brighton Musical Festival, which was just a few months away, had established a new category, theatre design. He wanted to do the set design, and asked if I would be interested in doing the costume design for a combined entry. Since entering was free, and the accepted pieces would be exhibited in the famous Brighton Pavilion, I agreed.

Paul had chosen Weber's opera *Der Freischütz*, convinced (rightly) that nobody else would think of choosing it – and also that the jury would be unlikely to know much about peasant costumes of Central Europe in the eighteenth century.

I had never heard of Weber or of his Freischütz. Paul played the opera (in German) over and over, until I finally convinced him that I had 'gotten the feel' of the visual passion Weber demanded. (I said this most convincingly, without the foggiest idea what I was talking about.) Luckily, Paul had the complete libretto also in English.

Unluckily, it listed a complete cast of dozens, each of whom would require some sort of costume.

I completed forty-three costume designs in glorious Technicolor with swatches of suggested materials attached; whilst Paul constructed elaborate models for some half-dozen set changes. The work stretched into two months of long evening sessions in Paul's studio.

To our delight, we were awarded first prize at the Brighton Musical Festival. Our victory convinced me of my professional path: I was destined to become a stage designer. Assuredly, one of Britain's finest!

I went to see Miss Coke, and told her of my decision. I was taken aback by her lacklustre response, and assured her that I really was serious about 'the theatre', and that the Brighton certificate had only strengthened my resolve. Miss Coke replied that she was more than pleased at my winning such a prestigious award, but only wondered whether the award wasn't more for the quantitative nature of my entry, than for its qualitative properties?

I, however, was not to be deterred, and wrote off forthwith to London, for brochures to both the Slade School of Art and Central School of Arts and Crafts. I waited impatiently for their replies.

By timely coincidence, an advertisement concerning auditions for the chorus of *The Gypsy Baron*, an operetta by Johann Strauss, appeared on the college notice board, not long after. The advertisement gave date, place and time of the auditions, as well as promising 'most liberal remuneration' for successful aspirants. Experience would be helpful, the small poster stated, but was not essential.

This, it seemed to me, was an omen. Quickly, I copied down the details. The auditions were scheduled for the following two evenings. I decided to go to the first audition, to beat the hundreds I was sure would apply.

We were about fifteen prospective choristers, male and female, at the first audition. Of these, a dozen were lined up under the sign that read SINGERS. The three of us remaining stood under the NON-SINGERS sign.

The casting director came on stage, looked our group over, and nodded to his assistant, a young lady of about eighteen, with a cigarette dangling from her lips, a notebook under her arm, and a chewed pencil in her hand. Then, with a visible shudder, he went over to the SINGERS group.

The assistant opened her notebook and said, 'You three give me your names and telephone numbers. Then stick around. It's pretty certain that you're hired, but we have to see who else is coming later this evening. But it looks good. We need ten hussars.'

I waited nervously. They only needed seven more. What if, in the next batch of prospective hussars, all were taller than me?

Like every English theatre, the Theatre Royal had a backstage bar, 'The Single Gulp', to which I repaired. I ordered a pint of bitter with a Melton Mowbray pie, and waited for the inevitable news that the casting director had found ten taller (and much more English) applicants.

At around 11 p.m. the director's assistant came into the pub.

'Good job you're still here. The others have all gone home. We thought you'd buggered off, and I was going to phone you. You are one of our hussars, and you can buy me a beer. My name is Josie and your name is Frank. Rehearsal at ten sharp in the morning.' She drank her beer, said, 'Ta-ta then!' and vanished.

Rehearsals took all of one week. The stock company's players were familiar with their parts, as *The Gypsy Baron* had already been playing for two months, in various towns. The chorus only had to learn half a dozen reprises, and rehearse their blocking with the seasoned players.

We appeared on stage some four or five times. All we had to do was follow our fearless leader, Ottokar, who would parade us to our proper positions on stage. Twice we had to shriek our rousing hussar marching song, which went – as I remember it – something like this:

> With love and wine the world goes round,
> Where gay hussars are found!
> This talent is peculiar
> To every brave hussar!

The first week of the play went well. The *Brighton* and *Hove Herald* gave us a sparkling review, and each performance drew a fuller audience than the preceding show. The stock players were happy and even started to talk to us local amateurs.

The Gypsy Baron himself was played by a Hungarian tenor, whose stage name was Laszlo Radetzky. The Baron was the romantic lead. Laszlo was a bit short and a mite dumpy. But he had a golden voice and a captivating smile.

The lovely Arsena was called Millie backstage, though the program listed her as Elizabeth Marlow. She had a toothy smile and sang nicely, with just a trace of a Lancashire accent.

The third star was an actor called Peter Penn, who played Ottokar. Ottokar was more or less the villain of the piece. The role required a baritone. Penn, however, had a high-pitched speaking voice – which did not quite go with his athletic physique and chiselled features. He was crowned with golden hair, and his cavalier moustache was better suited for the role of the naughty younger brother than for that of the villainous swordsman. Worse, he was unable to sing a single note.

This knotty point was solved by simply arranging things so that Ottokar never sang when he and the Gypsy Baron were on stage together.

How was this going to solve the problem of Ottokar's tin ear?

Simple! Laszlo would situate himself backstage in line with Peter, and sing Ottokar's arias, which Peter would credibly lip-synch. The amazing thing was that Laszlo's range was so wide he could go from tenor to baritone with ease. The other amazing thing was that Peter's arias had received more enthusiastic reviews, in the course of this tour, than had Laszlo's. Much to Mr Radetzky's amusement.

And no one would have been any the wiser, had Peter not fallen in love in Brighton.

The object of Peter's affections was one of the hussars: a handsome young man who had only just started studying music at the local conservatory. It transpired, alas, that this young man was simply not a 'gay' hussar. And this unrequited love became a devastating blight on Peter, a.k.a. Ottokar.

Trouble of another sort started toward the end of the second week of our engagement. We still had not been paid one penny, and the local cast was beginning to get hostile toward the repertory company. For the second Saturday's performance, the chorus came on stage with teeth bared.

Then Peter Penn made a fatal mistake. He had marched us on stage, and – as he always did – proceeded to inspect his regiment, front and back, whilst we shrieked out our famous marching song (*With love and wine the world goes round ...*). Only this time, all reason deserted him. As he passed the backside of his favoured hussar, he gave it a gentle pat.

Now, the 1940s in England were still the Dark Ages as far as homosexuality was concerned. It was both misunderstood and feared – especially by young men. And the reaction was swift and emphatic: *'Don't touch me, you bloody pansy!'* hissed just loud enough, unfortunately, to be heard by everyone in the theatre.

Everything stopped. The chorus stopped, the orchestra stopped ... but the audience kept going, right out of the theatre. The runaways were all parents with their children. Their only stop on their mad dash out was at the box office, where they successfully demanded their money back. With one act still to follow, the curtain went up on a hall that had lost a third of its spectators.

The next day, the local press laughed the matter off, after they had interviewed a pale and tremulous Peter Penn. He had somehow managed to convince them that his scabbard had inadvertently struck the young man as Peter had passed behind him. And that the poor fellow, quite inexperienced in the ways of theatre, had naturally assumed that he had been assaulted. Which had certainly not been the case.

Peter's own weapon, he assured the reporters, had at no time been drawn.

Luckily, the episode had a positive effect on attendance. The house continued to be filled. But Ottokar was never the same again. Peter began to drink – in such great quantities that the manager of The Single Gulp demanded he be barred. The director refused, stating that he'd sooner have an inebriated Ottokar than none at all.

Ottokar's big scene opened with the Gypsy Baron wooing Ottokar's paramour, the fair Arsena. At one point, the Gypsy Baron was to look stage left and sing:

> What rival enters now the field?
> 'Tis Ottokar, who stands revealed!

And thereupon the Gypsy Baron would flee stage right.

Ottokar would enter stage left. He'd look around, and look around, and finally see Arsena on the balcony, where she had been for at least ten minutes. (By now, it was estimated that Laszlo would have had enough time to get around to backstage left.) Ottokar, still stage left, would then lift his arms and eyes toward Millie and begin to sing:

Arsena, your faithful lover calls,
For soon the twilight falls ...

And so on.

The second performance following the buttock incident started well enough. But Peter went back to the pub, midway, to drown his sorrow. It must have been pure theatre instinct that alerted him that Laszlo was singing his cue.

Ottokar staggered in from stage right. He swayed around, and swayed around, then lifted his arms and started to 'sing' immediately, oblivious to the fact that he was holding sway over the wrong part of the stage. Unfortunately, his voice rang out from stage left.

The fair Arsena, meanwhile, was desperately trying to signal her suitor as to where his voice was coming from, by frantically waving to the other side of the proscenium. By the time Peter managed to stagger over – all the time feverishly lip-synching – one could no longer hear anything over the crowd's boos and hoots of laughter.

The curtain came abruptly down, and a desolate-looking director appeared. He held his hands up for silence. Finally, the audience settled down and our director cleared his throat. He was about to speak, when a torrent of tears came pouring down his face. Then he simply shrugged his shoulders and, without a word, walked slowly off stage right.

* * *

In spite of the debacle of a curtailed season, and my first encounter with the greatest social taboo of the times, my three weeks as a thespian reinforced my conviction that my path lay in stage design.

I decided to see Mr Salis-Benney, director of the Brighton College of Art, on the off-chance that, not knowing me, he'd be more sympathetic than Miss Coke had been. He wasted no time, and said that if I was certain that the theatre was for me, I should 'have a go'.

And since Brighton did not have a theatre department, he even went so far as to recommend the Slade or Central, both in London (and both jolly good art schools, he said – 'though not quite as good as a fine art college like the Royal College of Art'). He gave me permission to use his name as a reference, and advised me to write to both schools as soon as possible.

In April of 1946, then, with Mr Salis-Benney's encouragement, I wrote to Mr Polunin at the Slade; just to be safe, I also sent off an application to Miss Cochrane at Central. To my delight, I not only received prompt replies from both schools, but was given interviews – which, by coincidence, were two days apart.

My mother telephoned her sister, my Aunt Mitzi, who now lived in Kew. It was arranged that I would take the train to London the day before my first interview and stay over for the three days.

I hadn't seen the Weinigers (Aunt Mitzi, Uncle Viktor and my cousin, Erika) since 1937. I only vaguely remembered them, since they hadn't lived in Brno. The only time we used to see one another was at the annual family get-together at my grandparents' large house in Miroslav.

Uncle Viktor had owned a vineyard in Moravia, and on fleeing to England with his family, in 1939, he'd had no difficulty obtaining employment with one of England's most respected vintners. By the time that I became their three-day guest, he had become chief cellarman. Erika had completed Pitman's and now worked in the foreign department of ICI. Aunt Mitzi's job was to rule the Weiniger household, to proffer advice, and to mete out appropriate admonishment about anything to anyone under her roof. But it was an affectionate home.

The house was warm in both summer and winter. The kitchen was cozy and always open for business. There was none of the British restraint that we, in Hove, had studiously affected. Uncle Viktor was a portly man, who always shaved yesterday and tomorrow, but never today. He was coarse of manner and kind of heart. He asked ridiculous questions, which the next day became serious food for thought.

But he never asked me any prying questions about Newfeld family matters. His probing had all to do with decisions I had made regarding myself. Where Mike and I barely communicated – not that Mike seemed to communicate much with anyone in our clan, in deference to the British policy of non-intervention – Uncle Viktor took it upon himself to put me through the third degree on each of my visits to Kew. And there would be many, in years to come.

Neither of my art-school interviews was quite what I expected. Mr Polunin and Miss Cochrane were poles apart. Polunin was short, taciturn and very Russian. He conducted the interview in one corner of a studio filled with students, all chattering away, none seemingly working. He vocally hated my whole portfolio and sneered at my *Freischütz* drawings, pointing out their shortcomings to the delight of his suddenly silent entourage of students.

I protested that my costume designs had won first prize at the Brighton Musical Festival.

'*Brighton Music Festival?* Of course! Why not? We'll let you know.'

And that was the end of that interview.

Miss Cochrane was tall, plump and veddy English. I was ushered into her chambers, which looked more like the set for *Blithe Spirit* than an art-school office. She offered me a cup of tea and two digestive biscuits, then asked why I wanted to become a stage designer.

Luckily, Miss Coke's analysis of my motives – and Mr Polunin's analysis of my portfolio – had prepared me not to again blurt out the fact that I had won first prize at the prestigious Brighton Music Festival. I mumbled a number of rationales in as earnest a voice as I could manage.

Next, we went over my portfolio, which she found to be quite interesting. (In later years, as an art teacher, I employed the same phrase – 'Well, you do have some interesting pieces' – whenever I was faced with work of a quality about which my 'kind' nature led me to prevaricate.) Miss Cochrane thought that I might well fit in, without too much difficulty, at the first year level.

'I'm sure that you will hear from the Registrar's office shortly.'

Back in Hove, my mother listened carefully to my account of the London trip. She advised me not to say too much about my future studies, until I had received a firm acceptance. 'Sometimes, painting the Devil on the wall is the best way of making sure things don't work out. Wait till you hear before you announce that you are leaving. Which brings me to something else. Mike and I are leaving for Holland. He's been offered a job flying with KLM, the Dutch airline. He will leave in June to start work and to find us a place to live in Amsterdam. I will follow no later than at the beginning of August.'

'Good heavens! What if I'm not accepted? I've only got two terms of art school under my belt.'

'We talked about that. We thought at first of selling Waterloo Street; but we've decided to hold on to it for the moment. If you go to London, we'll rent it out. If you stay at Brighton College, you can have the place – rent free, of course. Perhaps we can sublet the upper two floors, which would bring in some extra income. Anyhow, there's time. So let's wait until you hear from one or the other place. You do think that one of them will take you, don't you?'

* * *

As it turned out, in 1946 AD, I got accepted left, right and centre.

First, I was accepted by both art schools. Even though the Slade was the more prestigious of the two, I decided on Central, as being more fitting to my 'provincialism'. (Frankly, Polunin and his disciples had scared the dickens out of me. Miss Cochrane's hospitality seemed easier pickings.)

Secondly, I was told by the Reverend Canon Tomkinson – vicar of St John's in Hove, where I had been a server – that the Church of England was seriously considering awarding me a scholarship to study at Cambridge. Apparently it looked quite promising; and if I should be invited to go somewhere for the summer, I would be well advised to accept. (This had all come out of a visit to the Bishop of Chichester that the vicar had arranged for me two months earlier.)

All of this sounded puzzlingly cryptic. But I decided, the more irons in the fire the better for my impending orphanhood.

Thirdly, I received a letter from the National Association of Boys' Clubs, the NABC, with an offer to teach arts and crafts at Ford Castle, near Berwick-on-Tweed, during the summer. The letter also stated that I came recommended by the Bishopric of Chichester. That offer I accepted with alacrity – particularly since the letter also mentioned quite attractive remuneration. (The incommodious fact that I was only a callow student, myself, who had hardly yet learnt any art – let alone become qualified to teach it – I brushed aside, and decided not to mention it in any correspondence.)

First, I told Reverend Tomkinson that I had accepted the offer to teach at Ford Castle, and that I was really pleased to take the summer job. He, too, was pleased.

Secondly, I phoned Miss Cochrane and said that I was delighted to have been accepted by the theatre department, but that I would have to arrange for a government grant (which I didn't expect would be a problem). I asked what the deadline would be for confirming my attendance. She told me that the school would have to know by mid-August.

Finally, I wrote a most humble letter to the Bishopric of Chichester, thanking the bishop for the summer employment that his good offices had arranged for me. And closing by promising to do my very best at Ford Castle, et cetera, et cetera.

* * *

Ford Castle was a much more significant institution than I had imagined. The place really was a castle, with turrets and such, situated some ten to fifteen miles north of Berwick-on-Tweed. The summer course was designed to offer young apprentices four one-week workshops on a variety of 'useful subjects', including typography, drafting, basic bookkeeping, 'arts and crafts' (which was me), and various other 'worthwhile pursuits'. There were well over eighty apprentices – all from Yorkshire and Lancashire, it seemed – who had gladly enrolled for the full four weeks.

The staff consisted of eighteen to twenty people, including the matron, kitchen staff, superintendent and janitorial crew, plus some eight instructors and the Reverend Berners-Wilson, director of the course, accompanied by his charming and proper wife.

The arts-and-crafts facilities were amazingly good. There were donkeys, drawing boards, reams of paper, easels, paints of various sorts – powder colour, poster colours and watercolours – india inks, brushes, pencils from 2H to 6B, pen-holders, drawing nibs and calligraphy nibs, two pottery wheels, one clay bin filled with fresh clay, a small kiln and a loom, as well as a few pieces of equipment I wasn't able to identify. Some of these I was never going to use, because I didn't wish to; others I had no intention of touching, because I didn't know how. The ratio was about one I-didn't-wish-to, to eight I-didn't-know-how.

We, the faculty (how impressed I was to bear that title so early in my career), arrived at Ford Castle two days before our charges were expected. The first evening, we had a get-together session before dinner. To my surprise, I was the youngest instructor by at least ten years – a fact not lost on my fellow instructors, who sent various patronizing remarks my way over the course of the evening.

The first week saw all of six NABC-ites register for arts and crafts. But the week went quickly and we parted as good friends. The second week, the arts-and-crafts group grew to twelve; and the last two weeks saw even more apprentices registering for my artsy-craftsy course. Much to my amazement, the course went well, and without any of the sneers and jeers I had anticipated my students might suffer from their peers, for selecting a 'sissy course' like art.

I spent several pleasant evenings with the Berners-Wilsons. I learnt that the Reverend had been the Eton College Padre for a number of years before taking over Ford Castle, and that both he and his wife were amateur musicians. He, in turn, ferreted out a good deal of my own history – from my ambitions in life, to my feelings of guilt regarding the fate of so many of my relatives, all the way to my relationship with Mr Macpherson. He was well informed about my tenure as server at St John's, and even about the potential offer of a scholarship to Cambridge.

The evening before my departure he invited me for a farewell chat. He came to the point immediately. He told me that Reverend Tomkinson had strongly urged Chichester to provide me with the wherewithal to study theology at Cambridge. Was I aware of that? If so, what were my feelings about it?

I told him that I had realized that the Church could not be interested in providing funds unless that led to some sort of calling, or at least to a commitment to an ecclesiastical future. I said that I had been thinking about it a great deal, but still had not made up my mind.

We must have talked and debated for two hours regarding the signs and portents of a 'true calling'.

Finally, he said, 'Of course, I knew about the scholarship before you got here. And I believe that you would make an excellent minister. In fact, you might even become one of our better ones. But I suspect that in time you would not be a truly happy minister, let alone a happy person. I also believe that you will make yet a better artist, but probably not always a happy one. But you must make your own decision. I intend to write the bishop to the effect that though you would make an excellent member of our ministry, I feel that you would serve us all better by staying in the arts.'

* * *

In the summer of 1947, I went to visit my mother and Mike in Amsterdam. Their apartment was quite lavish, as befitted the home base of a transatlantic pilot. It was located in the outskirts of the city, on a street called Jasonstraat near the Stadionweg, which was one of the routes from Amsterdam to Schiphol Airport. The place had three or four bedrooms and two bathrooms, permitting visitors and hosts complete privacy.

Duke, who had moved to Holland with my mother and stepfather, gave me a tumultuous welcome. Contemptuously abandoning his kitchen-corner basket, he ensconced himself on the bed in my room. When Mike ordered him out of there, he bared his teeth and growled, which made his change of quarters official for the duration of my visit.

My visit turned out to be much longer than any of us had planned.

I spent the first two days exploring Amsterdam. On the first day I went into the Rijksmuseum and also visited the Vincent van Gogh Gallery, like all good art students. On the second day, round about lunchtime, I wandered into the august Schiller Hotel, on the Rembrandt Plein. Mike had recommended it. I had never seen so many paintings in the same place, other than in a gallery. The paintings were all elaborately and expensively framed. In the lobby and main lounge alone there must have been fifty or sixty canvases. In most cases, the many different-sized paintings were hung, one under the other, from the ceiling down to the wainscoting. There seemed to be no rhyme or reason to their grouping. Whoever had acquired them had singularly eclectic tastes in art.

I was wandering around the open areas, nursing a glass of Bols gin and periodically chuckling at one painting or another, when a thin, white-haired man spoke to me.

'You find some of the paintings amusing?'

'I suppose so. But in a nice way.'

'What does that mean?'

'Well, they represent such a variety of taste. I wonder how many people were responsible for buying them.'

'Do you know something about art?'

'Not yet.'

'Are you an artist?'

'No. Why do you ask?' It was only at this point that I realized we had been speaking English from the first. How did the man know I came from England? 'Actually, I am an art student from London.'

'Then why did you say "Not yet"?'

'Because I have only studied art for two years. Which is just long enough for me to know that I don't know very much about art.'

The gentleman laughed. 'That was a good answer. Perhaps we'll meet again. I am here quite often.'

That evening, Mike said to me that there was a flight leaving, from Schiphol, for Prague the next morning. As far as he knew, the flight had not been filled, and he thought he could get me a 'Free-2' on it. A Free-2 was a complimentary ticket given to KLM employees or family members, if there was space available. Was I interested in visiting Czechoslovakia?

★ ★ ★

I phoned Brno from Ruzin Airport. My father was out, so I left a message in my version of the Czech language to say that I would be arriving that evening. Public transportation, even two years after the war, was not particularly efficient in Czechoslovakia. By the time I got to the Prague railway station, it was close to three o'clock. The next train to Brno was scheduled to leave at 5:30 p.m.

By coincidence, the only other passenger in my second-class compartment was a young man with a large portfolio. As the train pulled out of the station, some forty-five minutes late, my travel companion made a remark which I didn't quite understand. I replied that my Czech was pretty bad, since I hadn't spoken it for over ten years. Could he say it again, using simpler words?

He replied in fairly fluent English: 'I said that the only thing we miss about the Germans is the way they ran the railway. You are English, yes?'

'Yes and no. I was born in Czechoslovakia, but my stepfather is English –' (I decided that 'Scottish' would be too complicated), 'so now I am sort of English.'

'You have English papers?'

'Well, I am travelling on a Free Czech passport issued by the Beneš government in London. My passport has a permanent British resident visa in it.'

'I have never heard of that. What does it look like?'

I pulled out my passport and showed it to him. He then pulled out his own passport and showed me the French visa in it.

Then I asked him if he was an artist. To which he replied that he was in his second year at the École des Beaux Arts in Paris, and was on his way home for the summer holidays. I told him that, by coincidence, I was also an art student, in my second year. But in London, not Paris.

The train stopped at every station that it passed, and by eight o'clock seemed to have travelled only a very short distance. When I mentioned this, my travel companion said that I had caught a local train, and that I wouldn't get into Brno much before 11 p.m. It seemed that I could have caught an express train which, while it left Prague half an hour later than the one I had taken, got into Brno at least an hour sooner.

By this time, the carriage had filled up, and the temperature inside was climbing. Although I'd removed my jacket, sweat was finding every convenient trail down my body. I had been on my way since seven o'clock that morning. I could feel myself getting very tired.

We chatted for a while longer, mostly comparing notes about our respective art schools. Then my travel companion shared his French bread and salami with me. One of the other passengers insisted we have some of the genuine Hungarian slivovitz – which every Czechoslovak seemed to carry – that he had produced out of his leather briefcase. My friend, the art student from Paris, announced that he was getting off at a place called Humpolec, and asked that someone wake him, should he fall asleep.

I was in an empty train compartment when I was woken by the conductor, who kept shouting, 'Brno, Brno,' and pointing vehemently to the platform. I staggered out of the station, luggage and jacket in hand. When I looked at my watch, I was dismayed to see that it was past midnight.

There was no way I was going to start pounding at anybody's door at that time of night. I saw a hotel – Hotel Grand, which I hoped did not mean Grandly Dear – opposite the station, and made my way there. Fortunately, the night clerk spoke English. He had a room for me, and asked me to fill in the register. Then, as clerks do at every hotel in Europe, he asked for my passport. I reached for it in my jacket pocket. And found nothing.

Two policemen arrived within five minutes. After the hotel clerk had translated the fact that my passport had disappeared, the officers took me over to the station master. Luckily, the Prague train had finished its day's run at Brno. Unluckily, even though we searched through the train, compartment by compartment, the passport remained lost.

We next went to police headquarters, where the duty officer seemed very skeptical, until I showed him my KLM ticket, made out in Amsterdam. He made out a report, and suggested I go to Prague and get myself a new passport from the British embassy.

'Are you not going to try to find who has taken it?' I asked, in rather mangled Czech.

'That would probably be useless. I imagine we will announce it on the state radio and offer a reward. But don't expect too much. Any passport is worth 100,000 Kč these days.' All this said with a smile and a vigorous shaking of his head.

The next morning, I made a collect call to Amsterdam. By happy chance, Mike answered the phone, not my mother. I gave him the glad tidings, and told him that, this being a Saturday, I intended to go to Prague the next day and hit the British embassy first thing Monday morning. Mike told me which hotel to stay at in Prague, and added that he would have some money waiting for me there. Also, he said, if there were any problems at the British embassy, I was to get in touch with the Dutch embassy, who would have been contacted by KLM by noon on Monday. I was more than surprised at how good he was at handling emergencies.

Then I took a taxi to my father's apartment. I decided to say nothing of my adventure; I did mention, however, that I would only be staying overnight. My father didn't even question this. In fact, he appeared relieved that my visit was to be a short one. He said that we would have a good lunch at his favourite restaurant to celebrate our reunion.

The reunion was strained. We seemed to have precious little in common. He was obviously ill at ease with me. I was certainly uncomfortable with him. He was more of a stranger than I wanted to admit to myself. Both of us were hesitant to demonstrate any affection. Perhaps there was none. He was embarrassed by his reduced financial status – and obviously did not realize that his son, the art student, knew no other kind of financial status.

My father wore his good suit, a well-tailored, light grey one, very clean and carefully ironed. We had just started on the main course – Wiener schnitzel for me, and Debreziner sausages for him – when the radio in the dining hall announced, *Anglitzky student, Frantisek Neeyoufeld* ...

My father's knife slashed into his juicy sausage, and a stream of grease squirted onto his front, darkly staining his shirt, tie, and well-tailored light grey suit – which no longer looked very clean, nor particularly well-ironed. 'You had your passport stolen?' he whispered, in German.

I nodded.

'How could you do that?' He called for the bill, paid, grabbed me by the arm, and never let go until we were back in his apartment.

There, I told him the whole story of the train ride, the police search and my phone conversation with *Pane* Mike Macpherson, all of which he punctuated with frequent groans of *Nur ein Idiot!* and 'Only an artist!' Whereupon he granted that I had done all that could have been done. He added that he wished he could help, but these were no longer the old days. All he could do was give me one piece of advice. Most of the police were Communists; all of the police were anti-Semites. The less contact I had with them, the better it would be.

In July of 1947, political instability was more than evident in Czechoslovakia. Prime Minister Gottwald, a Communist, was firmly in command; the Communist Party held the majority in the House; and though the country had a coalition government, Czechoslovakia was being forcibly and inevitably pulled into the Communist bloc. Armed Russian soldiers were everywhere.

At nine o'clock, Monday morning, I was at the British embassy. The consular section did not open until ten o'clock. I seemed to be the only customer. I was given a green card with the number 1 on it, and told to wait. The waiting room was fairly large, with several rows of chairs facing a solitary desk. The desk had a stack of forms, as well as more of the cards with numbers on them. The cards seemed to come in two colours: green, like mine, and red.

At ten o'clock sharp, an imperious young woman sat down at the desk. I was still the only supplicant. She spent some five minutes rearranging her papers, and then called out, 'Number one. Please come up.'

On being asked the reason for my visit, I tried to explain what had happened. She stopped me rather abruptly and handed me a form: LOST OR STOLEN DOCUMENTS.

I filled it out to the best of my abilities. There were several questions that perplexed me. With trepidation, I took the form back to the desk and asked if she could help me.

To my surprise, the imperious young woman suddenly became quite human, and looked over the whole form. Then, taking a new form, she said, 'Let's have another go at it, shall we?'

The room was still empty, and during our 'redo' she got me to tell her the whole story, starting from Amsterdam. She asked if I had any other ID on me. All I could show her were my KLM ticket and my Commando Old Comrades membership booklet. This, by pure chance, I had put in my toilet kit, which I had fortunately packed in my suitcase back in Amsterdam.

'Let me call one of the consular officers. Tell him your story, and be sure to let him know how come you are still travelling on a Czech passport, when you've been naturalized as a minor.'

The young consular officer seemed singularly bored by my story. He wrote something on the form I had handed him. Then he put it into an official-looking envelope and told me to take it back to the lady at the desk. He was most standoffish about the whole matter. On top of which, he so resembled the 'Beasts of Bradfield' that I would not have been at all surprised if he had gone to school there. Still, I asked him his name, and for some reason thought to write it down.

When I returned to the outer room, there were about twenty people sitting there. The reception desk was now occupied by a new lady. She motioned me to put the envelope on her desk, and waved me to a chair. By now, it was well after noon. At two o'clock I was still sitting there.

I decided I might as well ask how long I would have to wait. I went up to the lady at the desk and politely asked whether it would take much longer for my 'matter to be resolved' – which I thought sounded most professional. She asked me my name, and flicked through a sort of exercise book. She picked up the phone, called out a number, and after a minute said, 'Righto.' Then, turning to me: 'We should have an answer for you in a week or two. Please give me your address and telephone number in Czechoslovakia, where we can contact you. If you haven't heard anything within two weeks, give us a call.'

By the time I got out of there, it was obviously too late to go to the

Dutch embassy. I decided to go back to the hotel, in case there were any messages there for me. Indeed, there was one waiting: from a Mr John McCordick of the Canadian Consulate.

I phoned him at once and he told me that my sister, Dorrit (who at this time was living in Czechoslovakia, and was a friend of his) had called and apprised him of my bad luck. He wondered if I had already been to the British embassy and how I had gotten on there. I told him that they thought the matter would take two weeks. He then asked me if I knew who was handling my case.

When I gave him the name I had written down he said, 'That jerk! Look, I'm in the same building. Give me fifteen minutes and I'll try and find out what is going on. Stay in your room till I call you back. Okay?'

McCordick phoned back exactly fifteen minutes later. He told me that he hadn't been able to speed things up. He advised me that things in Czechoslovakia were in a bit of a state of flux, and that two weeks might not be advisable. My best bet would be to phone the Dutch embassy in half an hour, and make an appointment. I said I could do that immediately. He replied that half an hour would be much better, and hung up.

When I called the embassy, I was put through to a receptionist. Upon hearing my name, she told me that I was meeting the ambassador at ten the next morning, and that the gate would be expecting me. I could see the *Daily Mirror* headline: FATE AT THE GATE.

To my happy surprise, the meeting with the Dutch ambassador proved to be civilized and comforting. He mentioned that a Mr Raeberger from KLM in Amsterdam had called him. Unlike my father and other advisers he listened to my dire tale without interjecting 'Only an artist' or 'Only an idiot'. Instead, he patiently let me recite my lament, before pulling out the requisite form, which he asked me to fill out. Then he said, 'We are going to issue you a "Nansen" travel pass. But the Czech Home Office will have to endorse it. I have spoken to a colleague there and he will look after it on the spot. They have to charge something like a hundred korunas. Do you have enough money?'

I nodded, and thanked him profusely.

'Nothing to thank me for. My son is also a student and I know these things can happen to students. You seem to make easy prey. Now, while your papers are being made out, we shall have a second breakfast. Then you will have to go.'

Back at my hotel, I had word from Mike: 'I will fly to Ruzin tomorrow morning. I want you at the airport by ten-thirty at the latest. Make absolutely sure that all your papers are in order. See you then.' And he hung up without so much as a goodbye.

I was at the airport by nine-thirty. (There was no way that I was going to give my stepfather any more ammunition.) The KLM plane arrived on schedule, and when the crew disembarked, I was surprised to see that Mike was the ship's captain; he habitually flew only transatlantic routes.

He came over to me and said that we were scheduled to fly back to Amsterdam in ninety minutes. He told me to go through Czech customs and emigration right away. That way I'd be in the departure lounge, which was international territory, if that meant anything. At least there, if something did go wrong, there would be time to work out some sort of contingency plan.

'What could possibly go wrong now?' I said.

But things did go wrong. When I got to the emigration booth, I was told that the 'Nansen' pass needed an exit visa. I was supposed to have received this at the same time that the travel document was endorsed. He was sorry, but I would have to go back to the Foreign Office for the endorsement.

When I slunk back to Mike, he roundly cursed the Czechs and – to my utter surprise – reassured me that it wasn't my fault. Not only did he not blame me, he refused, under any circumstances, to let me go back into Prague. He told me to wait, and disappeared into the area reserved for aircrew and personnel. Ten minutes later he returned with a small suitcase in hand.

By this time, the airport on the arrival level was fairly empty. The volume of air travel in 1947 had still reached nowhere near the level it had been at in prewar Europe.

Mike led me to the single public toilet provided, and locked the door from the inside. Producing a KLM steward's uniform, he told me to put it on. 'This should fit, more or less.' He handed me an ID card – the type one clipped to a lapel – then produced a razor and a pair of cuticle scissors. Needless to say, the photo on the ID card was of a clean-shaven man.

When I had finished removing two years' hard work, Mike arranged the ID card so that it was angled toward the buttonhole of the lower lapel. Then he produced, out of nowhere, some sort of flower, which he put into the buttonhole so that it partly obscured the card. Finally, he gave me a pair of U.S. aviator sunglasses to wear, and told me to pull the peak of my cap well down. He looked me over, nodded, and said, 'They won't look at us that closely; they never do, as long as they see a uniform. But if they do, at worst I guess you will have to spend some time in the Czech army.' Seeing my face, he added, 'I'm joking. Don't worry. Then we'll just bribe our way out of Czechoslovakia.'

Casually, we made our way past a bored-looking soldier, with me nattering away in what I hoped sounded like Dutch. Mike kept himself between me and the soldier, and cheerfully said to him 'Nazdar, tovarish!' Which made the young Czech roar with laughter and wave us through.

Twenty minutes later, we – the flight crew – boarded the plane. And twenty minutes after that, the thirty or so passengers came aboard. After a last visual check by two Czech uniforms, we were cleared to prepare for departure. Finally, we took off – with the whole flight crew breathing a sigh of relief.

The recriminations on Jasonstraat went on for over three hours. Even Duke decided to growl at me. To my relief, my mother announced that it was now too late to start making supper. In any case, she supposed that I had been sufficiently lambasted to last me a lifetime. And, since she thought it best to forget about the whole mess for a while, she proposed that we go to the Hotel Schiller for dinner. We even ordered a taxi (whether to celebrate my safe return or to afford a better opportunity than would a public streetcar for further censure was not clear to me). My mother asked if I still had any of the money that Mike had sent. When I nodded, I was appointed host for the evening.

We had barely ordered dinner when the tall, white-haired man whom I had met during my previous visit to Schiller's appeared at our table. He greeted us, and asked if I was enjoying Amsterdam.

'I am, thank you. These are my mother and stepfather, Mr and Mrs Macpherson. I'm afraid that I don't know your name.'

'Of course not. We never got round to that, the other day. It is Schiller.' Turning to Mike, he asked, 'You live in Holland?'

'Yes. I work for KLM.'

Turning to me, Mr Schiller now asked, 'And how long are you visiting for?'

'I really don't know. But no more than a week or two.'

'Well, next time you intend to visit, phone first, and I will show you my real collection of paintings.'

Then he left. Once he was out of earshot, Mike turned to me and laughed. 'I think he likes you.'

'How do you mean?'

'In the biblical sense.'

We finished an extravagant dinner, since I decided to be totally magnanimous with Mike's money. Finally, I gestured to the waiter to bring me the bill. He came back a moment later and said that our dinner had been looked after by the hotel.

On the way home, my mother said that Mr Schiller's etchings would need to be very, very good before she would be willing to pay the admission price.

The next day I took the train to The Hague and went to the British embassy there. I went through the whole explanation of my lost passport once again. And once again, was given the form with the heading LOST OR STOLEN DOCUMENTS. Only this time I left the embassy as soon as I had handed in the form, and caught the next train back to Amsterdam.

Four weeks later, we still had not heard from The Hague. We had, however, received a visit from the police. The inspector was very polite, and most sympathetic when told of our lack of communication from the British. He pulled an official-looking rubber stamp and ink pad from his briefcase, stamped my 'Nansen' pass, and announced that he had extended my visitor's visa for another four weeks. He hoped that we could get the matter straightened out by then, since he was not authorized to extend my stay beyond that time.

During those weeks, I got to know Amsterdam. At first, I covered the usual tourist haunts from the Leidseplein to the red light district – strictly as a sightseer, in both cases. Then I started sketching in the markets and non-touristy parts of the city. I even dared to return to the Schiller Hotel, where, with virtue intact, I was introduced to some of Amsterdam's artists.

Among them was a young Indonesian illustration student, with the unlikely name of Lisabeth. She escorted me round the city's art-

and bookstores and even posed for me in her small studio. We became close friends – and liked each other well enough not to let our eventual relationship spoil the friendship.

There happened to be a bakery opposite the Macphersons' apartment building, which started baking at 3 a.m. One night I went over and asked if I could sketch them at work. The bakery agreed, and I spent the next few nights there, and liked what I had done.

When I showed the drawings to Lisabeth she asked if I had ever thought of switching from theatre design to book illustration. I said the idea had never occurred to me, and wondered why she asked. 'Because they look like illustrations for a book,' she said. 'Listen, Frank, just forget I asked and carry on with your stage design. It's none of my business. I'm not even qualified to give advice!'

Finally, the 'Newfeld affair' was brought up in the House of Commons by our opposition MP. He soundly berated the Home Secretary for the incompetence of his department and reminded him that this latest victim was not only a British citizen, but had been attached to the British Commandos during the war!

Within two days of that brouhaha, I received a phone call from The Hague instructing me to get back to England within twenty-four hours. And to call in the flight number as soon as I knew it. The embassy gave me both a day and a night telephone number, and said that I would not require any visa, as long as they knew what flight I was taking.

Mike arranged for me to get on a 'tulip flight', leaving for Gatwick that night. We arrived at around 4 a.m. Waiting for me were two CID officers, who drove me straight to Scotland Yard. There, I was given a cup of tea and two biscuits, and told that everything was going to be all right.

They did, however, have a few questions, with which they hoped I would be able to help them. First, how did I get out of Czechoslovakia?

I told them the whole story, not leaving anything out.

Second, would I try to remember, with their help, certain details of the passport that had been stolen?

When I said I wasn't certain that I hadn't just lost it, they said they were damn sure it had been stolen on the train to Brno.

Essentially, what they were interested in were details such as torn pages or coffee stains, and any visas, immigration stamps, or money-exchange notations that might have been in the passport. One of the officers patiently explained that though the photograph and particulars about age and height could easily be changed, it was just not practical for a forger to change each page. Such seemingly picayune details were thus the most important for them to list in their report – though privately, he said, he was certain that the passport would already have been used, and there was little chance that it would even still exist, at this point.

When I wondered why it had taken so long for my matter to be resolved, the same officer told me, 'We couldn't figure out how we got two applications from two different countries for the same travel document. We were certain that this was some new swindle to get a passport with a British resident visa. Nobody even entertained the thought that Mr Macpherson and KLM might have gone into the people-smuggling business.'

One Sunday, about a month after my return to London, Mike appeared out of the blue at Ladbroke Grove, my flea-bitten digs in Notting Hill Gate. We went out for dinner, and he broke the news that not only was he leaving KLM, but he and my mother were leaving for Canada. The move would be soon, and they hoped that I would also consider going. He added that KLM would fly me over for free – but I would have to make the decision by the end of the week.

I thought about it for a couple of days, whereupon I decided that this really wasn't such a great dilemma. I liked theatre, but this past year of study had convinced me that stage design was beyond me; also, I had begun to feel that Lisabeth was right: my costume designs looked more like illustrations for a book than designs for a play. Finally, the passport misadventure had left me wary of distances: that between London and Amsterdam was daunting enough. The idea of coping with another misadventure, with my mother and Mike close to four thousand miles away, was frankly frightening. I phoned Amsterdam and announced, 'I'm coming too. You lucky people.'

4. RELIABLE TOY

We arrived in Toronto in the third week of October, 1947, and checked in at the Hotel Victoria on Yonge Street. The Hotel Victoria was owned by the family of Mike's navigator at KLM. When the KLM contract had ended, he and Mike had decided to start a bush airline. They had made all the arrangements back in Amsterdam.

The hotel had a grand staircase, a tiny elevator, and Victorian-style rooms with velvet curtains and ornate furniture. The beds were waist high. The rooms were pervaded by an old-time opulent mustiness, and the lights flickered incessantly. But it was well located, right in the heart of the city – where, it seemed, all the lights flickered in 1947. That was the Canadian way – or voltage – we were told.

We stayed at the hotel for two weeks, until my mother and Mike found rooms in a boarding house located in the northern part of the city, on Russell Hill Road, near Casa Loma – the Neo-Ghastly turrets of which were a handy point of reference for a stranger with little or no sense of direction.

After the two glorious weeks at the Victoria, the rooming house was a kind of purgatory. It was miles away from the city's core, and eons away from most creature comforts. Although breakfast was provided, tenants were forbidden to cook or even brew tea or coffee in their rooms; neither radios nor gramophones could be operated after 11 p.m., and the heat – or lack thereof – was controlled by the landlord. Visitors were not permitted in the rooms; instead, a public (and rather dreary) parlour was provided, in which one could 'entertain' one's guests.

I applied at the Ontario College of Art and was granted an interview despite having arrived some six weeks into the semester. After viewing my portfolio, however, the department head recalled this obstacle. He suggested that I reapply the following year, and in the meantime take some evening classes, possibly at one of the technical schools.

When I reported this to my mother and Mike, they said that there was nothing for it but for me to look for work. 'Like the rest of the world,' Mike added.

The next day, I bought a *Toronto Star* and carefully scanned the want ads. There it was: just the thing!

Toy Manufacturer Requires Artist. Good working conditions and excellent prospects for talented and conscientious young person! Experience in the Toy Industry not necessary. APPLICANTS MUST BE TALENTED AND AMBITIOUS! The successful applicant will receive professional training and full company benefits from start of his/her employment. Interested applicants should telephone for an appointment.

The ad was signed by a 'Reliable Toy Company' on Wellington Street. I telephoned immediately, and was given an appointment with 'Ronald, Vice-President, Production', the very next day.

Armed with my art-school portfolio, I arrived at the Wellington Street plant some ten minutes early. I was aware that I would probably have to wait to see Mr Ronald, who was surely a busy man. Still, I decided to go in.

At the receptionist's desk I explained that I had an appointment with Mr Ronald, but was a bit early. She smiled at me, and flicked a switch on her intercom: 'Hey, Ron, there's a young man here to see you. I'll send him in, okay?' This seemed to me a rather familiar way in which to address a vice-president. But they did a lot of things casually in Canada.

Mr Ronald turned out to be a corpulent, middle-aged gentleman, who smoked a cigar of commanding proportions. He motioned me to a metal folding chair and handed me a questionnaire. With the back of his hand he made just enough space on his crowded desk for me to fill out the form. Name, age, sex, address, next of kin, previous employment, and 'any criminal record'. But nothing to do with education, exhibitions or awards.

After filling out the questionnaire, I handed it back to Mr Ronald, and told him that I had brought my portfolio.

'That's good. Can you paint?'

'Yes. I took painting at both the Brighton College of Art and Central School of Arts and Crafts in London.'

'London has an art school? I didn't know that. I thought they only

— 58 —

had a county fairground.' I didn't quite grasp this. 'Well, good. Do you paint fast?'

'Average, I suppose. Would you like to see my portfolio?'

'In a moment. Are you a neat painter?'

'I suppose I am. I work in a realistic style. Would you like to see my portfolio?'

'Not yet. Can you work without supervision?'

'Actually, I prefer to work without supervision.'

'Do you mind supervision?'

'Not really. I find it can be most helpful in working out problems at my present stage of development. Would you like to see my portfolio?'

'That won't be necessary. You're hired. We'll start you at $15 a week, and it's a five-day week, eight hours per day. Okay?'

Clearly I had misjudged Mr Ronald. Without even seeing my portfolio he recognized talent. *This* was a sensitive person. And $15 a week! That came to over three guineas.

'Thank you, Mr Ronald. I'll work hard, and you won't regret hiring me.'

'That's good, kid. Take the service elevator to the fourth floor. There'll be a young lady waiting for you. She'll be your boss, and she'll tell you exactly what she wants done. And call me Ron, eh?'

The young lady's name was Vi, and she was at least ten years older than my mother. Her hair was in curlers and she wore a pair of powder-blue pants, elasticized at the waist and ankles. A paint-spattered man's shirt and a cigarette, grafted to her lips, completed the image.

She was waiting for me with a small pushcart, on which I could see four cans with a paintbrush beside each. Two of the cans appeared to hold white paint; the third can contained bright blue paint, and the fourth, shiny black paint. The brush beside the first white can was a fairly large, flat, V-shaped, hog's-hair brush; the second can of white paint boasted a size zero, short-handled brush. The blue can had a round brush, about a size six, and the black can had a smaller round brush. The paint was oil-based and fairly thick. In addition, there was another large can with a piece of masking tape stuck on it: 'Varsol'. A bundle of rags was secured to the pushcart handle, over which a lab coat was slung.

Vi led me to a large room – a very large room – with long rows of dolls' heads fixed on wooden pegs, about level with my chin. Each head had beautiful red lips, rouged cheeks and delicate eyebrows, as well as a coiffure – these came in different colours – protected by a miniature shower cap. There must have been three hundred of these disembodied French aristocrats. All sightless!

'Your job is to paint their eyes.' Vi explained the modus operandi. 'I'll be back in a while to see how you're doing. But if you run into any problems just yell "Vi!" – and me or somebody'll come to see what's up. Okay?'

The modus operandi was as follows. First, I was to take the large V-shaped brush and, with two deft strokes, paint in the whites of the eyes. This was to be done to all the dolls in the first four rows. Then I was to go back to the start and, using the second can and accompanying paintbrush, apply a nice blue circle over each white – which by then would have dried. Following that, I was to repeat the procedure with the smaller round brush, this time painting small black pupils into the middle of the now-dry blues. At each colour change, the just-used brush was to be thoroughly cleaned in the Varsol solution.

Finally, I was to take the size-zero brush, and deftly ping in a tiny white highlight on each pupil. Where to put it, was left up to my artistic judgment. After all, had I not gone to the Central School of Arts and Crafts in London?

Highlight complete, I was to proceed to the next four rows, and start all over again. This would allow 'another crew' to remove the heads from the first four rows and hang the next set of heads, which I was not to touch, under any circumstances.

I felt flattered to have advanced to the status of a 'crew' so rapidly.

I took over the controls of the pushcart and entered my studio.

I was just completing the first batch of dolls' heads when Vi came in, took a quick look, and said that it was time for lunch.

I was perplexed.

'I suppose nobody told you to bring lunch? Typical! Well, there's a greasy spoon across the way, and you can get a pretty good sandwich and a Coke for just forty-five cents. But don't be more than thirty minutes.'

As it happened, I didn't have forty-five cents to spare. But I went out anyhow, if only to plot my escape. Painting those endless eyes had become a nightmare.

Obviously, I could not resign. That would mean facing my

mother's concern and, worse, Mike's sneers. I had to get fired! But how? Vi had just congratulated me on my job – 'real neat, if a bit slow' – and told me that everybody was a bit slow to start, but that I'd get the hang of it in no time. After a week, she said, I'd be able to paint eyes in my sleep. (Or, I thought, in my padded cell.) Then the solution hit me. I could hardly wait to get back to work.

I was back with ten minutes to spare, and was just about to start when Mr Ron stuck his head into the room. 'That's what I like to see, kid! Enthusiasm! Vi has given you a pretty good report, and we think you'll do well here. Carry on!'

And carry on I did.

I started the first row in the prescribed manner, but as soon as I got to the second row of dolls' heads, I instituted the 'Kid' Procedure. Instead of starting with the white paint, I applied a careful coating of black. On my second round, I painted the irises white, and on my third round I applied the pupils: a beautiful, bright blue.

I was just completing my fourteenth head, with masterly highlights in ebony, when Vi came in. She took one look, and screamed.

Thus ended my career with the Reliable Toy Company.

* * *

By the time I reached Yonge Street, some five minutes later, relief had turned to doubt. And as I waited at the streetcar stop, doubt turned to panic. *You idiot! What have you done? How stupid, stupid, stupid, can you get? How utterly idiotic!*

At this point, an elderly policeman – at least fifty years of age – materialized. 'What's the problem, son?'

I'm going to be arrested, I thought. I've run afoul of the Canadian law.

The only thing I could think of that was worse than being arrested was having to face the Macphersons, so I decided to get the whole thing off my chest and make a clean breast of it. I told the policeman the whole story, including, in all its detail, my heinous act of sabotage.

Rather to my puzzlement, the cop started to laugh. 'Things can't be that bad, son. Why don't you go across the street to that big store, Simpsons. It's Christmas time and they always need extra help. Go to their personnel department and ask for Mrs Pritchard. Tell her Angus sent you. And cheer up. I'm sure it'll all turn out.'

I thanked him – more for not arresting me, than for his reassurances – shook his hand, and even waited for the traffic light to turn green before crossing Yonge Street at full sprint. I went into Simpsons and gasped.

Simpsons was the biggest and most luxurious store I had ever been into. Certainly, there was nothing like it in Brighton, and even though I had never dared to go into any of the swell shops in London, I was sure nothing there could beat Toronto's Simpsons. How would I ever get a job here?

But I found the personnel department, and the receptionist found Mrs Pritchard, who said that if 'Angus' had sent me, then she would have to interview me.

She took me to an impressive office and asked me to fill out a questionnaire. It was certainly more extensive than the one at the Reliable Toy Company. It was divided into three parts: FULL-TIME EMPLOYMENT/PART-TIME EMPLOYMENT/SEASONAL EMPLOYMENT. Mrs Pritchard directed me to fill out the 'Seasonal Employment' section, which had a number of headings: Student (area of study, year, institution); Military Service (branch, rank, etc.); Sales Experience; Reason for Application; Interests and/or Hobbies....

I filled out the questionnaire. Mrs Pritchard next asked how long I had been in Canada (three weeks); why I wasn't at art school (I arrived in Canada too late to get in); where I had worked before (Reliable Toy); how long (three and a half hours); and did I know anything about classical music (yes, I had taken both violin and piano lessons; what I neglected to add was that I had been seven years old for the former and eight years old for the latter, and that both teachers had given up on me with regret and relief).

Mrs Pritchard thought a minute and then said that she was sending me to see a Mr Stevens on the third floor. She amended my application to read, 'Full-time Employment Recommended'.

Mr Stevens, a tall, waspish gentleman in a grey suit and gold-rimmed glasses, was the manager of the third floor. He mentioned that Mrs Pritchard had phoned, and that a Mr Bull, the manager of radios, musical equipment and records, was on his way over. They were thinking of starting me in one of his sections.

When Mr Bull arrived – a shortish man with a kindly face – he asked me which composers I liked. I rattled off my complete repertoire of classical composers' names: Beethoven, Bach, Schubert, Chopin, Rimsky-Korsakov, Stravinsky and Tchaikovsky. My list seemed to impress him.

He then asked if I was familiar with contemporary popular music. I said that I knew of a few musicians, like Benny Goodman and Glenn Miller, but I certainly was in no position to discuss them intelligently.

'I suggest we put Frank on the classical records counter,' he said. 'I am still short one person, with the Christmas rush about to start.'

'I agree,' replied Mr Stevens. 'Well then. You will start at $22 per week plus one percent commission. You will get your base pay every two weeks, and your commission once a month. We work nine to six every day except for Fridays, when we work on alternating eight-hour shifts, since the store is open from nine to nine.'

To Mr Bull he said, 'Newfeld can have Tuesdays off, to start.' And then, turning to me: 'Mr Bull will introduce you to your section head when he returns. He is on sick leave at the moment, so until he comes back you can report to Mr Bull. But remember that

CASA LOMA

Mr Bull is a very busy man. We are both glad to have you with us, here at Simpsons. You may start tomorrow. Good luck.'

I returned to the rooming house on Russell Hill Road and found both my mother and Mike at home. They asked if I had been hired by the Reliable Toy Company. When I nodded, they asked for how much. I told them $15 per week, and they both agreed that seemed pretty good. Mike asked what my job would involve. I replied that I would be selling classical records, unless I was needed on the popular record counter.

'Selling records at Reliable Toy?'

'Not exactly. I was offered a job at Simpsons – for $22 a week. I start tomorrow and have to be there at ten to nine. Can somebody set the alarm for seven?'

★ ★ ★

With that, I started five happy and – except for one isolated incident – fairly uncomplicated months.

The record section staff seemed to be made up entirely of out-of-work musicians, music students, and opera singers between engagements. No one was greedy for commissions; no one was looking for promotion; no one had any illusions about the earth-shaking importance of the job. But no customer was ever ignored or neglected. You were expected to pitch in and help with everyone else's sales, without ever claiming a piece of the commission – and this we all did cheerfully. Lance, the section head, returned one week after I joined the group, and it was clear that the mood of the section echoed his philosophy of life.

At the end of my first month, I was overjoyed to find a commission chit for $11.75 in with my regular pay – an extra half week's wages! For me, this was a fortune. Now I would be able to buy some decent Christmas presents, and have money left over to buy a new shirt and tie.

That evening, I announced that I would be able to just about pay my own way from now on.

My mother looked at Mike with a smile. 'I might as well tell him. We've been looking for a place with a bit more privacy and space. One that's more conveniently located. Well, we found a place yesterday and were going to tell you about it during the holidays. It's right on

Bloor Street, near a Dovercourt Road, and we're moving in on the first of January.'

'I guess I'll have to start looking for a place at once. That's in less than three weeks.'

'No, no. It's a big apartment over a jewellery store, with lots of space. There's a room for you; we never even considered that you wouldn't be moving in with us. And the rent will be cheap.' Which was the nicest thing Mike ever said to me.

Certainly, getting to and from work would be a lot easier from Dovercourt, since it meant changing streetcars just once. Toronto was cold that winter and there was lots of snow, even as early as December. Each streetcar had a driver, and a conductor who dished out tickets and transfers and whose job also included keeping the potbelly stove well supplied with fuel, and the streetcar floor liberally strewn with sawdust. You could purchase streetcar tokens from young ladies, well-muffled against the frigid weather, at most major streetcar stops. This meant that the driver did not have to wait with the centre door open whilst passengers fiddled with change.

The new apartment had three bedrooms, plus large living and dining rooms, a kitchen with a breakfast nook, and a tiny den which Mike claimed as his own. There was, of course, only one bathroom: this *was* 1948. The place was clean – and, as my mother said, the jewellery business is seldom a very noisy one. Even if it is Jewish!

There was a movie theatre one block away, which had double seats up in the balcony – a boon for serious petting – and 'china' days once a week, where they actually gave away genuine china dishes, in the floweriest patterns imaginable.

To cap it all off, in January I sold an album to a young pilot officer in the Canadian Air Force, and on her third return to augment her music library, we made our first date. We went dancing at the Masonic Temple on Yonge Street and were getting on well together. Unfortunately, after only one visit to the double seats in the balcony, either her Presbyterian upbringing or her Presbyterian-minister father doomed any further chance of connection, let alone communion.

At work, things continued to go well. I got to know Lance, the section head. He, like most of my co-workers, was an out-of-work musician. He had played with some of the best-known big bands, and knew an amazing number of people in the industry. When the big bands came to Toronto – and all the big American bands played at the Palais Royale on Lakeshore Road in those days – Lance invariably had tickets, and more often than not invited me along.

So I not only heard, but also met, Stan Kenton, Spike Jones and even Peggy Lee. (She was booked for two weeks at the Casino Theatre opposite the old City Hall). Lance insisted that it was just a matter of time before he'd be back in harness himself.

One day near the end of January, he told me that he'd been clean for over six months now, and he wasn't going to be around Simpsons much longer. In fact, he had told Bull as much the week after the Christmas holidays.

Mr Bull called me into his office the very next morning. Lance was already there. Mr Bull said they wanted to move me into the stockroom. 'We want you to keep stock, and also to immediately take over the buying for the classical music counter.'

'Is this a demotion?'

'Let me finish. Standard stock items are flagged in the stock-card Rolodex for both classical and pop inventory. Those we think you can handle by yourself from the word go. As far as the classical is concerned, we think you can take over the buying of new products. As for the pop material, we don't think you know it well enough – at least not yet – to decide on new releases. So there you will carry out Lance's decisions. But you will immediately start attending all internal buying meetings and demonstrations. And no, this is definitely not a demotion.'

'But with commission, I'm making almost thirty dollars a week.'

'During the season you are,' said Lance. 'But you ain't gonna make anything like it during the doldrums, which should start just about now.'

'Still,' Bull interjected, 'we don't want you to suddenly go home with less than you have been. So I am prepared to authorize a raise of five dollars per week. I think that's fair.'

'Trust me, Frank. Take the job. You won't regret it.'

At the end of February, Lance was still around and I was still in the stockroom, getting more bored by the day. Admittedly, the February doldrums hit our section hard; some days the total sales for both pop and classical amounted to less than fifty dollars. On certain days, even this was better than the sales of record players; the department could finish the day with more machines than it had started with, because of the liberal returns policy for which Simpsons was famous, even back then.

But I really was not happy working in the stockroom. I missed chatting with the customers and gossiping with the opera singers. I felt that I would gladly go back to $22 for a change of scene.

One afternoon, Lance came into the small stockroom office and announced that he felt lousy and had to go home. He wasn't sure he'd be able to come back for a day or two, but he thought that most things were looked after and would go smoothly. One thing he had over-looked was ordering *The Teddy Bears' Picnic* for Easter. This was our major seller at Easter time. So would I look after that, and increase this year's quantity to fifty records. That was the only thing that needed to be done immediately. Anything else could wait until he was back. He looked terrible, and I was convinced that we wouldn't see him for at least a week.

I told him not to worry and that I would call RCA right away, and send out the order first thing in the morning. We had run out of order forms the day before and I hadn't gotten round to filling out a requisition for another batch. (In certain respects, Simpsons was very much like the British army. You had to fill out a form for everything.)

Not more than five minutes after Lance left, Mr Bull came into the stockroom carrying a Simpsons bag, and carefully closed the door.

This seemed too much of a coincidence. I surmised that he had somehow found out about Lance's 'sickness', and was going to ask me all sorts of questions.

I decided that I would simply deny any knowledge of any problem that Lance or anybody else in the department was thought to have contracted. (And there were quite a number of our orchestra members with every conceivable sort of problem.)

'This has to be strictly off the record,' he began. 'But I understand you really want to be an artist. So I thought you might be the right person to come to.'

He paused.

I thought to myself that he was going about this very carefully. I liked Mr Bull, and had always found him to be a kind person, who stood up for the people working in his department. But still, he was management, and if push came to shove I figured he would take management's view of Lance's 'sickness'. The best thing to do was to play dumb, and in the worst case develop a sudden toothache which would force us to terminate the meeting.

'Frank, you do understand what I mean by off the record?'

I nodded.

'Well, you know my name is Bull,' he reminded me. 'What you probably don't know is the fact that I'm a bit of an artist myself.'

Now he's trying to ally himself with me, I thought. This was pretty cunning. I would have to be extra careful.

'Let me show you something,' he continued.

He opened the Simpsons bag he had been carrying, dug inside, and produced an eighteen-inch plywood carving of a very bellicose bull standing on a woodsy-looking base on which were emblazoned the words 'THE BULLS'.

'I carved this myself,' he announced. 'I know it's not much, but my wife wants to hang it by our cottage mailbox. I wonder if it's not too much of an imposition to ask you to paint it for me? Of course, I'll pay for the work and the materials. I hope I haven't offended you. If you prefer not to do it, I'll understand. Look, Frank, I know it's a heck of an imposition, but I mentioned that we had a young artist working for us, and the wife insisted I ask you.'

I was dumbstruck.

'Never mind. I should never have come to ask this. Forget I ever came into the stockroom!'

'No, not at all! It's no problem, and I'd be delighted to do it. But I can't charge you for the work. Just tell your wife she owes me some home-baked cookies.'

'At least let me give you five dollars for materials,' said Bull, much relieved. 'Now, let's go and get a cup of coffee in the cafeteria. I think it's time for a break.'

The next morning, when I came in, I suddenly remembered *The Teddy Bears' Picnic*. I went to my desk, intending to telephone RCA and alert them about the order, when Mr Stevens suddenly appeared.

'I understand that Lance has phoned in sick. Do you happen to know anything about that?'

I mentioned that he had looked terrible the day before, and had gone home just before closing. Beyond that, I assured him, I knew nothing. But I said that, considering the way Lance had looked, I wouldn't be at all surprised if he would be away for more than just a day.

'That's too bad. I hope it won't be anything too serious,' he ventured. 'I assume that everything is under control. I would have waited to speak to Mr Bull, but he won't be here till noon and I'm going to be in meetings all day. So please phone him at home and bring him up to date. Let him know the message about Lance came to me by mistake. Thank you.'

Then I noticed that a fresh supply of order forms had been placed on my desk. Well, I thought, eventually they would let me order the bloody *Teddy Bears' Picnic*.

I phoned Mr Bull, who didn't seem at all happy that Mr Stevens had visited me. Then I started to fill out the order form.

I had barely gotten halfway through when one of the divas came in and asked me if it was true that Lance had 'fallen off'. When I nodded, she said, 'No wonder, after the news he just got.'

'What news?'

'You don't know? The Yanks turned down his application for a work permit. And without a green card no band will touch him. I guess he's stuck here.' As she left my cubbyhole she sniffed, 'And we'd all of us better make damn sure he doesn't get fired!'

I went back to filling out the purchase order, and had it almost finished when Mr Bull appeared. He took off his overcoat and sat down.

'I decided I'd better come in before anything else hit the fan. How sick is Lance and how much does Stevens know?'

I filled him in as best as I could, and told him that, as far as I knew, Mr Stevens had no more idea of what was wrong with Lance than I did five minutes ago.

'Can the section manage without him for a couple of days?'

'I'm pretty sure we've got everything under control. Lance told me exactly what has to be done until he comes back in a couple of days.' (Or a couple of weeks, I thought to myself.)

'Well then, I'll leave you to it. If you need me to do anything, come and tell me in person. But don't use the phone.'

At this rate, I was never going to get the *Teddy Bears' Picnic* order off to RCA. All there was left to do was to fill in the number of records and sign. Quickly I did this – before anyone else could come into the stockroom – grabbed one of RCA Victor's pre-stamped envelopes, shoved the P.O. in, sealed it and put it down the mail chute.

Our ailing section head returned ten days later, looking twenty pounds lighter and four shades paler. He was welcomed back like the prodigal son. And though he moved a bit more slowly and deliberately than did the old Lance, and spoke barely above a whisper, he took full command in his usual style as though nothing had happened.

Three weeks before Easter I received a phone call from receiving, saying that a shipment of records had arrived from RCA Victor. They asked what we wanted done with it.

'Send it up.'

'Are you sure? It's a bit bigger than your usual shipments.'

'That's okay. I know all about it. Just send it up.'

An hour later, the shipment arrived. Four cartons on a dolly were wheeled in.

Then four more cartons arrived. And another four. And more, until there were twenty cartons strewn about the record department.

'What is going on? What is in these boxes?' asked Lance – his whisper replaced by an anguished rasp.

He looked at the labels. Every carton was marked 'TEDDY BEARS' PICNIC / 25'.

'God, how many did you order?'

'Fifty!'

'Check your P.O. What does it say?'

'Five hundred,' I replied – my whisper putting Lance's rasp to shame.

'Oh boy!' sighed Lance. 'Well, let's leave it until I get back. Bull wants to see me. I guess he wants to bring me up to date; and I suppose he wants me to bring him up to date. I don't suppose that'll take that long. Then we can figure out our plan of action as far as the *Picnic* is concerned.'

Lance came back about an hour later, and said that he had been brought up to date; and had heard all about the meetings which I had been forced to endure. Also, it seemed, he had heard that nothing too disastrous had happened whilst he was sick. For which he was grateful.

'And now we are going to initiate the greatest sales campaign the Canadian record industry has ever witnessed,' he said. 'Get me one of the cartons, Frank.'

Over the next three days we saw very little of Lance. But, as though by magic, every radio station in Toronto suddenly began to play *The Teddy Bears' Picnic* at least once an hour. And each time they played it, they credited Simpsons and only Simpsons as the place to go and get it.

After ten days of this, Lance came into my office with Mr Bull and said, 'Why would you only order five hundred of a surefire winner? That shows that you still have quite a bit to learn about the music business. We think you should consider ordering another batch. But perhaps you could err on the cautious side, only because it's getting closer to Easter. What a coincidence, that the deejays all discovered *The Picnic* at exactly the same time.'

When they had finished laughing, Mr Bull added, 'As it's Easter, we figure that another three dollars a week would help with the Easter eggs. You'll find it in your envelope from the next pay on. And take the rest of the day off, after you've placed the order.'

I took the Bloor streetcar home that afternoon feeling quite pleased with myself.

As we passed the movie house across from Christie Pits, I saw a large banner which proclaimed: MENACHEM BEGIN SPEAKS! – TODAY AT 3 PM! – ADMISSION FREE!

I looked at my watch: it was three o'clock on the dot. The streetcar stopped.

I got out, crossed the street, and went into the movie house.

In 1948, the Israeli artist Ludwig Blum
painted my portrait in Jerusalem.

5. NEWFELD/SORBONNE, PARIS

had heard of Menachem Begin, of course, but all I really knew about him was what I had read in the papers, which portrayed him as a terrorist – ruthless, and contemptuous of human life.

His appearance was not what I had expected. He was short and very thin. Spectacles and protruding teeth gave him the look more of a scholar than of a man to be feared. With him on the stage stood four Levantine-looking men, in black leather jackets, with crossed arms and threatening scowls. Beside them, he looked vulnerable and alone. But he certainly was a firebrand!

In the next two hours, I learnt more about Palestine than I had in six months of English and Canadian press reports on the 'situation in the Middle East', which had mostly praised the forbearance of British troops stationed there under trying conditions.

The Arab Legion, British Occupation Forces, the Palestine Police, the Mufti, the Bevin Policy, Acre Prison, Irgun Zvai Leumi, Herut, Haganah, the Balfour Declaration, Cyprus internment camps, Tzofim, Lochamei Haghetaot (Fighters of the Ghetto), military tribunals.... Some of these names were new to me; others took on new and freighted meanings.

As Begin's speech went on, even the word 'assimilation' got a guilty ring about it: we, in the comfort of Canada, had been blissfully unconcerned about the imminent upheaval in the Middle East. We, in the comfort of Canada, had ignored the lesson of the Holocaust. We, in the comfort of Canada, had best be aware that without the State of Israel, history could repeat itself. That, in essence, was Begin's message.

But he had touched a chord within me. Ghosts of aunts and uncles, of cousins – boys and girls – flashed before my eyes. My aunts Minna, Yelli, Gretel, Reggie and Sofie; both uncles Leo; Uncle Alois; and Uncle Hugo, who had been a Rittmeister in the Austrian army during World War I, and still hadn't been spared; also Stefan, Peter,

Two aunts killed in the Holocaust. Grete (left) and Yelli (right).

Irene, Trude – playmates of mine and Dorrit's from trips to our grand-parents' farm in Miroslav. All had perished in the name of racial cleansing. They ranged in age from six to eighty-plus years. History could not be allowed to repeat itself.

As we stood and applauded, a table and two chairs were brought onto the stage. Begin raised his hands to quiet us. 'Those of you who will fight for Israel, and have had some military experience, come forward now and sign our covenant. Those who can't, please sign a pledge and participate in the coming battle that way. I thank you in the name of Israel. Shalom!'

There was a shuffling of feet and a murmur in the hall, but no one made a move to go up to the stage.

Then, to my surprise, I found myself climbing on stage. I sat down at the table and signed up, to a round of applause. It was fearfully easy: like painting the dolls' eyes at Reliable Toy. My bravura started a stampede of idealists: four more would-be freedom fighters – or foreign legionnaires, or future heroes, as you prefer – ascended the steps.

The meeting broke up and the movie house emptied quickly, except for the volunteers – the 'brave five' – the Irgun bodyguards, and a pair of local gentlemen. Begin, by this time, had also disappeared. One of the local gentlemen then turned to us and said that we would be contacted by telephone within a few days. He emphasized that this was not a game. We were *not*, did we hear him, *not* to tell anyone about going to Eretz Israel. Not even parents or girlfriends. We were even to avoid contact with one another, in the event that we had been friends or acquaintances before 'this day'.

Next, he gave each of us a number to dial in the event that we weren't home to receive the phone call. In which case a message would be left for us, saying that Joshua had called.

Our return call should be made from a phone booth.

Looking around furtively, the five of us left. I caught the next streetcar and went home.

* * *

One evening two weeks later the phone rang. Mike came in and announced that it was for me.

'Who is it?'

'I have no idea. He didn't say.'

I went to the phone and said, 'Yes?'

'You don't know me. But I believe you went to the Christie Pits theatre two weeks ago, and I wonder if we could meet early next week at the Zionist Organization of Canada building on Spadina. My name is Gelber.'

I agreed, and the following Tuesday, at exactly ten o'clock, I reached the front desk of the Zionist building and asked to see Mr Gelber.

'He is in the boardroom. Let me take you to him. He is expecting you.'

Mr Gelber shook my hand, asked me to sit down, and came straight to the point. 'How much do you know about the Irgun, and what precisely made you decide to join up with them?'

I confessed that I didn't know too much about the Irgun. I told him that I had some military experience and felt that I could be of use to Israel in the inevitable upcoming fight with its Arab neighbours.

'Are you a Zionist?'

I admitted that I wasn't, but felt it was probably time to become one. I told him that we – my mother, sister and I – had spent the war in comparative safety in England. Meanwhile, over twenty of our relatives had died in the camps. That was the main reason for my decision to go.

'But why choose a right-wing, extremist, terrorist group?'

Gelber then proceeded to give me a lesson about the Irgun Zvai Leumi – acknowledging their heroics against the British occupation, but condemning their many acts of mindless brutality.

He went on to recite the Irgun's political agenda, outlining the goals they intended to pursue, with all means at their disposal – as they had vociferously proclaimed – once the State of Israel was established.

None of this sounded too good to me.

'Mr Begin led us to believe that his fighters were all that stood between the Arabs and the Mediterranean Sea.'

'There is also the Haganah,' he said. 'It is the regular army established by the Israeli government in waiting. Do you have any objection to joining the Haganah, instead?'

'Not really. In fact, I would prefer to be with a legitimate, as opposed to an underground, group. But how will I let the Irgun know?'

'We will do that,' he said. 'Don't you worry. Now I want you to meet two friends from Israel. They will, in all likelihood, ask you a few questions. I have to leave now, but I am sure that we will see each other again.'

The session with the two Palestinians – or rather Israelis (I would have to get used to the idea that calling them Palestinians was a Galut habit) – was surprisingly brief. They asked if I had any documents from my British army days.

When I produced my Commando Service Certificate and my Old-Comrades Association book, they said they didn't need to see anything else. They were happy to welcome me to the Haganah.

One of them introduced himself as Amitai, and said that he was to be my liaison, and would be in touch with me as soon as he had arranged my doctor and dentist appointments.

When I said that I would give him my address and phone number, he replied that he already had them.

Then he asked if 'Mike' had any idea I was going to Israel. This question shook me. Obviously, I was joining up with a bunch of consummate professionals.

I assured Amitai that nobody had any inkling I was anything other than an art-student-in-waiting. At this, both Israelis pricked up their ears and conferred in Hebrew. Amitai asked me to jot down some details of my previous art education. 'We think we will get you a letter of acceptance to one of the fine-arts programs at the Sorbonne. That will make a perfect cover for you should the French Sûreté or anyone else ask awkward questions on the way.' He paused. 'Is there anything you want to ask?'

'Only about the doctor/dentist visit. Is this an enlistment checkup? Because I am really in very good health.'

'No, of course not. But you will have to get a number of inoculations before going to the Middle East, and we want to complete any dental work that needs doing over here. Our local dentists are the best; they are all volunteers eager to do their bit for Israel. You will get VIP treatment, free of charge. We'll call you. Shalom.'

As I left the boardroom, Mr Gelber reappeared, with one of the other four 'Irgun Irregulars'. We greeted each other somewhat cautiously. Mr Gelber said, 'You met at the movie-house Irgun-show. Let me introduce you properly. Perry Covent, Frank Newfeld. You're both going to Eretz Israel shortly, so you should get to know one another. Frank, why don't you wait in the lobby? Perry won't be more than ten minutes, and then he can give you a lift.'

Secrecy, where art thou? Obviously not in the ZOC building.

I was curious to know what Mr Covent's contribution to the war effort might be. He was around twenty-five years of age, quite tall, with a full head of curly blond hair, and a frame a full twenty pounds overweight. He certainly did not look military.

Half an hour later, he appeared.

'Let's go. I'm absolutely starving. There's a nice little restaurant on Bloor near Bathurst, and we can walk over. I'll leave the car here. We won't find a parking spot any closer.'

As it turned out, Perry was a pleasant fellow, generous of both opinion and pocket. Over lunch, which was breakfast for me and an impressive stream of dishes for him, I acquired a full intelligence dossier on 'Covent, Perry' – which convinced me to reciprocate with as little information as possible on myself.

He confided that he was a pilot, and though he had no military experience to speak of, he had been intending to ferry bombers over for the Irgun. I was surprised that the Irgun even had an air force! He went on to say that the Haganah, having gotten wind of this, had immediately contacted him and made a counter-offer which was much more interesting.

When I asked him why he had come up to the stage and signed up, he replied that it had been a charade, pre-arranged, to persuade others to enlist.

He was charming. He was amusing. He was a master of small talk. He had a car and he paid for lunch. Actually the car belonged to his mother, but since she didn't drive, he had full charge of it. I was most impressed when the car turned out to be a large 1947 Pontiac with velvety seats and a radio that had speakers front and back.

We exchanged telephone numbers, and Perry announced that he would arrange a double date with two sisters he knew well. As he drove off, he called out that he would phone me.

That same evening, he telephoned to say that the 'heavenly twins' were dying to meet me and that he would fetch me the next day around seven-thirty in the evening. When I asked him what they were like, he said: 'They are very nice girls. Maybe a little older than me, but real nice. What's more important, they are ardent Zionists, and when I say ardent, I mean *ardent*. If you know what I mean.'

The next day was quite unexceptional at Simpsons. All I had to do was book in the new shipment of *Teddy Bears* – still selling – and book out the records sold Monday and Tuesday. Business was brisk, and our record-studios, where customers listened to their selections, had waiting lines for a good part of the afternoon. Even the 'divas' were occupied, so I had the stockroom to myself. The silence was golden, the solitude a luxury. I had time to think about the events of the last few days.

I decided that perhaps I hadn't made such a terrible mistake. In fact, this could turn out to be the most salutary rash decision I had ever made. For the first time since my impulsive climb up onto the stage at the movie house, I came to terms with my volunteering.

By the time I was ready to leave work for the day, I was ready to leave for Israel.

Perry appeared at exactly seven-thirty, smelling of Brylcreem, cologne, and testosterone. He came up to me and sniffed. Then he shook his head and asked if I had any aftershave lotion. When I nodded, he suggested that I use it.

On the way over, Perry told me that the twins lived by themselves in the upper half of a duplex owned by their parents, who occupied the lower apartment. An excellent arrangement, he declared. Perry rang the upstairs doorbell, and a small man wearing a yarmulke opened the door to the downstairs apartment.

A woman's voice came from behind him, 'Who is it?'

'The suitors!'

'So mind your own business!' she told him.

By this time, one of the twins had opened the other door; she quickly ushered us upstairs, where her sister waited. They really were identical twins – indistinguishable one from the other. But 'heavenly'? They were, to put it kindly, unattractive.

The evening started normally enough. A table had been set for four, with wineglasses and two lit candles. On a small side table I could see an open bottle of Chianti. The ladies brought out a big bowl of spaghetti and meatballs, and an even bigger bowl of salad. One twin coquettishly put a large helping of food on Perry's plate, whilst the other did the same for me, in carbon-copy manner.

Then they poured us each a glass of wine, each twin wiping a drop from the bottle neck and licking it off her finger, in what was meant to be a sensuous move. (The whole evening, in retrospect, seems like something straight out of *Tom Jones*.)

After dinner, we chatted a while in their living room, which was connected to the dining room by elaborate French doors. One of the twins told us they really liked living alone together. In fact, they had so much space that each had her own bedroom. Which made entertaining much easier. Then Perry remembered, apropos of nothing, that they had a marvellous dance routine, which they had to show me.

'Of course we will.'

First, they insisted on clearing the dishes, 'because we'll need both rooms.' They tittered. 'Then we'll have to change. But it won't take us too long. We won't have that much to change into.' Titter, titter. 'You gentlemen can wait in the dining room.'

When they had gone, Perry said to me, 'We are set for the night. Which one would you like?'

'Is there a difference?' The prospect of 'liking' one or the other was distinctly unappealing to me. Worse, I was convinced I would insult my chosen twin by my predictable lack of ardour. I had to escape. Graciously. Perhaps I would think of something during the performance.

Then began a strangely hypnotizing performance, which would have been quite erotic had the 'heavenly twins' not been so much like characters out of the Grand Guignol.

The performance was impressive, but the sight had not been pretty. Perry and I applauded with gusto. One of the twins linked her arm to mine and whispered: 'My sister and Perry want to be alone for a while. I think we should go to my room so that they can have a bit of privacy.'

'That's a wonderful idea!' I announced. 'But I'd better phone home first to check if I had any *special* telephone calls. Though I most certainly hope there won't be any.'

'Of course,' my twin replied, in a conspiratorial tone. 'Use the phone in the hall.'

I went to the phone and dialled, with my other hand holding down the two disconnect-buttons. I counted to ten. 'I hope you weren't busy, but I wanted to check if anybody had called.' I paused for a few seconds. 'No, don't give me his phone number. I'll get it later.' I paused again, then continued, 'He asked that I call back as soon as possible? Hm – that important! I'd better come home. Thank you.'

Then I said 'Damn', and returned to the room. 'I have to leave. I can't tell you what it's all about, but believe me, I wish I hadn't phoned.'

To my dismay (I was already feeling guilty), my twin insisted on wrapping a piece of strudel for me to take home. She said that she understood, and just knew there would be 'other times'. Perry wondered if he should drive me home. He seemed relieved when I said that I would take the bus to the nearby streetcar terminal, and that there was nothing to discuss.

On the bus, I laughed so uproariously that the passenger next to me decided to move to another seat. The other passengers fell silent and looked at me with marked apprehension.

My mother used to say to me, 'Do not paint the Devil on the wall.' I might have remembered this. The very next day, there really was a call to arms. Only it did not come by phone.

The next morning, at around ten o'clock, with nothing much to do in the stock room, I was out front talking to Lance. There were no customers about and the record-department divas had finished dusting and tidying up. Then, of all people, Amitai appeared. He browsed around for a while, not making any attempt to come near me. I decided to wait and see what would develop. Finally, he went up to one of the salesladies, with a selection of records. She took him to one of the booths where he settled down to listen to one of the records.

As soon as his saleslady disappeared, he re-emerged, strolled over to me and politely asked if I could help him. We went into his booth and both bent over the record player, pretending to examine it. 'This is a bit sooner than we had hoped,' he said, 'but you'll have to hand in your notice. One of the people scheduled to leave with the next group cannot go. We want you to take his place. The ship sails from New York in ten days, and there are lots of things to be done. How soon can you get off?'

'I suppose I can give notice today, and ask to work Tuesday of next week. That'll mean that I can finish on Friday. But what do I use as an excuse?'

'That will do, I suppose. Tell them that you've been awarded a scholarship to study in Paris. We should have something on Sorbonne stationery here by next week.'

'Okay. But won't they wonder why I would have to leave now? No university semester starts in May!'

'I don't think they will even ask. But if they do, tell them you had to enroll in a crash course in French.'

Amitai took his selection back to the sales desk. He bought two records, thanked the diva and me for our help, and left.

My leave-taking from Simpsons turned out to be quite easy. There were no probing questions. I received my last pay envelope, with Mr Stevens' good wishes, the following Friday, and was happily surprised to find over one week's holiday pay included.

But the last ten days in Toronto were hectic. There were several briefings at the ZOC offices; there were long visits to the Haganah dentist, crammed together in none too painless a fashion. ('What those English dentists do to people is unbelievable.')

The day before my train trip to New York, the volunteer doctor administered my final set of shots. ('You will probably have a bit of a reaction to these, because I had to lump a number of vaccines together. You might get a temperature. But I had no choice, the way the Haganah manages to screw things up. I imagine you'll be fine in the morning.')

That evening, I had 'a bit of a reaction.' I collapsed on my bed for an hour, then struggled to get up. I had to get my stuff packed. I had my train ticket; a manila envelope containing my boat ticket, 'Sorbonne letter', and itinerary – carefully composed to resemble a typical student's travel guide; as well as my British passport, complete with visas and money. I had an address in Brooklyn to which I could resort, in the event that I missed 'our man' at Grand Central Station. All I had to do was throw some clothes in a suitcase, set my alarm clock, and sleep off this damn temperature. Check off the list I had made of 'things to do in the morning', and get to Union Station by eight o'clock! Only I hadn't counted on my mother, who suddenly appeared.

'It's after nine o'clock, and I wondered if you were hungry. You've been asleep for over three hours.' Then she looked at me more closely. 'What is wrong with you? You're running a temperature. Look at your arm! You've had some sort of injection. You aren't taking drugs?'

Then she saw my suitcase, which I had left open on the floor. 'You've had vaccinations! Where are you going? You're going to Palestine!' Then, shouting to Mike: 'I told you two weeks ago that something funny was going on, with all those strange phone calls and that odd fat fellow he's been meeting lately. Well, he's certainly not going anywhere – I can tell you!'

We all started yelling at one another, and the argument might well have gone on all night except that I fell asleep. The alarm clock woke me at five-thirty.

To my relief, I no longer seemed to have a temperature. I had only the haziest recollection of what I had said the previous evening. I saw, however, that my suitcase was neatly packed, and my portfolio – labelled 'NEWFELD / SORBONNE, PARIS' – propped against a chair.

We parted on good terms, with tears all around, and a hundred-dollar handshake from Mike.

6. GRAND ARENAS

mitai was in the main waiting room at Union Station when I arrived at a quarter to eight. With him stood four men, two of whom I thought I had seen at the ZOC on Spadina Avenue. He waved me over and introduced me to them. One was from Toronto – an Al Stitz – the other three were from Montreal.

Two of the volunteers from Montreal I subsequently got to know and love like brothers: Lenny Waldman and Meyer Naturman. The third man, with whom we all somehow managed to lose touch after the War of Liberation ended, was called Jack Kopstein.

To my surprise, Amitai said that it was probably safe enough for us to travel together, but that it would be wise for two of us to go to the dining car alone just before Niagara Falls. Once we had passed American immigration, it would be quite safe to 'stop playing Beau Geste'.

Then the gate to our platform was opened.

Amitai said 'Shalom, mazal tov!' and off we went.

The train ride proved most uneventful, the U.S. border inspection an anticlimax. When we reached Grand Central Station, our contact was waiting for us exactly where he was supposed to be. He recognized us even before any of us attempted to use Amitai's password, and whisked us off in a Nash station wagon, which was parked outside the station with a sign that read 'ON DELIVERY' stuck in the windshield.

Our destination was the Hechalutz Hatzair youth movement house in Brooklyn. We were taken to two rooms that had been prepared for us, then given a plain but filling meal and asked if we would like to clean up before going to Manhattan.

In lower Manhattan we were taken to an Army Surplus warehouse, where we were each fitted out with a pair of brand new U.S. Army boots of brushed brown leather, with attached gaiters; two pairs of heavy-duty, khaki cotton pants; plus two shirts, some heavy socks and a zippered carry-on bag. Someone asked if any of us needed underwear, but as far as I can remember no one took him up on that.

Then our 'driver' asked whether we had any American money. Most of us hadn't changed any funds; I hadn't even thought about that.

'You'd better. They much prefer U.S. dollars both in France and in the Middle East; they don't really know the Canadian dollar. Our exchange rate will be much better than at any local bank. In any case, your Canadian dollar is worth slightly more than the American dollar, today. Which'll make you feel like you've got a lot more dough!'

We sailed the next morning. I shared a small cabin with Lenny Waldman – deep in the ship's bowels. He knew quite a bit more than I did about Israeli life. His family had been active in the Zionist scene of Montreal, and over the course of our cruise he introduced me to the vocabulary I would soon encounter on a daily basis.

I had no real understanding of what a kibbutz was. I had never even heard of a moshav, a farming co-operative. I was surprised to hear that there were no more than 600,000 Jews in Palestine. I had never heard of Mapam or Mapai, the two major labour parties, nor of the Histadruth. Names such as Ben-Gurion, Weizmann and Myerson meant little to me, and familiar names such as Wingate and Robertson now took on new meanings.

When Waldman wasn't patiently imparting to me his knowledge of Israeli life, we were eating (I kept conjuring up 'My last meal!' – just about all of us were pessimistic when weighing the odds) or playing poker.

The several non-stop poker games set up in the lounge on the first evening at sea were the only shipboard entertainment. The second evening I decided to ask to sit in on the one which seemed most financially conservative. I figured that my training at my mother's Hove poker club – *Do not lose more than two pounds! Do not win more than one pound!* – should stand me in good stead.

The players all looked like kind, grandfatherly gentlemen. One of them asked me why I would want to play with *alte kackers* like them. I replied that their game had the lowest stakes, and I figured I wouldn't get burnt too much.

After playing for an hour, during which time I was careful not to win more than a couple of pots, I realized that they really were kind gentlemen, though none of them could play poker too well. I also found out that they were all Jewish, and going to Paris on a fall-fashion buying trip.

During a break in the action, one of the players mentioned a rumour going around the ship, that a group of Haganah soldiers was on board. Had I heard anything about that?

I replied that I hadn't heard a thing, but would be surprised if there was anything to the scuttlebutt.

The poker players exchanged sly glances, laughed and said, 'Of course not.'

Over the next three days, I had astounding luck at the poker table. After Lenny and I finished packing on the night before disembarking, I checked my bankroll and found that I was $150 richer than I'd been when I embarked, in spite of bar bills, cigarettes and poker. I must have won close to $200! (Or perhaps, I thought, the *shmatte* industry had subtly contributed $200 to a worthy cause.)

On our arrival in France, things went as smoothly as they had in the U.S. The French customs and immigration officer accepted my story at face value – in fact, he seemed bored by my letter from the Sorbonne – and ushered me out with an impatient wave of his hand.

By the time I found my suitcase on the wharf, a group of about eight young men was gathered around two French-looking gentlemen. The group included Al Stitz, Lenny Waldman and the other two Montrealers. They waved me over and we all piled into three taxis, which took us to the nearby railway station.

In Paris, we were driven directly from the station to the famous Moishe's Restaurant. We were treated to a sumptuous feast, and encouraged to take seconds of everything. We were each given a carton of cigarettes of our choosing (Camels or Gauloises). Then one of our hosts told us the next part of our journey would be to Marseilles. And that it was time, apparently, to catch our train.

★ ★ ★

The Haganah camp was situated on the outskirts of Marseilles. It was called Grandes Arènes.

It should have been called Gritty Alcatraz.

Grandes Arènes – or Grand Arenas, as we all called it – consisted of two sectors, divided by a tall fence. The whole stockade was enclosed by eight-foot-high concrete walls, with lethal-looking shards of glass embedded in the tops of them.

The place was an all but forgotten DP camp, one of many put up after World War II all over Western Europe. Our side consisted of four or five barracks, a large dining hall and a rather ramshackle house used as an administration building and as a billet for the Israeli *madrichim* (counsellors, agents, or scrutinizers, as you like) who ran the place.

The other side of the fence contained a similar number of barracks. As we soon learned, these still housed a mix of liberated concentration-camp inmates – not only Jews, but also White Russians, Ukrainians and Gypsies – who were now being looked after by the Haganah, whether for humanitarian reasons, or just to provide a credible cover for an underground passage to Israel; the fact remains, the Haganah was caring for these people, when no one else seemed to give a damn.

The barracks were sparse accommodations at best. The building we were put in had been whitewashed – obviously quite recently – and boasted some twenty army cots with a thin, rolled-up mattress placed at the head of each one. Beside each bed, built into the wall, was a box-like structure made of concrete, about two feet square and two feet deep. The front of the box was left open, and there were two shelves built in. Someone had thoughtfully provided a long wooden table, as well, decorated with vulgar multi-lingual and multi-orientational carvings, along with four dilapidated, but thankfully undecorated, chairs. And that was the extent of our furniture.

'You all have suitcases with locks in which to keep your personal belongings,' we were told. 'In any case, you won't be in Grand Arenas long!'

The first two days passed without incident. In fact, they passed without anything being told to us, or done for us, or done to us. Though we were fed – something that barely passed for food. The madrichim kept as far away from us as possible. Our barrack was just about fully occupied; my travelling companions and I brought the Canadian contingent up to eight. We were all very young; the oldest, Lenny Waldman, was at most twenty-six. My passport gave my age as twenty-one, but I had just celebrated my twentieth birthday.

Amongst the other eight occupants of the barrack were a pukka British army officer type, whose name we never did discover, accompanied by an English springer spaniel; and a young Cockney hairdresser by the name of Viddie Sassoon, who was there with his cousin Manny, an accountant.

Add to these three South Africans, only one of whom – a Zvi Green – was prepared to fraternize; an Irish mercenary by the name of Sean, who was 'cairtain he'd be moerdered boy the Wogs before the Jews would have a charnce to paigh him, God bless them!'; and a tough little man by the name of Robert Klaper, an ex-marine commando, whose ethnology was a mystery.

The three 'old' Canadians – they had been in Marseilles for almost a week – were all Westerners: Jack Katz, Max Robinson and Joe Steinberg.

On the third day, our barrack was finally assembled, and welcomed by the commandant of Grand Arenas. His name was Shmuel and he was a university student from Palestine, who had been studying political science in Paris. The Haganah had conscripted him earlier that year and commissioned him to take over Grand Arenas from the more than willing local French authorities. He was accompanied by the other madrichim. One of them was a doctor. Two of them had been conscripted like the commandant, and like him were ill at ease in regard to their duties, given their admitted lack of expertise. There was only one Israeli with any knowledge of weaponry or explosives. He was a member of the Irgun, whose presence in a Haganah camp was never explained. It was obvious that the other four were a bit uncomfortable in his presence.

The commandant explained that we would be shipped out as expeditiously as possible. When asked what he meant by 'expeditious', he replied that he could not predict. He admitted that the Royal Navy was causing havoc with the Haganah's attempts at running its blockade. Just about every ship was intercepted, and the human cargo interned on Cyprus – under conditions, unfortunately, that could only remind them of Nazi concentration camps.

Only those volunteers with priority qualifications, such as navigators and pilots, could be flown to Israel for the time being.

Coming back to the subject of Grand Arenas, he had some bits of information for us; also, there were a few 'touchy points' he wanted to discuss.

Point 1: the Arabs were also using Marseilles as an embarkation port, and their camp was within half a kilometre of our own. Both sides had guaranteed the local authorities that there would be no martial activities or violent incidents – this in return for the laissez-faire attitude of the Marseilles gendarmerie. Still, he cautioned us to be on the alert outside of our camp, and reminded us that the sympathies of the Zouave regiment, stationed in town, naturally lay with their Moslem kinfolk. He added that there had already been two incidents resulting in knife wounds. Luckily, the police were not involved in either, as the fights had gone unreported.

Point 2: he had been informed that the distribution of funds was running behind schedule and that he would have to cut back on rations. (There had already been some audible moaning on the part of certain volunteers concerning the mess hall, in matters of both quantity and edibility.) Because of that, he wanted to sound out our feelings on the Haganah's lifting the 'out of bounds' restrictions on going into town. Only, of course, as far as the *machal* (overseas volunteers) group was concerned. That way we could supplement our reduced rations as we liked or were able, without the appearance of any inequity of food-distribution among the residents of the camp. Not surprisingly, this proposal was unanimously endorsed.

Point 3: there were now some twenty to twenty-five raw recruits from North Africa and Europe in the other barracks. It was feared that they were beginning to feel the confinement and inactivity, and thought that the situation might be alleviated if they could receive some elementary military training. (Even if the 'training' was not all that productive, as such, it might at least make them feel that they were learning something, and not again sitting in a concentration camp.)

Which brought him to his questions: was there anyone among us who would be prepared to become a madrich? He would have to be able to speak a bit of French. What would be really helpful was some knowledge of Czech, German or Russian, as well. Failing that, Yiddish would probably do. Also: could we plan a simple training program to take place both within the camp and in the hills around?

He explained that he was asking us because word had gotten around that some of us were professional mercenaries; he believed that both the North Africans and the Europeans would be eager to be trained by us. And the Israeli contingent was far too busy with the day-to-day affairs of the camp to provide the training themselves. And the inactivity was frankly turning into belligerence, especially with the North African contingent.

We all immediately looked toward the 'pukka officer type' with the springer spaniel. He looked back at us with alarm and disdain, and snorted at Shmuel, 'Don't be ridiculous. I certainly did not volunteer for that sort of nonsense! The very idea! Either you fly me and Lady to Israel within two days, or we are going straight back home!'

At this point, Lenny Waldman kindly volunteered my services, and before I could gather my wits and also threaten to go home, the meeting broke up.

Shmuel thanked me for helping out. He added that I could start in a day or so, and thought I might like to come to their quarters after supper that evening and listen to the broadcast from the UN, where they were voting on the establishment of the State of Israel.

I hadn't realized that this was the 15th of May.

* * *

The news of the establishment of the State of Israel had been posted in the mess hall by the time we trooped in for breakfast the next day. This explained all the yelling and rejoicing that had been going on in the camp since early morning.

At breakfast, a young lad – from College and Spadina, by the sound of his accent – asked to sit down at our table. He explained that he had arrived with a group well ahead of ours; all the others in his group had been shipped out ten days prior to our arrival. For some reason, only he was left. Would we mind if he moved into our hut?

He seemed very young – he could not have been more than eighteen – and very lonely: vulnerable, in spite of his six-foot-four frame. He had probably never before been away from home.

Kopstein asked him if he had any Canadian or American money left, to which he replied in the affirmative. 'Then, sure, move your stuff over, and stick close by.'

Fifty plus years later, I *believe* the youngster's name was Abe, but I can't swear to it. I do, however, remember that we nicknamed him 'Li'l Abner' because of his height, and also because of a short ditty he composed, which he soon had all the Anglos in Grand Arenas singing – to the annoyance of the Israelis, and the amusement of everybody else:

> If your name is Abie,
> Join the Jewish Navy!
> Fight, fight, fight for Israel!

Oh you sons of Moses,
With your Jewish noses!
Fight, fight, fight for Israel!

That morning, the machal group decided that from then on we would eat only a European-style breakfast and a very light lunch in camp, and eat suppers in town. This would help, slightly, to alleviate the problem of the meagre rations, and would also bring much-needed relief to our digestive systems.

And while we were on the subject of food, Max Robinson suggested that we take it easy with the camp coffee, since he suspected that the MO was likely in charge of the mixture, in order to keep the inmates' enthusiasm to a nice minimum.

Obviously, we couldn't invade Marseilles en masse without attracting a bit too much attention. It was therefore agreed that we would split into two or three groups. Klaper asked if he could join the Canucks off campus; the Brits and Afrikaners formed another contingent, with our Irish mercenary. The springer spaniel and her master labelled the whole business futile machinations since, in any case, they would be leaving in two days' time.

I spent the rest of the morning exploring the rocky hills beyond the camp's perimeter. The Irgun madrich offered to show me around, and pointed out areas which would lend themselves well to training. In the afternoon, Shmuel came to fetch me, saying that he wanted to show me the 'other side' of Grand Arenas.

The 'other side' was distressing. Men and women were housed separately. There were no children. Complete silence hung over the whole enclave. People shuffled rather than walked, and smiled wanly at Shmuel as they passed wordlessly by.

'Once upon a time they used to ask me of any news. But by now they don't bother. Some of them have been here since 1946. They think that the world has forgotten them. I do, too. Heaven knows what will happen to them once we leave.'

'Aren't you going to take them to Israel?'

'The few Jews that are still left here, of course. But lots of the people here are Gentiles, who have gotten lost in Hitler's madness. We can't take them – that's not our job. The way things are going, I don't know how much longer we'll be able to feed them, never mind take them to Israel. The UNICEF shipments ceased some time ago. I have no idea why. Hopefully by mistake. Though I doubt it!'

I returned to my barrack feeling depressed, and guilty about my carping regarding the conditions that we, all volunteers, were being forced to endure. The idea of eating out now seemed self-indulgent. But I still wanted to go.

That evening we split into two groups, one of four and one of five, Al Stitz having decided at the last minute not to go. We showered, dressed in our most civilian-like clothes and departed. My group included Waldman, Naturman, Robinson and Klaper. My friend from the Irgun had given me the name and address of a good restaurant, and had told me that a full meal would not cost more than four or five dollars, including wine and tip. For some reason, I was appointed secretary-treasurer for the evening. Each partner gave me ten dollars' worth of francs, and we agreed to settle any discrepancies on our return.

The meal was delicious. So good, in fact, that we added course after course, drank two huge carafes of the house wine and finished the feast off with a double brandy. I dreaded to look at the bill when the maître d' finally brought it.

To my surprise, the whole affair only came to the equivalent of twenty dollars. I was sure that the restaurant had made a mistake and undercharged us. But when the maître d' came to collect the bill, he gave me back the tip I had included, saying, 'Merci, mais non. Moi-même, je suis juif, aussi.'

'How the heck did he know we were Jewish?' asked Naturman – who could well have been the inspiration for the second verse of Li'l Abner's ditty – once we were outside on the street.

We decided to look around Marseilles for a while, seeing that we still had pocket money. Admittedly, the town did not resemble the one in *Beau Geste*; the only thing Hollywood had gotten right was the fact that the French Foreign Legion still made its headquarters here. But the town did still have something of the character of Arles in some of Van Gogh's paintings, especially where its bars and billiard parlours were concerned: a rough and colourful place, which breathed more the Middle East than the south of France.

Still, I can't say that, at the time, I wished I had brought my sketchbook along. That part of my life was already beginning to feel as though it belonged to a different era.

After stopping off at a couple of bars, we decided it was time to make our way back to camp. The only problem was the total absence of taxis; and we certainly didn't want to have to ask someone which streetcar went to the Haganah camp. Klaper said that this did not present any problem, since he knew exactly how to get to Grand Arenas. He assured us it wasn't more than a fifteen-minute walk.

After about twenty minutes, we began complaining that this was becoming a route-march. All except Klaper, who said that we would probably have been home by now, had it not been for our drunken dawdling. At that exact moment we spotted a small amusement park on the other side of the road.

You couldn't truly call it an amusement park. Rather, it was a collection of about twelve booths, most of them offering games of chance, two of them offering games of skill: a shooting gallery, which guaranteed cuddly pink and blue bears as prizes; and a game in which you threw three tennis balls at a pyramid of ten tin cups and had to knock over all the cups to win a plaster-of-Paris figurine of a hula dancer.

We decided that the shooting gallery was most definitely our speed. After all, we weren't going to throw tennis balls at the Arabs.

Winning entailed shooting an air rifle loaded with half-inch darts to which tiny flight-feathers were attached. Fifty sous bought you ten shots, and five bull's-eyes got you a very small bear. Ten bull's-eyes got you a giant bear, and there were four gradations of bear-size between.

You won nothing but ridicule with four bull's-eyes or less.

Max Robinson went first, and came away with just one tiny pink bear after shooting three rounds of ten shots each. I followed, and chose the same rifle Robinson had used. I knew exactly what that air rifle would do, having scrutinized Max's souvenir-target. The rifle shot low and left. One giant bear was as good as mine.

I swung the rifle up to my shoulder and squeezed off ten rounds of rapid fire. I put the empty rifle down on the counter. 'There you go. That wasn't hard. Somebody please ask the carny to bring back my target while I go and pick out my teddy-bear.'

I found the very bear I wanted. He was the second from the right on the back wall: impressively big, and the only one with purple fur and smiling face. Then the carny brought back an unblemished target. How he managed to switch cards with the five of us watching, I will never know.

The group asked whether I wanted to win another bear, but since it was getting late, I thought it best that we get going.

As it turned out, Grand Arenas was less than five minutes away – though we had somehow managed to reach it via the back gate.

* * *

The nightly trips of the machal contingent to the eateries of Marseilles continued quite happily. But we had now been in Grand Arenas for the better part of three weeks, and the deplorable conditions of the camp were getting to us. Frankly, we were about ready to rebel, and the Israelis knew it. We had said farewell to a small but steady stream of people who either held commissions (the English twerp and his dog) or were destined for the Air Force (Zvi Green and Vidal Sassoon). Both Robinson and Steinberg were gone. Robert Klaper had also left – like the others, quietly in the middle of the night.

On top of the unpredictability of life in Grand Arenas, there was the fact that every English-language newspaper painted the gloomiest picture of Israel's chances of surviving: Egypt, Transjordan, Iraq, and Syria had mobilized, and were far superior in both equipment and manpower; Egypt had already made serious advances in the south, and had come within twenty or so miles of Jaffa; Transjordan's Arab Legion, commanded by Glubb Pasha, had not only crossed the Jordan River, but taken the Old City of Jerusalem, and come as far as Latrun on the east. All this made worse by reports of atrocities, and of an Arab 'no prisoners' policy.

Still, most of us seconded Li'l Abner: 'If I've got to eat my last meal, can I at least have it in Israel rather than Marseilles!'

Then, one afternoon, Waldman came back to the barracks and told me that most of the remaining Canadians were shipping out the next day. I knew nothing of this, and an alarm went off in my head.

'How come I haven't yet been told? Am I going?'

'I really don't know,' he answered. 'You'll have to ask Shmuel. He wants to see you in any case. He said he had something to discuss with you. Maybe that will clear things up. But I wanted to let you know that some of us are going into town for a last bash and we can't do so without our treasurer. Don't let the Sabreh momsers keep you too long. We want to get to town no later than seven.'

The meeting with Shmuel was brief but unpleasant. It seemed

that I was staying. One of the Sabrehs had been recalled to Israel. (No explanation, why.) That left them short one madrich. Which meant that I had been elected.

My protestations fell on deaf ears. They had a war to win, and since I was in the Haganah I would do my part wherever Shmuel thought best. I would immediately move my gear into the administration building, where I could have the departing madrich's room.

Shmuel dismissed any further discussion of the matter by saying that he and the other Sabrehs weren't any happier than I was that I would be hanging around. So he would do his utmost to ensure that my departure was given top priority. 'For the sake of my own sanity,' he said.

After the dinner, a taxi dropped us off at Grand Arenas. We walked toward the barracks, Waldman and I lagging behind.

'I'm sorry you're not coming with us,' he said. 'I'm sure I'll see you in Israel before you know it. Take care and good luck.'

The next morning, they were gone.

* * *

And three days later, the roof fell in. An eight-year-old boy at the Jewish orphanage was found murdered in the hills behind the camp. He had been sexually assaulted and horribly mutilated.

Naturally, we suspected it was someone from the Arab camp. As did the Marseilles detectives. The deputy chief of police, one of our few local sympathizers, kept Shmuel informed daily. But after four days they were no closer to finding the killer than the day the boy had been found.

Then, on the fifth day, whilst we were doing some sort of drill, the MO came and asked me to right away come with him for a meeting with Shmuel.

Assembled for the meeting were Shmuel, the camp commandant, the other Israelis, and Nissim, my 'assistant madrich' from Casablanca. As soon as I saw their gloomy faces, a bad feeling came over me.

Shmuel motioned the doctor and me to sit down, and said: 'We know who raped and killed the orphan. Nissim came to tell me a few minutes ago. Unfortunately, it is one of Frank's men. The North Africans suspected him, because of his odd behaviour. They think it likely that he volunteered because he had to leave Casablanca, not because he was a Zionist.'

'Why the hell didn't they tell somebody?'

'They wanted to make sure. Frankly, they don't really trust us Ashkenazis. Anyhow, they persuaded him to confess early this morning, and they've got him locked in the infirmary. I haven't seen him yet, but I understand that they didn't really need to lock him up – he's in no condition to go anywhere. But I've got to inform the deputy chief of police. I wanted to tell all of you first. I imagine we'll have flics all over Grand Arenas. I don't expect it to be pleasant. That's all.'

The Marseilles authorities wanted nothing to do with the affair. They made only one condition: get the murderer out of Marseilles – dead or alive, they didn't care – within twenty-four hours, or they would shut down the Haganah operation in Grand Arenas immediately.

That evening, Shmuel convened a trial in typical Haganah style: a wooden judge's table, bare but for a prayer book with a revolver on it. The trial lasted less than fifteen minutes. The prisoner pleaded guilty, the verdict was death. The sentence was to be carried out in Israel. The three North African witnesses nodded approval.

After the trial, Shmuel pulled me aside. He told me that I was leaving that night with my prisoner. A Haganah plane would be arriving from the Trieste area (a second Haganah camp was there) around two in the morning. We were to be met by our own military police on landing in Israel. That would be the end of my involvement in the matter. I would be taken to a place called Teletvinsky, which was the Haganah induction centre. He thanked me for my help at Grand Arenas.

Then, to my surprise, he gave me a big hug. 'All the best, *chaver*. Shalom!'

A street scene in Jerusalem, 1948.

Dizengoff Street, the main thoroughfare in Tel Aviv, 1948.

7. RAOUL

I arrived at Sarafand in June of 1948, exactly one week after reaching Israel, and officially became an officer of the Yechidat Siur Agaf Modiin, which roughly translates as 'the reconnaissance section of army intelligence service'. Not that being an officer in this unit really meant too much, since, as far as I could gather, there were only officers in the unit. Rodrigues, the French officer who had interviewed me at Teletvinsky, turned out to be the CO, and also the only one who appeared to know what this top-secret unit was all about. Certainly I had no idea, and neither, it seemed, did the other sixteen members. Nor was our CO inclined to tell us anything at that time.

Sarafand was a former British Army camp located some twenty minutes from Tel Aviv, consisting of forty to fifty Nissen huts, an HQ building and two mess halls, plus a number of administrative and auxiliary buildings, and one rather grand movie house. (Later, I found out that my father had been the Free Czech Army sergeant in charge of this cinema during World War II.)

It was a great sprawling place, which the local British area-commander had turned over to the Arab Legion just before the end of the British Mandate, preceding the declaration of the State of Israel in May. Sarafand commanded a strategic position, with Latrun to the southeast, and Rehovot on down to the south. As soon as hostilities officially began, the base was attacked and partially surrounded by what was later reported in the foreign press to be an overwhelming force of Palmach commandos. After a fierce bombardment, the Arab Legion CO had taken advantage of an escape route that the Israelis had 'inadvertently' left open and, in the face of the 'overwhelming forces' arrayed against the defenders, had managed to evacuate Sarafand with minimal losses to his troops. The story I learned on arrival was quite different: the Palmach had mustered a force of just eighty seasoned commandos, a few three-inch mortars, and a large number of noise makers. The escape route was purposely left open.

The hut where I was billeted already had two residents: a Belgian by the name of Yitzhak Mohrer, and a young American called Yossie who, like the rest of us, didn't know a word of Hebrew; he claimed to be a lapsed Southern Baptist. Neither of them knew exactly what the unit was all about, but they both had military pasts more interesting than mine.

Mohrer had been a British Navy Intelligence officer during the war, and was some sort of codes-and-ciphers expert. Though Belgian, he looked like a Grenadier Guard officer and spoke rather upper-class English, without a trace of an accent. Before the war, he had been an agronomist. Yossie, who never did tell us his real name (though we called him Yoskeh), had been a U.S. Ranger in the Japanese theatre of war for only a few months in the late part of World War II – but in that short time he had managed to collect two Purple Hearts and one Distinguished Service Medal. He insisted that he was a just a professional mercenary (albeit unpaid): '… a goy who feels much more at ease with your Arab cousins than with you Jews.' But in fact he was more of a staunch Zionist than either Yitzhak or I.

Yossie already had his posting; he was going to join a Druze unit, which was intended to operate behind enemy lines in the northern theatre, from the Galilee to the Golan, and specifically to harass el Kaukji's brigade.

Neither Mohrer nor I had any idea of why we'd been picked, or of where we'd be posted. But at least we were both members of the Chosen People – which probably wasn't much to crow about, considering the troops gathered against us!

The second-in-command of Yechidat Siur Agam was an American, like Yossie – but unlike Yossie he was very Jewish. His name was Aaron; he hailed from Brooklyn and sported a maroon velvet yarmulke. He had apparently been a member of the OSS, and was the personification of the rough and tough professional. The Israelis were in absolute awe of him, and he told us in no uncertain terms that he wasn't going to take crap from anybody, least of all us!

Let me tell you about one other member of our happy little group.

This was a Basque by the name of Raoul, who was reputed to have been brought along – unfortunately not on a leash – by our commanding officer. Raoul stood over six feet of vindictiveness and mean temper tall. Added to his charming personality was the fact that he had been an assassin in the Spanish Civil War – and he seemed to sympathize more with the anti-Semitic aims of the Spanish Inquisition than with the aspirations of the Haganah. Each encounter with him turned into a confrontation, in which Raoul would issue threats of physical harm and sneers of derision, coupled with imputations of military and sexual shortcomings on all our parts. Just spying him coming towards us made Yitzhak and me wheel about and go off in another direction.

By and large, the members of our unit kept to themselves; as I got to know the rest, however, it became apparent that each one had some particular lethal skill. It seemed our unit was to serve as a sort of repository of expertise: we were each to be made available to different units, as and when we were needed.

The first week was spent in briefings, the drawing of equipment, a series of minor military tests – weapons checks, unarmed combat and so forth – and the issuing of uniforms. (Well, really the only bit of standard uniform was a French Foreign Legion–style hat, but made of soft khaki and with a fold-back neckcloth; for the rest, the clothes and army boots I had gotten in New York were deemed more than good enough. No need to waste Haganah's budget!)

We were each issued a Thompson submachine gun – at that time, an unheard-of luxury in the Haganah – which proved to be a bit of a dilemma for me. I had mentioned to Rodrigues, during our interview, that I had spent some time on the weapon-training staff of No. 6 Commando. The problem was that I had never handled, let alone stripped, a Tommy gun.

In No. 6 Commando, our automatic weapons were all nine-millimetre, which was the standard German Army ammunition size. Even though No. 6 Commando never did work behind enemy lines – and therefore could have easily obtained .45 ammo throughout the war – we all were issued Sten guns, and most officers carried liberated Lugers or Schmeissers, rather than British Army issue. (The official rationale for this was that, if need be, we could scavenge German ammo and it would fit our weapons; the unofficial rationale was that certain German weapons were far superior to ours.) I decided to quietly figure out the Tommy gun in private, rather than let Rodrigues and company know that their 'weapons expert' was less than they had hoped for.

Unfortunately, that gun would play a horrible part in coming events.

I had brought three personal items with me to Israel. They were items I felt would be of great strategic value to me in my role as a heroic machalnik: one, my green beret, which would let any hostile know that I meant business; two, my paisley silk scarf, which I had never dared wear in No. 6 Commando, but which was similar to the ones sported by Major Price and the Lieutenant-Leppard brothers, whose sartorial improvements to army uniform I had always envied; and three, my Commando knife, which I had never handed back in.

On the third day after I arrived at Sarafand, we were taken to the local firing range, where Aaron asked to be shown our small-arms skills. He produced a Ross rifle that looked as though it dated from World War I and, calling me forward, thrust an ammo clip into my less than eager hand. Here was yet another weapon I had never seen before. Still, I managed to load the clip, and fired off one round at the target. The butts signalled that I had gotten an inner, but was not in the bull's-eye. 'Just shoot off the whole damn clip,' Aaron sighed, 'and let's see if it's the rifle or you.'

Well, I pulled the trigger, and nothing happened. I tried this a few more times. Then Aaron came over and whispered, 'Try cocking the fucking thing! What sort of rifle did you use in the last war?'

'Something called an M1. You may not know it, but it reloads automatically. I believe it was made in the U.S. It was standard issue for Nos. 6 and 10 Commandos.' This I 'whispered' back, at the top of my lungs. Then I pulled back the bolt, shot after shot, and angrily fired off the whole clip – every round, by sheer luck, smack in the bull's-eye.

With that I hoped the day's trauma was over and done with, but I hadn't counted on Raoul. He was next, and grabbed the Ross rifle. But instead of pointing it at the target he suddenly pointed it at me and demanded to have my paisley ascot.

I told him that I couldn't let him have the ascot since my mother had given it to me as a going-away gift.

His demeanour changed in a flash. He threw his arms around my neck and with crocodile tears in his eyes told me that he would never take *anything* which my sainted mother had given me – not *even* something as beautiful as my ascot. At which witticism Raoul and the whole company roared with laughter.

And then, for once, I had an inspiration. Taking my not-as-yet-used-for-killing killing knife, I cut the paisley scarf in half along its length and gave one half to Raoul, saying that I thought my mother would have wanted him to have it. (In truth, I had bought the scarf at Marks and Spencer for five bob; I doubt my mother would even have remembered it.)

Raoul threw his arms around me once again and, with real tears this time, kissed me on both cheeks. He solemnly put on his half of 'our' paisley scarf. Then, turning to the assemblage of our fellow military specialists, he pointed to me. Looking straight at Aaron, he proclaimed that I was his only true and treasured friend, and that nothing had better happen to me, since the perpetrator of insult or injury to me would be harming not just 'Franco, el canadiense', but Raoul Mano also!

The following Sunday, Yossie, Yitzhak and I were called to Aaron's office and told that he was going into Tel Aviv that afternoon, and that he would give us passes if we wanted to drive into town with him. Furthermore, he knew some charming young ladies, and would be happy to arrange a 'farewell dinner' for eight.

Back in our barracks, we decided that Aaron's invitation must be a hint either that the three of us were being sent off on a mission – secret and important, of course – or that we had flunked out of Yechidat Siur Agam.

At six o'clock on the dot, we set off in Aaron's personnel utility vehicle, the three of us sitting in the back, where Aaron had put two benches. We picked up four very real ladies, who had memorable figures, but not very memorable names. Three of them jumped into the back with us and divided Yitzhak, Yossie and me between them.

Aaron drove us to the Gat Rimon Hotel – which was, in 1948, the ritziest hotel in Tel Aviv. We had a splendid meal, complete with appetizer, main course, dessert, wine and brandy. Dinner was served by two waiters – in tails yet. The place was filled with very wealthy and very American-looking guests.

Our four new friends seemed as ill at ease as we were in the luxurious surroundings. It turned out they were all members of a southern kibbutz named Tzilim. They were on leave from the Givati Brigade, one of three crack Palmach brigades that had forced back advancing Egyptian and Arab Legion troops, when these had gotten within twenty miles of Tel Aviv, before the current ceasefire.

Sitting at the next table was a robust and important-looking man in an almost Savile Row uniform, who seemed to be more interested in our conversation than in what was going on at his own table. As we were having coffee, he strolled over and said that he couldn't help but overhear us speaking English, and wondered where we were from. Aaron introduced each of us by country and name, then asked the Savile Row uniform who he was.

'I'm from Toronto, Canada,' he said, 'and my name is Ben Dunkelman. I've put together a brigade of machal – well, mostly American and Canadian – volunteers. And I am still looking for a number of NCOs and officers. What unit are you fellows with, may I ask?'

At that time, except for the military police – called Mem Tzadikim, an acronym for Mishtarah Tzvait – whose members all looked more British than the British, nobody here wore any insignia; ranks hadn't been given out yet, and you simply took people's word as to their standing.

Aaron replied that we were with a newly formed unit, and that unfortunately – since none us of spoke Hebrew – we didn't rightly know its name. (Though Aaron had managed very well earlier, with our four ladies, in something that sounded very much like Hebrew to me.)

'From your conversation I could tell that you have all seen military service. The 7th Brigade is still short a few officers, as I said, and I feel sure that you chaps would really fit in. Also, we probably have the best ordnance and uniforms in the Haganah. Think about it, and if you decide to join my brigade contact the town-major. He'll know all about it, and will look after the transfers without any problems, and arrange transportation for you chaps the same day.' He smiled.

Aaron thanked Dunkelman profusely and walked him back to his table, promising to seriously think about his kind offer. He then returned, bearing gifts of fine Cuban cigars – further incentives – for each of us.

What I didn't know until later was that Dunkelman – a wealthy Torontonian, whose family owned Tip Top Tailors – was justly famous. He was a dedicated Zionist, and had had an illustrious military career. He was a former major in the Canadian Army who had received numerous medals, including the DSO, for extraordinary bravery during World War II. In Israel, he had already distinguished himself in planning and overseeing the construction of the Burma Road; he had also been second in command to Yitzhak Rabin of Har El, or the 10th Brigade, and ops officer for Jerusalem in the early days of the siege. Later in the War of Liberation he would oversee the capture of Nazareth, without any damage to either Christian or Moslem holy sites; but his brigade would suffer grievous losses during the recapture of Latrun.

That night at the Gat Rimon, however, I was thinking mostly about the cost of the evening, and getting more anxious by the minute. I still had about $80 left, but I really didn't want to spend it all on the damn dinner.

(I should tell you that Israeli army pay in those early days was all of two *lirot* a month, though there was talk of a living allowance for overseas volunteers; this was supposed to be brought into effect in a month or so.)

You can imagine my relief – as well as Yitzhak's and Yoskeh's – when Aaron announced that dinner was on the unit. At that, Yitzhak leaned over and whispered to me, 'God, we are being posted and we're all going to be killed. Only this time the condemned men aren't just getting a last meal, but a last lay also!'

We piled back into the pickup, and Aaron announced that one of our dates had invited us to her parents' home for a farewell nightcap. Our new hostess giggled that her parents just happened to be abroad. The car had barely taken off when my date took my hand and placed it on her left breast, kissed me and whispered – in unison with her two friends, who appeared to be mouthing a similar script to Yoskeh and Yitzhak – 'Can you feel my heart?'

She then put her hand on my pants, precisely where my 'private' part was growing rather public. It took but a few minutes of this before I felt I was losing control, and pulled her hand away in a vain attempt at decorum. But too late! The damage was done, and I could feel it spreading. What to do?

I had to get away, or besmirch the reputation of the Yechidat Siur Agam – and become the laughing stock of Sarafand!

'Stop the car,' I yelled. 'I have to get back to base!'

I explained that I had suddenly realized I had left my Tommy gun on my bed, and that I had to get back before it was stolen – if it hadn't been stolen already. Yossie – the idiot – argued that he had checked our barracks and hadn't seen anything lying around. Yitzhak, who was easily the smartest of us, said that it would be better for me to go rather than spoil the evening with my worry.

I jumped out of the pickup, my French Foreign Legion cap acting as sporran.

Then, with head hung low, I made my way to the main Egged station. By eleven-thirty I was back in Sarafand.

On reaching Sarafand, I heard gunfire in the distance. The sentries all had weapons at the ready; they barely glanced at my papers, and jabbered away in Hebrew, pointing toward our compound. I said 'ken, ken' (yes, yes), which was about the only Hebrew I could remember, and hurried toward the area of our hut, the sentries yelling 'loh, loh' (no, no) after me.

I was in no mood for an argument, nor for a lesson in Hebrew, and so decided to ignore them. But the closer I came to the hut, the louder was the sound of gunfire, and it began to sound very much like automatic gunfire.

At that moment the awful thought struck me that perhaps I was being punished for my lie, and that it was my Tommy gun I was hearing. But what was it firing at?

I raced to the hut, tore into our room, unlocked my locker and breathed a sigh of relief. My submachine gun was exactly where I had stowed it. But then I realized that Yossie's locker had been forced open, and that there was no sign of his weapon.

Just then Rodrigues came racing into the room. 'Thank heavens you're back. Raoul has gone quite berserk and is shooting up the place. He's already badly wounded two people, and is yelling that everyone except the Canadian Francisco is trying to kill him.'

'What the hell am I supposed to do?' I asked. 'It isn't my Tommy gun!'

'Actually, he has two Tommy guns – one of them from your barracks,' replied the CO. 'But I have decided that you're the only one who can approach him. If you can distract him, I'll disarm him. But at the moment no one can get anywhere near him.'

'We're really not such good friends. I doubt he'll let me get close. He'll probably shoot me just for the heck of it.'

'*Malheureusement*, it's a chance I will have to take.'

'Can't you find someone more qualified to distract him?'

'There is no one better qualified. Nor anyone willing. Now, let's get started before someone else gets hurt.'

Reluctantly, I put on my paisley ascot. I strapped my knife onto the back of my belt, so that it couldn't be seen from the front, and – barely keeping from throwing up the Gat Rimon dinner – walked slowly toward Raoul.

He was standing between the two end huts, a Tommy gun in each hand. As I got closer, I saw that he was sheet-white and had obviously been shot in his left thigh, which was bleeding profusely.

'Who the hell shot you?'

'Mem Tzadikim, before I get gun from your room. But I careful not take your gun. Now they too frighten to come shoot me!'

'You can't stay here, you're bleeding to death. Why don't you come into my barracks and lie down. I promise nothing will happen to you, and I'll get Rodrigues to call the MO at once.' I took a step closer.

Raoul smiled at me, put down one of the Tommy guns, and put his hand to my cheek. Just as he was about to say something a shot rang out.

Raoul crumpled to the ground. He was dead.

Behind him stood Rodrigues, his Luger still smoking.

Then Rodrigues put his fist through the window of the Nissen hut. He said softly, 'Please, put the Tommy guns somewhere safe and report to me in the morning. And get somebody to fix the window. *Merde!*'

Kibbutzim in the Jerusalem Corridor.

8. THE BURMA ROAD

The next morning I went to our headquarters and reported to Rodrigues' office. I was obviously expected, and his clerk told me to go to Aaron's office and wait there.

I had barely sat down when Aaron came in and said, very quietly, 'I heard. It's a bitch. The powers that be have already heard all about last night, and are having second thoughts about the whole fucking unit. They are certain that the CO has put together a group of pathological misfits, or worse, and are threatening to call off all planned operations and disband the unit. Rodrigues has convinced them to go ahead with two operations – one of which happens to be the one we were sending you on – as proof that the Raoul affair was an isolated incident, and the rationale for the Yechidat is still completely valid. The catch is that you have to volunteer for it. I just wanted you to know that, before we go into Rodrigues' office, because he isn't permitted to mention the condition to you.'

Great, I thought. That's really giving me a lot of choice in the matter.

But at least I'd be able to get out of this lunatic asylum, and that morning anything seemed preferable to staying at Sarafand.

Rodrigues greeted me with seemingly genuine solicitousness, and said that he would have given anything to have the previous night's misadventure turn out to be nothing but a bad dream.

Having gotten that out of the way, he proceeded to describe the job they had for me. Apparently I was to go to Jerusalem, report to the *Mikafed*, or commander, of the Jerusalem garrison – a man called Bar-Nun – at his HQ in Machane Schneller, and map out Arab Legion defensive positions around the Jaffa Gate.

He then asked me if I knew anything about street fighting. To which I replied not really. I explained that No. 6 Commando had cleared the Wehrmacht out of Osnabrück, and that I knew the details of that action. But the fighting there was mostly from cellar to cellar, since the Germans had constructed a network of underground passages from one fortification to another. So I guessed it was more like under-street fighting – and with very heavy casualties. Did this count?

He nodded, a bit impatiently.

Then he asked if I knew about enfilade fire emplacements and how such positions were established. I replied that I knew the principle from the *Small Arms Manual* used by the British Army (or rather, not used too much, since every Intelligence Service in the world was known to have a copy).

Rodrigues hoped that Glubb Pasha also had a copy, and was still using it.

I then asked why on earth the Haganah would want to send someone like me to Jerusalem. Surely their local people would be more familiar with the terrain of the place, and know the psychology of the Arab Legion far, far better than any one of us *machalnikim*.

To my surprise, Aaron answered, 'We're pretty sure that these are simply put-up tests to see if our people are really pros, or are just a bunch of impostors. Yours is the easier of the two jobs. Yossie has the real shitty one! The Druze have sent back his two predecessors in body-bags.'

At this point the CO asked me if I had any reservations about the mission and I shook my head, very much against my better judgement. We shook hands, and repaired to Aaron's office to put together all the bits and pieces of the 'mission' (otherwise known as the unit's final exam, my potential unmasking). Not surprisingly, most of the documents were already in a file on Aaron's desk.

'This is your ID for the job. We've made you a *seren* for this one. That's more or less a captain in the Haganah. We're issuing you a sidearm' – it was a Czech revolver called a Narodni Podnik – 'which you will please bring back to me. You are also delivering a jeep to Machane Schneller, which you'll pick up here on Shabbat. Your papers say that you are going to Jerusalem for personal reasons. You'll be briefed by Mikafed BarNun. You're now on leave until Friday evening, but must be back before sundown. You will join a convoy to Jerusalem, which is leaving Sarafand at 600 hours sharp on Saturday. We are going to give you some hotel vouchers, and you're also getting a pay allowance of twelve lirot for the leave. Pick them up from the paymaster after you're packed.'

He paused. 'Look, I'm sure you'll be okay. The Haganah certainly doesn't want any Anglos killed for nothing. That wouldn't be good for fundraising in either Canada or the United States. Now, is there anything you need in the way of equipment?'

'Just a good pair of brothel creepers,' I said. 'My boots are too bloody noisy.'

I packed some clothes for my leave and left the rest of my gear, including a small portfolio of drawings that I had done in Marseilles and Israel, in Yitzhak's care. Then caught the afternoon bus to Tel Aviv.

I found the *malon*, the hotel, to which I'd been directed. It wasn't quite as luxurious as the Gat Rimon; actually it was a dump. But it had an excellent location, not five minutes away from the seafront – it in fact overlooked the wreck of some sort of landing craft. (Later, I found out that the wreck was that of the *Altalena*, an Irgun ship which had tried to run the arms embargo agreed to by Ben Gurion, and put into effect while negotiations during the first ceasefire were under way. The *Altalena* had been blown out of the water by the Haganah shortly before my group had reached Israel, and had become a major *cause célèbre*.)

The hotel, like all but the priciest hotels in the Middle East, had no air conditioning. Every morning both I and all the bedding were covered with a gritty layer of sea-salt/body-sweat. Still, the place was clean, and the sheets were changed almost daily.

On top of that, my host was friendly and informative. And like all Israelis in 1948, he was fascinated and sincerely touched by the coming of the machalnikim from the 'west', completely of their own accord – as opposed to the DP's, who had had little choice in the matter (though this distinction seemed somewhat callous to me).

He and his wife laid out an itinerary that took me beyond the usual Hayarkon and Dizengoff Street tourist haunts, and included a list of restaurants owned by 'honest *vatikim*', old-timers or settlers, who would be more than equitable in their charges.

On hearing that I had been studying stage design, they made a number of phone calls to members of the Tel Aviv theatre and art communities. Unfortunately, I was not able to meet with the local artists, but at least I established contacts which would later stand me in good stead.

Because of the scanty army pay in those early days of the war, service-people had bus privileges and could ride anywhere for free. I decided to take a long bus tour the next morning and sightsee around the city.

I got on at the nearest bus stop and sat down next to an elderly gentleman, who struck up a conversation.

I explained that I could speak neither Yiddish nor Hebrew. This led to a long series of curious yet kindly questions in English, which my new friend spoke remarkably well.

What did I know about Israel? Why had I come to fight in a war so far away from Canada? Did I intend to stay in Israel after the war was won?

I was heartened by the news that we were going to win this war, after all.

By now all other conversations had ceased, and my fellow passengers were not just listening, but joining in with comments and questions of their own. Finally, he asked me if I had any relatives in Israel.

I replied that I wasn't sure, but I thought an Austrian cousin of mine had come over by herself with the last Youth Aliyah allowed out before the Nazi Anschluss. My new friend asked what her name was. 'Israel is a small country,' he said. 'Perhaps I know her.'

'Her name was Irene Steiner, but I really don't know whether it still is, or whether she has changed it to a Hebrew one. I have no idea where she might now be living.'

A young man sitting in the seat ahead of us quickly turned around. 'Her name now is Irene Rohr,' he said, 'and she is living in Jerusalem!' He got up, came over to my seat and gave me a hug. 'I know her quite well, I am married to her. My name is Gideon Rohr. Irenli will never believe this! Of course you have to come to Jerusalem as soon as possible and stay with us. I'm giving a concert here tonight, but I'm planning to go home tomorrow. I can't wait to tell Irenli!'

To say that I was surprised would be an understatement.

This was fast becoming like something from a B movie.

I wanted to tell him that I would be visiting them sooner than he imagined, but thought better of it. I took his address and telephone number and promised that I would be in touch at my first opportunity. By now we had reached my new-found cousin-in-law's stop, and he got off carrying a rather large violin-case.

The whole bus exploded in applause. Passengers came up to me to shake my hand, or slap me on my shoulder. My seat companion told me that my new cousin-in-law was indeed *the* Gideon Rohr. And that he was principal viola with the Israel Philharmonic, as well as a member of the famous Jerusalem String Quartet. And that everybody in Israel knew of him. And that I'd surely heard of him, even in Canada. And wasn't I lucky to have come to Israel. And when did I think I was going to Jerusalem to see my family? And was I aware that the Haganah had something called compassionate leave? And that there was an *afugah*, a ceasefire? And that not even the most important *macher* would dare not let me go now, before the shooting started up again?

I hadn't any idea what a macher was, but decided I'd better get off at the next stop, before things got any more complicated.

By now, I had no idea where I was. My plan was to cross the street and catch a bus going back the way I had come.

On first boarding the bus, however, I had asked the driver to let me off near the Gat Rimon, the only landmark in Tel Aviv I was sure of. Now, the bus came to a stop right outside the front door: a new service, the bus driver explained, reserved just for 'machalnikim', as of that morning.

By coincidence, on the sidewalk outside of the hotel, stood Lenny Waldman, the Montrealer with whom I had travelled all the way from New York to Marseilles, and who had left Grand Arenas a week before I had.

We greeted each other like long-lost brothers, and in unison proposed, 'Let's go in and have a drink.'

We went to the hotel bar, sat down, and ordered a cold beer each. Cold beer was something of which only the Gat Rimon appeared to keep a steady supply. In every place else, the English preference for tepid beer still prevailed.

Waldman was now with a Palmach unit, and had been sent to the Teletvinsky holding camp to pick up some other newly arrived recruits. Because of typical bureaucratic delays he had been given a pass to spend a few hours in Tel Aviv.

I mentioned that I had spent the previous evening with some girls from the Har El Brigade, and that they were members of a kibbutz.

Despite the shipboard primer on Israeli life that Waldman had given me, and a number of orientation sessions at Grand Arenas, I still wasn't sure what a kibbutz was. Art school and the army had provided me with little education about utopian ideologies; the closest I had come to communalism was a school project designing costumes for a mythical stage production of Ninotchka.

'Is a kibbutz something like a kolkhoz?' I asked him.

Apparently not. On the surface, the kibbutz-movements may have sounded totally communist, but Waldman's understanding was that communists weren't really favoured by most kibbutzim. In fact, some kibbutzim refused to admit Communist Party members altogether, because of the party's opposition to Zionism.

As it turned out, most of the members of Waldman's Palmach brigade – including his commanding officer – were kibbutznikim, so he had become something of an expert on the subject.

At this point, who would appear but my good friend Brigadier Dunkelman.

'Back again!' he said. 'I hope you've come to tell me that you want to join the 7th.' And, turning to Lenny: 'Didn't I meet you the other night? Have you also had some previous military experience? Where are you from? Have you been assigned to an outfit yet?'

Lenny responded laconically, 'No. Yes. Montreal. Unfortunately I am already spoken for. But can we offer you a beer?'

Dunkelman declined, wished us a good war, and hurried away.

Turning back to me, Waldman asked where I had been posted. On being told that I was with some peculiar intelligence unit, he told me that he, too, had been interviewed by Monsieur Rodrigues, but had decided not to tell him that he had held a commission in the Canadian army during the Second World War. Instead, he had suggested Rodrigues look out for me, who he thought would fit in rather nicely.

'Thanks a lot! With you as a friend, who needs enemies? Lenny, my vanity has landed me in some shitty situations, but none like the Yechidat Siur Agam, I can tell you. Do me a favour, don't recruit me for anything, anywhere, anytime again. Now, I've still got a couple of days of freedom left, so let's get drunk.'

Which we proceeded to do. The evening looked like it was going to dig a pretty deep hole in my twelve lirot.

Feeling fairly happy after a few drinks, I started to joke about Rodrigues and company, and proclaimed – too audibly – that the only sane member of the unit was a Belgian called Yitzhak.

At this point, a young United Nations officer, who had been sitting at the bar just a couple of stools away from us, said, 'Most of us Belgians are actually not quite sane. Are you sure your friend is Belgian?'

We were wary of United Nations people: we had been told that the UN only invoked a convenient ceasefire when the Arabs were in trouble. So his jocular remark received a rather cool reception from us both. Still, he introduced himself, as a Capitaine de Blocque, and insisted on buying a couple of rounds of Courvoisier – which was quite a bit more expensive than was beer at the Gat Rimon bar.

Since he didn't embark on any fact-fishing expedition, and since he appeared to be more sympathetic to our cause than he was to the Arabs', we began to relax. But we were relieved when he got up, saying that he had to go upstairs to pack, since he was being posted to Jerusalem the next day. I was even more relieved when he insisted on picking up the bar-bill before bidding us *au revoir*.

Shortly after, Lenny also got up, saying that he had better be going back to Teletvinsky, and to keep in touch.

* * *

On Saturday morning I reported, as ordered, to the motor pool at Sarafand and signed for a freshly painted jeep. As I went to move the seat forward so that I could reach the pedals, I found a blue United Nations beret wedged under the lever. I handed the beret over to the motor-pool *samal*, or sergeant. He growled, 'How the hell did they miss that? God, they're getting sloppy.'

I joined the convoy, which consisted of half a dozen trucks, each with heavily armoured windshields; one still more heavily armoured Egged bus; plus three escort jeeps carrying some twelve well-armed, rather bored-looking young men and women, all wearing black-and-white checkered *khuffiot*.

We sat there for about a half hour, until a small group of civilians arrived. One of the civilians was brought to my jeep. He climbed in, and introduced himself as Israel Gallili. He announced that he was to be dropped off at a place called Na'an. When I said that I had no idea where that was, Gallili smiled and told me not to worry. He wouldn't let me get lost, and it was on our way.

Then the convoy started off, with my jeep sandwiched between the last two escort vehicles. After a couple of miles my passenger initiated the usual Israeli third degree, asking me where I had come from, what I did in Canada, and what I hoped to do after this 'nonsense' was over; then what had made me come to Israel, what my military experience was, and how long I had been a Zionist. His questions were polite and friendly, but I could only answer briefly, since I was trying desperately to remember how to work the four-wheel drive on the jeep. But Gallili laughed and shook his great mane of curly, blondish hair when I told him I had become a Zionist the same day Rodrigues had told me I was leaving Sarafand. That turned out to be the full extent of our conversation, until we stopped in the town of Rehovot.

There, one of the escort vehicles drove up to my jeep, and one of the escort party changed places with Mr Gallili. The escort jeep drove off, and my new passenger told me that she would ride with me until her jeep had caught up with the convoy, probably at the start of the Derech Burma, the Burma Road.

I had never heard of any Burma Road in Israel, and wasn't sure that this wasn't another Sabreh put-down of an unnecessary and uninvited military *mumche* from North America. So I decided just to laugh, and to leave it at that.

I managed to find out that my new passenger's name was Tami and that she also was – of course – a kibbutznik in civilian life.

The countryside around Rehovot consisted of lush orange orchards and was gradually becoming more hilly. I could see a fairly large settlement on one of the hillier stretches, and observed to Tami that it looked rather lovely.

She replied, in her very limited English, that that was Kibbutz Na'an, which was Minister Gallili's home.

I wondered whether the title 'minister' meant he was pious or political, but discreetly decided not to pursue the matter further. Apparently, these kibbutznikim were machers – the word, I'd discovered, meant 'movers' – of more than just the military in this newly founded nation.

Soon the landscape became much more rugged, and we were obviously climbing. Then the convoy veered to the left and the highway suddenly turned into a dirt and gravel road, barely wide enough for two vehicles side by side.

The convoy came to a halt, and a member of the escort squad

came over to my jeep. He explained that we had now come to a rather 'nasty' part of the trip, and we would be sent off at irregular intervals. So, would I be ready to move as soon as he gave the signal. And would I please move off without delay. I would catch up with the vehicles preceding mine about two miles up the road, where they would be waiting for me.

I suddenly realized that Tami had gotten all her things together and was leisurely walking toward her original transport.

'Wait a minute! Isn't anybody riding with me, at least till we get to Jerusalem?'

The delegate from the escort squad shook his head. 'Impossible. We aren't going to the same part of Jerusalem, and the other vehicles aren't going anywhere near Machane Schneller. But you'll be fine.'

'No I won't! I have never – do you understand – *never* been to Jerusalem, and I can't read your bloody road signs. If road signs even exist in this country!'

'No problem. From where we leave you in Jerusalem, take the third turn on the left and make a right turn at the first crossing you come to. The *machane* is on the left, and you can't miss it.'

With that, a smile and a hand-wave, he walked back to his jeep and yelled over to me, 'When I blow my whistle, drive like hell, and make sure you're in four-wheel drive, else you will never make it up this part of the Derech Burma. And don't worry, the Arabs know full well that Jews are not allowed to drive on Shabbat. Nothing will happen. I can almost guarantee it!'

In the mean time, the other vehicles had all taken off and disappeared round a corner. Before I had a chance to ask him to come back and repeat his directions – since I couldn't remember a word of what he had said – the whistle blew. I took off in a swirl of dust and a screech of tires. I thought I saw the remaining escort party looking on, doubled up with laughter, but decided that it must have been my imagination. In any case, it was too late to regain my dignity. I had turned the corner and could not see anyone behind me.

I was certainly not going to try to put the jeep into four-wheel drive, since I had never managed to do it easily, even back in England. (In those days, the four-wheel-drive option was engaged by two floor-mounted levers, in a sequence I had never understood or mastered properly.) But the road didn't seem that bad – nor was the jeep going to be mine for much longer, so if I stripped its gears, it would be the new owner's problem!

I began to really hate this whole business. I had no idea where I was. I could not communicate properly with the Israelis. I wasn't sure where the Arabs were supposed to shoot at me from. And, worst of all, I had no idea how to get where I was going.

Finally, a thought made it through my hide of self-pity. I hadn't heard any kind of gun- or mortar-fire. And surely the Egged bus and the trucks would have been far more tempting targets than my little jeep.

Just as I was about to relax, I passed by a number of burnt-out vehicles pulled over to the left side of the road. They all had Hebrew letters followed by numbers painted on their hoods. This sufficed to make me put my foot back down on the accelerator. And I almost crashed into the back of the rest of the convoy, which was waiting round the next corner.

I later learned that the hills around the Derech Burma – it really was called that – had been pretty well secured for a long time: at least two weeks. I was fast learning that both distance and time were measured differently in the Holy Land. An enemy position two miles away was on another continent. Thus, except for the odd surprise-incursion by Arab irregulars, the Burma Road was generally safe to travel, even though Jerusalem was still, technically, under siege.

Upon my arrival, the convoy took off, and before we had gone more than a couple of miles we rejoined a proper highway made of asphalt.

The scenery was stunning. We navigated a serpentine road which climbed between high, terraced hills festooned with cypress trees and stone-walled vineyards, as well as the odd herd of sheep or goats, and the occasional small cluster of whitewashed clay buildings.

Up above, I could see the city, dominated by a golden-domed mosque and a number of church-spires. It was awe-inspiring, and quite un-Cecil-B.-deMille-like. The movies, up until that moment, had been my only visual source of the Holy Land.

Then, suddenly, we reached Jerusalem. The convoy drove along what seemed to be a main artery, but the group in the jeep in front of me pointed furiously to a street to my right. I pulled over, and they waved goodbye and drove off in the other direction.

There I was, all alone in Jerusalem.

Nothing really traumatic had happened on the trip. Still, I felt completely drained – both by the anticipated dangers that had never materialized, and by my growing sense that I had been the butt of Sabreh humour, in my breakneck drive on the Burma Road. I was tired, shaky, and needed a bathroom more than badly. On top of which, my stomach was roiling and my watch seemed to have stopped at 11.42.

I had no idea how long ago the thing had ceased working, so I didn't know whether I was ready to eat or to throw up.

I sat there, and in my mind went over the directions to Machane Schneller. Once I thought that I had them pretty much sorted out, I started the jeep and proceeded down the road.

I thought to myself that it might be smart to ask somebody how to get to the garrison. This proved to be somewhat of a problem, however, since the street was not only empty of cars or buses, but devoid of even a single human being. By now I was sure that I had passed a couple of turns on my right, and decided to turn off at the next street I came to.

There was the very one! It seemed a bit narrow, but at least it had a street-sign, in all three languages, which I unfortunately spotted too late to read.

The houses were all two-storey stone-block buildings – narrow and seedy in spite of the stonework. Each had tightly shut windows with metal bars and a heavy wooden door.

I still had not seen a single human being.

A couple of hundred feet further on, the street narrowed noticeably. Suddenly, windows were being thrown open. Shouts of 'Shabbos! Shabbos!' rang out all around me.

It hardly sounded like a greeting.

From the vehemence and vestments of the 'welcomers', it dawned on me that driving a jeep on a Saturday in this neighbourhood of Jerusalem was probably not a practice accepted too kindly.

'Bist a goy?' a voice demanded.

I made another of my famous 'to-be-regretted-as-soon-as-I-had-made-it' decisions, and shouted back, 'I'm afraid I am, old chap!'

A storm of household objects came flying at me from all directions.

Retreat seemed to be the only possible course. There was no room to turn the jeep around, however; I simply would have to back up all the way to the main road in as speedy a manner as circumstances would allow.

This I somehow managed to do, but not before a well-aimed brick had smashed the windshield of my (correction: the unsuspecting new owner's) jeep.

By now, it did not seem to matter. The whole trip had become a Grand Guignol skit, and any moment now the curtain was sure to come down.

I thought it prudent not to take any curtain calls, no matter how long and hard the applause.

I finally reached the main road, and was overjoyed to see a Mem Tzadik, who had materialized out of nowhere, thrust up one hand and with the other wave me over to the kerb.

After having checked my army travel documents and noted my 'that-day' rank, he actually saluted me. Now, this was the very first salute I had received – or, for that matter, given – in Israel, since I'd never been sure whether they actually did that sort of thing in the Haganah, and if they did it, how. Then, politely, in fluent English, the military police officer asked how my windshield had been broken, and whether it had happened on the Derech Burma.

I told him of my unfriendly reception and was then informed, with a laugh, that I had driven into the Mea Shearim quarter. This was Jerusalem's ultra-Orthodox district, where driving on the Shabbat was considered worse than sacrilegious.

Why would I have turned right, he asked, when Machane Schneller was 'over there', to the left of the road? He jumped into the jeep and laughed that I now had an escort just like Ben Gurion. He said he'd have me at the garrison gate in five minutes. He was as good as his word.

He shook my hand and, as he left, said, 'Tell them the windshield got smashed on the Burma Road. Everybody will be much happier!'

I checked in at the garrison, and was shown to the second floor of the building. That floor contained the CO's offices, and also what appeared to be a communications section. But for a couple of clerical sorts, and what was obviously the duty officer, there was no one around.

The duty officer seemed to be expecting me. He apologized, saying that BarNun had waited for me as long as he could, but had finally left. The Mikafed would now be away for two days, and until then he, the duty officer, would be glad to be my host. Unless, of course, I had other business in Jerusalem.

He was relieved when I told him that I had family in Jerusalem and would like to take the opportunity to visit with them, since I had not seen my cousin Irene since 1937. I showed him the address that Gideon had written out for me in Tel Aviv.

'Well, if I can't be your host, at least I will be your taxi driver,' he said. 'Here is our phone number. When you want to return to Schneller, just telephone and we will send someone to bring you back here. Let me take you to your billets, where you can leave your things. And then we can go.'

My grandparents' home in the Moravian village of Miroslav had been just thirty-five kilometres from the Austrian border. Two of my mother's seven sisters, including Irene's mother, Charlotte, had married Austrians. Twice each year, my grandmother – a formidable figure a little under five feet tall – used to convene a family gathering. This was faithfully attended (for who would have dared not come?) by all children and grandchildren, from near and far.

Irene was the eldest of the cousins, and I remembered her as tall, willowy and imperious. She had the world's most intimidating eyebrows (they were particularly so when raised)! When we children were by ourselves, she was the unchallenged leader of the pack. She was also the musical talent of the family, and had monopolized my grandfather's piano on each reunion.

Irene had towered over me in Miroslav. Obviously she had shrunk in the eleven years since I had last seen her!

In fact, I now stood a good three inches taller than her – but apart from that, my memories of her were accurate. She was willowy, she was imperious, she was still the leader of the pack – and she was now a piano teacher by profession.

Within five minutes it seemed that we had never been apart. The family relationship re-established itself without effort on either of our parts. In fact, it was now much closer than it had ever been in my childhood.

Upon first meeting, we had automatically spoken German, but

before very long Irene asked me if by any chance I knew English a little bit better than I did German? It was with relief that I found out her English was pretty well fluent. Which, as she put it, was just about the only plus that she had managed to get from the British occupation.

After about an hour of my telling them about my journey from Toronto to Israel, via New York, Paris – and especially Marseilles – Gideon asked if I had eaten.

Now, one fact that even I knew was that Jewish Jerusalem was still under siege. Just about everything had to be brought in from the north. The burnt-out vehicles which I had passed on the way up were evidence of the reality of the blockade. And though the current cease-fire allowed for set quantities of supplies to be sent through, I felt certain that some form of rationing would still be in force. So I declined, saying that they had fed me back at Machane Schneller.

'That is obviously not true!' proclaimed Irene. 'You never could lie convincingly. Anyhow, we have plenty of food, and even if you aren't lying – and we both know that you are – you will just have to eat again. Also, Franzl,' (nobody had called me that since Miroslav) 'you are filthy dirty. Go get washed, and by the time you come out dinner will be ready.'

I repaired to the bathroom. But when I tried to turn on the tap nothing happened. Then I noticed that there were about three inches of water in the bathtub. The water was barely tepid, but since on that evening Jerusalem was unpleasantly hot – and I figured it wouldn't be polite to make demands on my first visit – I decided to make do with the skimpy bath that they were offering.

The bath felt marvellous; and I finally managed to remove almost all memory of that day's trials and tribulations. I obviously had needed the bath, judging from the ring my cleansing had left on the tub. But when I tried to wash the tub, there was no water to be found, no matter which tap I tried. I even looked into the lavatory tank, only to find it empty.

Well, never mind, I thought. I would just ask for a bucket of water once I had finished my toilette, and that would be that. Simple!

'That certainly took you quite some time.'

'I know. But I've left a bit of a mess, and was looking for some sort of cleanser for the tub. Could you give me something with which to clean it?'

Gideon covered his face with both hands and Irene started to laugh. Then, Gideon got up and very slowly walked to the bathroom door where, wincing a bit, he peeked inside. He turned to Irene, nodded, and sat down with his hands once again covering his face.

Then he too began to laugh, and Irene joined in. Next thing, they were both holding their sides, and with tears rolling down their cheeks they roared with laughter. It was infectious! I joined in with uncontrollable laughter of my own. Finally, I asked, 'Why are we laughing?'

'You've just used up our week's washing water.'

This statement brought the three of us to our knees with laughter. I was the first to come back to reality. I felt terrible and cursed myself for being a total idiot. Why I wouldn't have guessed that water would also have had to be brought in was beyond me.

Then I had an idea. Surely Machane Schneller would have more water than a civilian home. And surely my friend the duty officer would be the very person to supply it. I asked the Rohrs if I could use their telephone. Irene and Gideon refused, saying that luckily the next day was Sunday, which was water distribution day. They still had plenty of drinking-water, which we could use for both drinking and washing. So I really hadn't done any damage at all, they assured me.

When I still tried to insist on calling my friend the duty officer, Irene said that it would be better not to be in his debt so soon, especially if I had come to Jerusalem for some silly military purpose. 'Better you put them in your debt first,' Irene advised. 'But now, let's eat.'

By the time we finished a rather cold supper, it was getting fairly late and the day's dramas were catching up with me. I figured that I was pretty close to outstaying my welcome and said that I should at least phone the garrison to pick me up.

But Irene would have none of that. Of course I would spend the night with them. There was plenty of room. And there was still lots of catching up to do. Hadn't I mentioned that Bar Nun wasn't going to see me until Monday? And, in any case, she wanted to introduce me to some of the city's artists.

She thought that perhaps I should phone my friend and let him know I was spending the night, before they sent a search party to Mea Shearim, thinking I had decided to pay a return visit! I should tell him that I'd get back to Schneller by myself, the next evening, some time after supper.

Soon after my phone call to Schneller, Gideon excused himself, saying that he had to get up early the next day and that, in any case, his English wasn't keeping up with the conversation. Irene and I stayed up – I had now gotten my second wind – talking about the family. Irene was more informed than I. Compared to other families, ours had not fared badly; but the toll was still grim.

Our grandmother had died in Theresienstadt, an internment centre, before 'relocation' – as the Nazis put it – to one of the notorious concentration camps.

Of the eight aunts, Mitzi was in London; Lotte (Charlotte, Irene's mother) had also escaped to England, but was now in New Jersey; Lorly was also in the U.S., teaching at the University of Pittsburgh; Poldi was in Sweden. Olga, however, had died in Bergen-Belsen, and Yelli in Auschwitz. Grete, who was single, had simply disappeared off the face of the world; she was last known to have joined up with partisans in the Tatras. Our uncle Leo – the lone brother, of the nine siblings – had been shot at the beginning of the German occupation, with many other 'traitorous' Czech politicians.

The cousins' fate paralleled that of their parents. Erica was in London; Lisl, Irene's younger sister, was in New Jersey; Hennie was somewhere in Sweden. Trude had died in Bergen-Belsen and Stefan, the youngest cousin, was transported to Auschwitz at the age of five.

My mother, my sister Dorrit, and I completed the roster. We, of course, had left Czechoslovakia two years before the nightmare started – and were just about the only ones on the Miroslav side of the family who had left 'normally', so to speak.

With that, we ended the evening, and finally went to sleep.

I woke to strong light; I had obviously slept in. My watch still wasn't working, though, so I had no idea what time it was, until Irene peeked into the living room: 'Time for lunch,' she announced. 'The water *malheur* is all fixed, so the bathroom is yours, but please try not to have another bath. We are meeting a good friend of mine, an artist called Pinsel, in half an hour.'

Ja'akov Pins, a Yacke, or German Jew, by birth – hence the nickname Pinsel, which means paintbrush in German – ran a private art school at his nineteenth-century house. Coincidentally, the house was located in the Machane Yehuda area of Jerusalem, not far from the Bezalel Art School. He was a short, intense man with one crippled leg.

This impediment had not stopped him from being in the Irgun – but he had fled the underground in utter disgust after the Deir Yassin massacre in April.

Over strong Turkish coffee, I was subjected to the usual amiable interrogation about my motives and my background. I also received a better education about the war for which I had volunteered than I had received in all the orientation lectures at Grand Arenas and the briefings at Sarafand combined. And all in a quiet and matter-of-fact manner, by a cousin and a new acquaintance who, by profession, was a kindred spirit. The fact that they spoke from personal experience made it all the more credible.

In Jerusalem, they had endured a great deal, they told me, the worst of it concentrated within the space of a few months.

Before the British had left, the Arab Legion, under Major-General John Bagot Glubb (Rodrigues's 'Glubb Pasha'), and led by British officers, had been allowed by the British Mandate Authority to assemble troops in a number of strategic positions in and around the city. The Legion – well trained and far better equipped than was the Haganah – had thus quickly occupied vital outlying areas such as Sheikh Jarrah and the surrounds of Mount Scopus. The worst defeats for the Haganah had been the loss of Latrun, which dominated a vital stretch of the Tel Aviv-to-Jerusalem highway – hence the Burma Road – and the capture by the Legion of the Old City.

In the month leading up to the current ceasefire (instituted on June 11th, and still in force now, in early July) over three hundred Jews had been killed, and thousands of shells sent into the New City. In the Old City, all but five of the twenty-seven synagogues had been destroyed. There had been widespread looting, as well as the desecration of holy books and other artifacts.

Amazingly, the Legion was not able to penetrate beyond the Old City. In fact, the Legion had been repulsed in even armoured-vehicle and tank attacks, such as the one on the Notre Dame Monastery, right by the New Gate. (Little did I know that I was to become uncomfortably familiar with that particular building on the morrow.)

Pins mentioned that Bezalel was closed for 'the summer or the siege', whichever ended first; else he would have taken me over to see the place and meet some of the local artists. He seemed genuinely interested in my interrupted studies in art. And though there were very few of his colleagues around – certainly none of the 'younger' ones – Pins thought he could at least introduce me to an artist by the name of Ardon, the director of the Bezalel, as well as to a painter called Ludwig Blum, who was quite fashionable (even if more than a little *kitschish*) – since Blum also happened to be Czech.

With that, the visit ended. Irene and I walked back to Rehavia, picking up some food and wine for supper on the way.

The rest of the visit passed very quietly, and finished with a promise of a proper party as soon as my *tafkid*, my task – whatever it might be – was concluded.

Then I telephoned Schneller.

* * *

At twelve o'clock noon we set off for the Notre Dame Monastery, which was to be our jumping-off point. My equipment consisted of my old mapping case, a dozen sheets of paper and a pair of beat-up binoculars, the last supplied by my friend the duty officer at Schneller. My Narodni Podnik revolver and my spanking new brothel creepers completed my 'battle gear'.

At the monastery, I was handed over to the recce sergeant who was to be my guide. Like Pinsel, he was a Yacke. His family had wisely escaped from Germany in 1934, and during the Second World War he had served in the Jewish Brigade.

He explained that we were going through the monastery up to a 'veranda', which in fact was a flat roof connected by other buildings to our objective. This was a three-storey bombed-out public building of some sort, from where we would have an excellent sight line to Arab Legion positions – he hoped. He added that once we were past the veranda we would be within earshot of the Arabs, and would I be as quiet as possible. Once we were at our observation point, he said, we would have to confine ourselves to using sign language. He had purposely chosen the hottest part of the day for my 'needless adventure'; still, he said, we were dealing with essentially British troops, and I surely knew that 'mad dogs and Englishmen....'

With that, off we went. Up several flights of stairs, until we reached a large room with about ten or twelve of our soldiers in it. The room had about four large windows leading onto the typical Jerusalem veranda-cum-rooftop.

My guide pointed to a large building about thirty or forty metres away, which had several smashed-in windows. 'That's where we are going. The Arabs can see us once we are about halfway across, but we should be okay at this time of day. But not a sound. And once we're in position, remember, only written messages or sign language!' All this was said in the most picturesque blend of English and German, which gave the injunctions all the more impact.

We went across the roofs in a loping crouch and took what seemed to me to be a bit of a circuitous route to our target. Still, we reached our goal without incident. I decided I had better have a look at the route back, before we went into the building. And found, to my consternation, that I had no idea which window we had come through. What was worse, there were several buildings that could be reached via the patchwork of rooftops. All of them looked alike to me.

We entered a blitzed building with gaping voids for floors, but with a narrow frame, about four feet wide, of jagged flooring running around each room. Looking down through the gaping hole, I judged that we were on the third or fourth floor of what must have been quite an imposing building. Amid the debris there were two or three chairs and a couple of footstools, all too dilapidated to have been 'rescued'.

We edged, or rather crawled, our way over to the 'Arab' side of the room, which boasted another row of windows overlooking a fair-sized open area adjoining a row of buildings facing our position. The recce sergeant pointed to the buildings and silently mouthed the word 'Legion'.

Then I saw my first Legionnaires. They certainly looked like professional soldiers! And there seemed to be an awful lot of activity, for siesta time.

I crouched by one of the windows, and tried to aim my binoculars at the buildings opposite in as covert a manner as possible.

When my guide saw that I was about to open my mapping case, he brought one of the stools over to me, to serve as a table.

The windows of the buildings were fairly bristling with Bren guns and all sorts of ordnance. I made a quick sketch of the area and then swung the binoculars to the left, where I could see what appeared to be another entrance.

What I saw there really confused me. Amidst a group of Arab Legion officers, most of whom looked very Caucasian, I noticed two officers with black berets. Urgently beckoning to my companion, I pointed to the bunch of officers, and wrote, 'Black berets = Brit. Tank corps. How come?' The sergeant shook his head and gestured that he didn't know. Then a thought struck me. I wrote: 'May be ops. preps. / not defensive pos.' This time he looked bewildered and wrote in the dust on the floor: 'Not understand.' Whereupon I wrote, '*Angriff Vorbereitung*. I make notes. We run!'

I was finished in a flash. I figured the Israelis probably knew all about this in any case. Then I quickly closed my mapping case, turned to let the sergeant know I was done, and knocked my binoculars off the stool. They clattered to the floor and then bounced down the void in the centre of the room, making enough noise to wake the dead.

Unfortunately, the noise woke not the dead, but a group of Arab Legionnaires. A detachment of about half a dozen men took off at the double, running toward our row of buildings.

We hurried – as best as we were able – to the window that led to our route back. The sergeant had cocked his Sten gun by this time. He snapped, 'Go, go, go.'

I would have been delighted to do exactly that, except for my unerring lack of any sense of direction. I simply had no idea which way to go, let alone which window I was to jump through once I reached the other side.

'*Geh, geh, geh. Die Arabern werden sofort rauf sein!*'

I sincerely believed he was right, and that we'd better get out of there.

'No, you go first. I'll bring up the rear.' To reinforce my determination I unholstered my Narodni Podnik, praying that I would not have to try to use it.

With my guide leading by about ten or twelve feet, we had almost gotten to the halfway point, when the Legionnaires burst out of another window onto the flat rooftops. Two of them started firing, while the others continued their pursuit at full pelt.

To my utter shock, I half turned and, still running, pulled the trigger of my revolver. To my greater shock, not only did the revolver work, but one of my pursuers actually stumbled, and they all came to a halt. In the meantime, 'my' sergeant had reached 'our' window, and was waving me on vigorously.

Our people were at all the windows, laying down a pretty good covering fusillade. The Legionnaires turned tail, but not before one of them threw a grenade. It landed within three feet or so of the window I had just reached. I froze – out of complete fright, not strategy – until the sergeant quietly picked up the grenade and said, 'He forgot to pull the pin.' Then he asked me if I wanted the grenade as a souvenir.

I declined, without thanks.

During the debriefing back at the garrison, I found out three things.

1. The ceasefire would end on the 9th of July, since the Arab High Command had turned down a Security Council request for an extension.

2. BarNun knew about the buildup; however, the news regarding the presence of the black berets was interesting. The two officers were more likely to have been Egyptians than Brits, and that pointed to the possibility of a coordinated action of some sort. So my 'trial by fire' had been of some military use, after all.

3. There was to be a last convoy before hostilities resumed; it would depart in two days' time, and I was scheduled to leave on it.

Since I still had time, however, they thought I might like to see Deir Abu Tor, another front-line position in the Katamon part of the city. They could schedule it for early that evening, which would then give me a full day tomorrow to spend with the *mishpacha* (that is, the family).

Actually, 'might like to see' was a euphemism, since the arrangements had already been finalized.

'What am I supposed to do there?'

'Nothing special. Just take a look, and meet some more of our people,' advised BarNun. 'But now, I am sure, you'll want to get cleaned up a bit. Akiva will drive you over once you are finished. Incidentally, I heard about you insisting on bringing up the rear today.'

Akiva left me at a sandbagged forward position located in yet another bombed-out house, which overlooked an open area with yet more Arab Legion troops in evidence on the higher ground. This position had obviously seen some heavy fighting in the weeks before, judging from the war debris all over the place. But for the moment all seemed peaceful enough, and I couldn't see anything of note. Nor, to be truthful, did I know what 'anything of note' might be.

I messed around for about twenty minutes, trying to look

sanguine and knowledgeable, and then announced that I had seen enough, and had better get back to Schneller. A young Sabreh said that he would take me back in a few minutes, and suggested that I wait outside, where it would be a bit cooler.

I had scarcely gotten outside when a United Nations jeep pulled up and discharged none other than our drinking companion from the Gat Rimon Hotel, le Capitaine de Blocque. To my surprise he recognized me, and said that this coincidence would have to be celebrated with a drink at the King David Hotel. How would I like to be his guest for dinner later that night?

I said that I was just waiting for a lift to my place and expected to leave at any moment.

De Blocque then parked his jeep about fifty feet from the house-cum-bunker. On his way into the bunker, he said that his inspection would only take about five minutes and he'd be happy to give me a lift. (Apparently, the UN was in the process of making inspection tours of every front-line position held by all of the belligerents, prior to the ceasefire's ending on the ninth.)

Sure enough, he came out within five minutes, accompanied by the young Sabreh, whose hand he shook. He then went over to his vehicle. When I mentioned to the Sabreh – who turned out to be in charge of the sector – about the ride offer, he said, 'Lama lo?' (why not?) 'Just be more careful what you say than he is. I will let them know at Schneller where you've gone.'

With that, I strolled over toward the United Nations jeep, and was within about twenty feet of it when there was a huge bang. Bits of shrapnel and masonry came raining over us. A mortar shell from the Legion sector of Abu Tor had hit quite close to de Blocque's jeep!

How the Arabs had mistaken a UN jeep for one of ours, and how they had managed not to score a direct hit, heaven only knows. But the damage was serious enough. De Blocque was bleeding profusely from one arm and the jeep's interior was pretty well ripped to bits. An Israeli soldier with a Red Magen David band on his arm had rushed over, and was attending de Blocque.

The bunker commander asked if I was okay, and when I nodded, said that it would be best if someone took me out of Katamon before everybody arrived. By then, I could hear ambulance sirens, accompanied by a lot of yelling across both lines.

I told my new guide where Irene lived, since I thought that that would be closer as well as easier to get to than Schneller. He agreed. As we ran through the narrow streets, somebody started pulling insistently on my left arm. In fact, whoever it was seemed to be digging his fingernails sharply into my biceps. I turned my head to tell him to bugger off, only to find that there was no one there.

Instead I discovered that my arm was bleeding quite nicely, and that something was caught in my left shirtsleeve. At this point I really did not want to get involved in any more problems. And since the bleeding seemed to be abating, I decided not to say anything and simply to clean myself up at Irene's place.

My escort left me at the Rohrs' apartment, suggesting that I'd better put something on my arm without too much delay.

As soon as I had gotten in, I asked Irene if I could use her bathroom and if she might find be able to find me some peroxide and a Band-Aid, since I had had a small accident on the way over. Giving me a rather peculiar look, Irene took me into the familiar bathroom and produced a first-aid box.

'Do you need any help?'

'No. I can do this by myself. It's nothing much, and I promise not to take another bath.' With that I ushered her out and gingerly took off my shirt.

It really wasn't much! All the pulling and blood had been caused by a metal splinter no more than an inch long, quite narrow but with a sharp point. With the aid of a pair of tweezers, the splinter came out easily. Then I used a lot of peroxide and finished up with a dab of iodine, which made me scream and brought Irene to the other side of the door, asking if I was all right. I assured her weakly that I was okay.

Next, I found a large Band-Aid which I slapped on my arm, and emerged. 'I'm fine,' I said, 'but your iodine has quite a kick to it.'

Irene handed me a shirt which she had been holding, saying that she figured I needed one and this was an old one of Gideon's, so it didn't matter whether I gave it back or not. Then she asked how much longer I was staying in Jerusalem.

I told her just a couple more days and that as far as I knew, except for one more short session with BarNun, I would be on my own time until then. Irene said that she had arranged to meet Pins and some other friends for supper at one of the designated restaurants near the Bezalel, since Gideon was away again until the next day. I would, of course, join them.

I begged off, saying that I would welcome a bit of time alone so that I could sort out my notes for tomorrow's meeting.

In fact, I didn't think the note-making was going to take too much time. But the day's events had taken their toll, and I couldn't face the prospect of dinner or company. Irene suggested that I lie down for a bit, and said she wouldn't be late.

I phoned Schneller and managed to get hold of Akiva, the duty officer. I told him that I wasn't feeling up to coming in that evening. He already knew about the de Blocque incident and asked if I had been badly hurt. I assured him that it was just a scratch, which didn't amount to anything.

He suggested that I report to the CO's office at eight the next morning. Since he couldn't see anything on the calendar, he thought there wouldn't be any problem – but I should have some notes ready to leave with Akiva, in case the Mikafed didn't have a chance to meet with me.

By now, all I wanted to do was shut my eyes for a while. I wrote 'Meeting BarNun / 8:00 a.m.' on a piece of paper, with a second note to Irene asking her to wake me up when she came in, and lay down on the couch. My arm had started to throb a little but wasn't really painful. And then I must have dozed off, because the next thing I knew Irene was shaking me awake.

'It's six o'clock and you have to go to a meeting at eight. And, incidentally, you look terrible!' With that she produced a thermometer and shoved it in my mouth. 'Well, you've got a slight temperature, but nothing alarming. Do you have to prepare anything?'

I shook my head. Mainly because I could not remember what I was supposed to make notes about. In the bathroom I felt a hard lump in my left armpit and took off my shirt. I groaned as I looked in the mirror. My arm seemed to have grown in width overnight. It also seemed to have gotten a real sunburn from shoulder to elbow. I did the necessary things in the bathroom, then went back into the kitchen and announced plaintively, 'I think I'm in a bit of a mess.'

Whereupon Irene requisitioned the telephone number to Bar-Nun's office and held an animated conversation in Hebrew with someone there. Then she turned to me and told me that they were sending a jeep to pick me up, and that they had said I should be ready in half an hour – which in Israel meant two hours, at the very least.

At ten-thirty, Akiva picked me up and said that the meeting had been postponed until noon, which would give me a bit more time to get my notes into a comprehensible form. Apparently, the convoy was still leaving the next day and I would make my full report to Rodrigues, but there were some minor questions that BarNun wanted to ask me regarding de Blocque. Akiva suggested that in the mean time it might be an idea for him to take me to the MO to have my dressing changed. He also thought that he could get me a more suitable shirt to wear, since Gideon's striped short-sleeved one, though very nice, was a bit unmilitary, even for the Haganah.

There was only a nurse on duty at the infirmary. She very gently took off my Band-Aid and swabbed off my 'puncture'. Leaving me with a glass of tea which she seemed to have ready, she took Akiva to the other side of the room where they held what seemed to be a rather earnest conversation.

The discussion was obviously about me, since Akiva kept glancing my way, each time shaking his head. Then he came over to me and told me that the nurse wanted the MO to look at my arm once my meeting was over.

Leaving the infirmary, I went to my room and made a jab at preparing something for the meeting. But I gave up after ten minutes, unable to concentrate. I decided that I might as well spruce up a bit.

Possibly then I would feel better and would be able to concentrate on preparing for the meeting.

I took my shaving kit and a towel to the bathroom – which reminded me of the boarding-school facilities at Bradfield College. I had just started to shave when Akiva came in accompanied by a gentleman in khaki shorts and a white coat, with a stethoscope sticking out of his coat pocket. He looked at me and said in English, 'I want you will come to my infirmary now before the meeting. I just need to check a couple things.'

Akiva nodded agreement and the three of us trudged back to the MO's office, where I was told to take everything off except my shorts, socks and brothel-creepers. I noticed that my arm had actually ballooned to double its normal size. Next, to my surprise, the doctor pulled down my shorts. He gently touched a new lump that had appeared on my groin.

He turned to Akiva and said something that made Akiva vanish at a good pace. Then he turned to me and asked how I had gotten scratched. I pointed to my trousers, which were brought to me, and pulled the shrapnel sliver out my wallet.

'Well, *gibor hatembil*, you now go to Hadassah. No more playing soldier for a while, I think.'

9. HOW TO BECOME
AN OFFICIAL WAR ARTIST

The next thing I knew, I was in an ambulance, accompanied by the medical officer and Akiva. I didn't feel all that good but I really didn't feel all that bad either. Still, I couldn't be bothered arguing about anything. I did ask the MO if I would be through in time for my noon meeting, and was told by Akiva that the meeting had been cancelled in any case.

At that point, I must have dozed off. When I awoke I was lying on a narrow bed, obviously in a hospital corridor. Somebody had taken off all my clothes and thrown a sheet over me. My arm and chest appeared to have been painted a hideous yellow. Around me stood the MO and two other men in white gowns and caps.

One of the men in white, who must have been well over six feet tall and had the build of a wrestler, said to me, 'We think it better for you to have small operation. My name is Rakovchik. I will be surgeon for you. Is not serious, not to worry. We only do it fast because I am not busy.'

With that I was wheeled into an operating theatre and a doctor put a chloroform mask on my face. When I came to, I was still on the operating table. Dr Rakovchik said, rather loudly, that everything looked fine and that I could go to my room. I swung my legs over the side of the table to get up, and was immediately caught by Rakovchik, who then carried me, like a baby, down a long corridor into a room, laughing all the way.

Sleeping that night was a struggle. My now really painful arm had been put into some sort of harness and had tubes running out of it. The tubes led to some kind of noisy apparatus on the floor. Finally, out of a combination of exhaustion and anaesthetic hangover, I dozed off.

I certainly had lots of attention, over the course of the next day. Nurses and interns popped in quite frequently. So frequently, in fact, that I became worried. I finally asked one nurse, whose face had become familiar to me, if I was extremely ill.

'No,' she replied with a big smile. 'But you're the first machalnik from Canada we've had, and everybody wants to take a look. But you are one of the easier cases. All that is wrong with you is a bit of blood-poisoning.'

This – combined with the fact that I really did not feel all that bad – reassured me, and I became more preoccupied with the fact that I was hungry. By the end of the day, with two substantial meals in my stomach, I was quite happy to be a guest of the house.

That changed around midnight, when I was suddenly woken by Dr Rakovchik and the nice nurse removing my bandages and doing something or other – I didn't inquire too closely – with my tubes. Rakovchik saw me watching and told me not to be alarmed. It seems there was a minor hitch, which he was going to fix right away. But they would have to take me back into the operating theatre. He muttered something to the effect that with my 'stupid piece of shrapnel' and home remedies, I was more trouble than I was worth.

When I came to again, I was back in the ward, and it was obviously daytime. My arm was once again shackled to the hoist and rigged up to tubes, but at least it sported a brand new bandage. Standing by my side was the nurse with the familiar face, holding a small metal tray with a hypodermic needle and a roll of cotton wool on it. 'Time for your needle,' she announced, pulling back my bedsheet and expertly jabbing my thigh. 'You'll be getting one of these every four hours. It must pay to be a Canadian machalnik.' This was clearly said without any malice, however, and was accompanied by a friendly smile.

The next few days were a nightmare, however. I could hardly keep any food down, and by the second day I had come to detest the injections. Everything seemed to go wrong. Twice the needle broke off, and by the end of the third day they had to move over to my other leg. The first one had become so hard that no one but my nurse with the familiar face was able to get a needle in without causing me excruciating pain.

On the fifth day life became a little more bearable, and I was able to keep all my food down. The injections had been reduced to one every eight hours, and Dr Rakovchik's daily visits had been cut to nil. However, I was still confined to my bed-and-breakfast-and-bedpan.

Two days later the hoist was replaced by a sling. A small cup had been taped to my arm by this point, into which the one remaining tube flowed. I was told that from now on I would eat lunch in the lunchroom on that floor, and that a nurse would take me there for the first meal or two. After a couple more days I was told that, in a week's time, I would be transferred to the Katamon convalescent depot – sooner, if they had room.

That same day Irene came to see me and told me that she had come by a couple of times, but not been permitted to visit. So the fact that she'd been allowed in must mean I was getting better. I agreed and told her that I was being transferred and to where.

To my surprise, Irene at this point said she had forgotten a prior engagement. She was glad that I was feeling better; and would come back the next day. Then she disappeared.

I decided to go to the lunchroom for a smoke followed by a bite of lunch. Putting on the threadbare dressing gown I had been issued, I went on my way. As I passed through one of the main wards – these held about thirty beds each, just like a British army hospital – I heard someone mispronouncing my name. Looking around, I spotted an arm in one of the beds waving me over. It turned out to belong to one of the North Africans from my platoon at Grand Arenas.

The North Africans and their fellow volunteers had left France by ship a few days after I was flown out, he told me, and had been posted to different units the day they reached Israel. He had been one of a group of about a dozen sent to the Jerusalem command. Four of them, he said, had been wounded the day the truce ended – six days ago, apparently. He also thought that one of them had been killed.

It seemed that the Haganah considered that the Grand-Arenas training had provided them with adequate mastery of the art of war! (I experienced only a few disenchantments with the ways of the Haganah during my time in Israel, but this was easily the worst: the whole thing reeked of cannon fodder.)

That day I had become a bit more aware of what was going on around me. The wards had filled considerably and I noticed a fair amount of sporadic gunfire. It then occurred to me that this noise had been going on for quite a few days, but had simply not registered with me until then. Both the nurses and interns had become more abrupt while performing their work. Even the nice nurse with the familiar face had become disinclined to visit and chitchat.

The next day Irene reappeared bringing a pack of cigarettes and a bar of chocolate. The latter was in a brown paper bag, which Irene flashed open and shut as though it contained gold. Where she had found a chocolate bar was a mystery.

She had scarcely sat down when BarNun and Akiva arrived, escorted by the head nurse of that floor. I introduced them to Irene, who said that they had spoken on the phone. Then the three held a spirited conversation which, of course, I could not understand. It finished with laughter and a lot of 'ken, kens', however, so I assumed the officers weren't there to conduct the meeting cancelled on the day of the ambulance trip.

Then BarNun asked if I was feeling better (yes) and if I needed anything (no). I apologized for causing so much bother, to which BarNun replied that I should get well quickly, so I could get back to duty. Then they all left.

A few minutes later the head nurse came in and told me that I would be transferred in another few days, but that I would be going to Beit Hakerem rather than to Katamon as had originally been planned. 'I guess it just shows that it is true what they say: it is good to know important people. You have *mazal!*' She shook her head.

* * *

I turned out to be the first machalnik in residence at the Beit Hakerem Convalescent Depot.

This made me more of an oddity than a celebrity. In the beginning the other patients viewed me with a fair bit of suspicion, mostly caused by a rather stupid wisecrack which I delivered during my first meal with the rest of the 'ambulatory residents'.

I was the last man to be brought down to dinner, and was put at the head of a long table, with six men on each side. I was introduced by the commanding officer of the depot as *haCanadi hachadash*, the new Canadian. The CO, a woman by the name of Miriam, must have been all of twenty-two years of age.

The mess group consisted of the walking wounded, all of whom had at least one body part bandaged or missing, or were armed with crutches. So I fitted in quite well, with my leper's bucket. The men were a mixture of ages and races. A number of them looked just like my Algerians from Grand Arenas. Most of the others were obviously Ashkenazi Israelis. Two of them – non-military – were ultra-Ortho-dox Jews, complete with side-curls and yarmulkes. And every one of us smelled like an uncollected hospital laundry basket!

I had barely started to eat – something unfamiliar that turned out to be eggplant, but tasted not too bad at all – when my neighbour asked me, in halting English, whether I was a Zionist. 'Not really,' I replied.

'Then why did you come to fight for us?'

'Well, for the money, I guess.'

Now, I assumed that my interlocutor would know that we got only two lirot a month from the Haganah, and would recognize my remark as a bit of sophisticated humour.

'The money? You are a mercenary?'

'Of course. What else?'

'Do you mean that if the Arabs had offered you more money, you would fight for them?'

'My God, I never thought of that. Is there a telephone in this place?'

All this was duly translated into Hebrew, and a loud hubbub ensued. Loud enough that Mifakedet Miriam reappeared. She was promptly engaged in a heated discussion, with everybody at the table remonstrating vigorously.

She gave me a disgusted look, and said a few words in Hebrew to my inquisitor.

He turned to me and said, 'Miriam say I should ask you how much we are paying you. And that I should tell you not to lie.'

'Two lirot per month.'

He echoed, *'Shte lirot le chodish!'*

Whereupon everybody at the table laughed, and the crisis was over.

The convalescent home was a two-storey stone house, which had been a school before the war. The classrooms on the second floor had all been turned into small dormitories, with four to eight ambulatory patients to each room. Part of the main floor had been transformed into two large wards for critical cases. The rest of the rooms were used as examination chambers, staff offices and an occupational therapy studio. There was a dining room and full kitchen facilities, which had been kept exactly as they were before the school was requisitioned.

Although rather spartan, the place was clean, the rooms pleasantly painted, and the furniture – obviously donated – homey and non-institutional. However, the dietitian seemed to only have a one-track solution to healthy eating: *eggplant,* in every guise and at every meal. After four days, during my daily session with Miriam – we all had a daily assessment with her – I asked whether there was any chance of a change of menu, even if only for one meal. 'The eggplant is really very tasty. It's just that we're basically not vegetarians in Canada. Please, don't take this as a criticism, but I would really appreciate something like bacon and eggs. Or the kosher equivalent.'

'So would I,' she said, 'but unfortunately we're living under a siege; so until the Haganah completely secures the Burma Road, we'll have to keep on eating eggplant. The school has left us a whole field of the things!'

At least I had the couth to apologize. I told her that I was an utter idiot, and I hoped she would ignore me.

'Well, you're wounded,' she said, 'and that has probably made you a little stupid. But I'm sure you'll be cured soon!'

Apart from the eggplant, life at Beit Hakerem was pleasant and for the most part peaceful. The mortar- and gunfire were at least five kilometres away – and I was becoming native enough that any military engagement not within a kilometre seemed of little concern.

One of my roommates, wounded in the losing battle for the Old City, was the brother of an Irgun fighter who had been one of the men held responsible for the hanging of two British sergeants in an orange grove during the Mandate. His brother had been summarily executed, without any investigation or formal trial.

My roommate's painful accounts of life during the last months of the Mandate, though obviously biased, provided me with a new perspective on the British occupation. How either Jew or Arab was treated seemed to have depended more on the sympathies of the local British commander or administrator than on logic or political propriety.

Many of my other fellow inmates also had stories of life in Palestine and the Middle East, which dashed my preconceptions about English fair play along with any images I had of Valentino-like desert sheiks. Any remaining notion I had that the Irgun were really nice chaps also flew out of the window and way over the eggplant field.

I settled into a vapid routine. After a week, I had become one of the old guard at the place. Healing was slow, mainly because of a lack of antibiotics. I was driven twice a week to the Hadassah Hospital to have my bucket emptied and to be examined by one of the doctors.

Apart from that, my time was my own. And I did absolutely nothing with it, except to look out of the window and feel sorry for myself.

In my third week at the place, for some reason, I decided to look into the occupational therapy room. They had a couple of small table-top looms, a bin with clay and three or four easels. But I couldn't see any signs of paper, paints or drawing instruments. Supervising the 'non-activity' was a small, dark-haired young man who, though burdened by a visible humpback, had an engaging smile. He obviously knew who I was, since he immediately addressed me in English: 'Is there some craft or project that would be of interest to you?'

'You don't happen to have any drawing or watercolour paper, or anything of that sort, do you?'

'Do you paint?'

'A little. I went to art school for a while.'

'We don't have any here, but I am sure that I can get you something by tomorrow. As it happens, I have to be at the Bezalel School of Art this afternoon. I'm sure they'll donate something.'

This launched, for me, a more productive sojourn at Beit Hakerem. The first time I sat down to sketch I attracted a small crowd, which quietly watched as I produced a fairly prosaic masterpiece. At the next assessment session, Miriam said that some of my fellow inmates had wondered if I would hold some art classes.

'I'm not trying to be coy,' I said, 'but apart from the fact that I don't know what I am doing when I draw or paint, I haven't the foggiest idea how to teach art.'

'Some of the men really want to have a bit of instruction. This is the first time that these patients have shown any interest in occupational therapy. Could you at least give it a try?'

And so started the Beit Hakerem Academy of Wounded Art.

To my utter amazement, we soon had an enthusiastic and fairly talented group working away. And to my surprise, I enjoyed teaching. The days settled into a steady routine. After breakfast, we would be given a quick checkup by the resident MO, after which I would get together with my 'students' for a three-hour drawing session. This would be followed by lunch, after which we all repaired to our rooms for a two-hour siesta.

Then I usually went for a short walk, most often to a nearby abandoned fig orchard: a good place to feast on figs and and flights of fancy.

From there I could see down to a valley and past narrow terraces of cypress trees to Arab vineyards and vegetable gardens; in the distance I could see a small, deserted Arab village.

After supper, we would collect in the occupational therapy room, where at least twice a week we were ably entertained by professional musicians or folk singers. Other evenings saw regular chess matches, and attempts on the part of various of my 'students' to teach me Hebrew. I was not a good student.

One of the entertainers was the daughter of the former director of the requisitioned school: a young girl called Sarahle, who played a mean recorder, and spoke English fluently. We became good friends. One evening she bullied me into writing a letter to my mother and Mike, just to let them know I was still around. Frankly, I had completely forgotten the world outside.

Writing the letter brought me back to reality. And I started a vigorous campaign to be sent back to active duty.

After I had been at Beit Hakerem almost a month, the MO changed my ambulance pick-up to just once a week. My arm was finally healing. And though Dr Rakovchik kept postponing the removal of my leper's bucket, he slapped me on the back, on one of my later visits, and said, 'Your cousin right, not let us send you to Katamon, Canada.'

'What exactly is Katamon?'

'Nothing! Is normally reserved for patients we not certain about.'

Only much later did I find out that Katamon was reserved for the terminally wounded.

Meanwhile, back at Beit Hakerem – with Jerusalem still under quasi-siege – the diet remained limited to eggplant. Eggplant sautéed, eggplant schnitzel, eggplant coq au vin, eggplant flambé, eggplant *shashlik*, eggplant pie, eggplant falafel, 'mystery (eggplant) pudding'. Our chef strove to concoct the most inspired culinary dishes, with only one stipulation: each and every one had to contain eggplant!

One day, in the second week of September, I returned from the hospital to find a truck parked outside the convalescent home. Miriam was arguing vigorously with a military anachronism: a small man wearing a British-style peaked officer's hat, with a profuse beard and the longest *paiyes*. With arms belligerently crossed, he was shaking his head and shouting *'trefe, trefe'* – among other words, none of which I could understand, but which didn't even sound like Hebrew.

By this time, the Burma Road had been secured, and supplies were getting through to Jerusalem as quickly as Middle Eastern efficiency permitted. Apparently, one of the trucks had been earmarked for our convalescent home. Among the goods unloaded were several boxes filled with cans of corned beef. Unfortunately, one of our two *yeshivah bochers* had phoned the local rabbinate, which in turn had gotten in touch with Machane Schneller – which in turn had been forced to send the garrison rabbi, with whom Miriam was now arguing.

The upshot was that all the food supplies were loaded back on the truck, and our chef had to go back to the challenge of daily (but kosher!) eggplant.

I was improving by leaps and bounds. One day Miriam informed me that the removal of my leper's cup had been scheduled. She added that this would entail minor surgery, and advised me to take a toothbrush in case of a delay. Then she said, 'You know that you will probably not go back to Yechidat Siur Agam. You've lost your *zug aleph* (A-1) rating. The army has recently started an education corps. I could get you in as an education officer. Would you be interested in transferring to it? You really worked well with the chaverim here.'

'Honestly, no,' I said. 'That would be a bit embarrassing.'

The next morning, I waited outside the depot for my ambulance. After half an hour, when it hadn't come, I decided to start walking. I figured that with my arm-sling it would be easy enough to hitch a ride to the hospital. After I had walked for about fifteen minutes, I realized I had not seen a single vehicle on the road. And it wasn't Shabbat.

Just then, a military police jeep drew up, with brakes screeching. Two MPs jumped out and demanded to see my papers, first in Hebrew, and then – when I told them I was machal – in English. I explained that my ambulance had not come to pick me up, and that I was on my way to the Hadassah.

'We'll take you there.'

On the way, I asked what was going on.

'There's a total curfew. Haven't you heard? Count Bernadotte was killed. It's been on the radio all morning.'

It was September 17.

* * *

A few days after Count Bernadotte's murder, I received my travel orders to 'Return to Unit'. I bade Beit Hakerem a final farewell and returned to Sarafand.

Yechidat Siur had changed dramatically during my absence.

I reported to the unit office only to find that I had a new CO, a gentleman called Palgy. I was told to report back to him the next morning at 800 hours sharp.

I returned to my old barracks, where I was happy to find Yitzhak Mohrer busy reading a Hebrew textbook.

'Are we learning *Ivrit*?'

Yitzhak looked up. 'Finally, he's here! Gad, I'm glad to see you. They told me yesterday you'd been posted back.'

'Who are "they"? I don't recognize a single soul.'

'No, everything has changed. Le Colonel Rodrigues has been fired – and is hopefully dead! Every one of the Foreign Legionnaires has gone, one by one. You and I are the last ones left. This is now an elite parachute outfit. Not only are we the only machalnikim, all the rest of the troops are *sabrehs*.'

I looked again at his book. 'Is that why you're studying Ivrit?'

'Mainly because I have no intention of jumping out of a plane, and want to be able to tell them that in their own language, if necessary.' Yitzhak looked at me. 'How do *you* feel about jumping out of a plane?'

'I may have lost my zug aleph, but not my mind. I'll try to get some answers when we see what's-his-name Palgy, tomorrow.'

The next day, both Yitzhak and I were told that the new parachute regiment had its full cadre of officers. Palgy suggested that we contact the machal office in Tel Aviv. He was sure that they would be able to find a unit that would be happy to have us. Of course, he *might* be able to use us in a clerical capacity – and *might* even offer us each the rank of sergeant. But then, he was sure we could do better elsewhere.

I decided that I would be happier elsewhere. Yitzhak agreed. Whereupon we were handed papers authorizing travel and ten days' furlough including hotel chits. These, with great foresight, had even been prepared.

With my package, I found two letters from the Macphersons. The second one was from my mother, telling me that my letter from the convalescent home had arrived just ahead of a letter from Perry Covent, in which Perry had written to say that I had died a hero's death in Jerusalem, fighting superior forces of the Arab Legion. He wanted her to know that my death had not been in vain, since I had surely prevented the fall of the city.

'Luckily,' my mother wrote, 'I opened your letter first, and realized that the news of your death may have been a bit exaggerated.'

When I told Yitzhak about Covent's cretinism, he told me that Perry had actually come to Sarafand, and stated that he had been informed of my death at Air Force HQ. And that as a friend of the family, he required my portfolio, in order to send it to Toronto. It seems that Rodrigues had told him that he needed official written orders before 'he would look for some damn portfolio'.

At the machal office, we were seen by a Giveret Ayala Zacks, a Sabrah married to Sam Zacks, a Toronto financier. In short order, she arranged an interview for both of us with the CO of Air Force Intelligence, an American by the name of Nat Cohen. The interview lasted about forty-five minutes, at the end of which time he told us to report back in two days, when he would let us know if we had been accepted.

We were billeted at the malon where I had stayed before. The hotel still supplied rough sheets plus a morning blanket of hot salt, courtesy of Tel Aviv's humidity.

Yitzhak and I both agreed that Cohen was a mensch, especially when compared to either Rodrigues or Palgy. And if Air Force Intelligence – the Chel Avir Agam – was half as simpatico as the CO, our lot in the war was undoubtedly improving. We hoped we had passed muster.

When we reported two days later, we were greeted by a very young Israeli officer, Carmi Tscharni, who said we were now part of his section.

We underwent ten days of intensive instruction in different types of intelligence gathering and analysis, and in coding and photo recognition, all at a very basic level. Then Yitzhak and I were formed into a 'team' supervised by Tscharni, linked to a field officer, and given half a dozen file folders for (possible phony) targets. After two weeks we were trusted with files of our own.

We actually made a very good team. Where Yitzhak was painstakingly methodical, I leaned toward intuitive analysis. I made lickety-split decisions – but Yitzhak put each of my instant insights through one of his sieves of consistent logic.

Carmi described the team as being composed of Newfeld, who by himself would decide to bomb a target before the war had begun; and Mohrer, who by himself would finally decide to bomb a place after the war was over. As a team, we usually hit the right button at the right time.

One of the very first files we were assigned was for Bethlehem. We were supplied with a fat folder of direct reports from field men, and accounts by friendly Bedouins. These were supported by more than fifty aerial photographs, most of which had been taken from a very low altitude – in fact, they were worthy of paparazzi! We found a trove of targets. All legitimate. All consecrated, religious shrines, worshipped by either Judaism or Christianity – and now converted into ammunition dumps or anti-aircraft defence locales by the Egyptian High Command.

Yitzhak made me go over my photo interpretations at least half a dozen times (I had impatiently elected myself the official aerial-photo interpreter of the team) before he would allow our findings official status in the file.

We handed the newly revised file to Carmi, who glanced at it and said, 'I'll get back to you on this. In the meantime, here's another potential target. It's a place called Bir El Hamma, which should keep Frank busy for two days,' and, turning to Mohrer, 'and you for at least two weeks. Which is when we'll need it.'

We finished off Bir El Hamma in about one week. From our perspective, the most interesting things about the place – a forlorn desert village, really just an oasis – were its strategic Negev location, and the nationality of some of the officers stationed there. Its location appeared vital to any breach of the Sinai – which explained the concentration of Egyptian armour in that dung heap. Also, there appeared to be quite a few 'European gentlemen' – soldiers of fortune – around.

At the end of that week, Carmi brought back the Bethlehem file. The file had a big red stamp in Hebrew on its cover. When I asked him if the stamp meant 'For Immediate Action', he replied, 'Well, not exactly. A better, if loose translation might be, "For Immediate Inaction". We can't touch it.'

'What's stopping us?'

'The Pope, among others. But you two did a good job on it.'

After preparing the two briefings, Yitzhak and I sat around HQ for almost a week with next to nothing to do. In fact, I started to doodle, and made a number of sketches of the Intelligence people working around the place. One day, Carmi strolled over and watched me sketching away. 'That's pretty good,' he said. 'I didn't know you could draw. But it hardly looks like the work of a gifted amateur.'

'You mean it looks more like the work of an untalented professional? You are probably right. I confess I spent a little time at art school. I sort of studied stage design.'

'No. I like your work. Listen, I am a poet. Or rather, I was, until this bloody war started. I've written a new poem which Ma'ariv is going to publish. How about doing an illustration for it? I'm sure they'll be delighted to publish it, and even give you a few piastres. I'll do an English translation of the poem for you.'

This duly became my first formal assault on the halls of illustration.

From that, Carmi brought me another commission, to design a set of Zodiac symbols for a newly established English-language magazine aimed at the *galut* and also serving machal. 'They are even going to pay you for them!'

After another three weeks at Intelligence HQ, both Yitzhak and I were posted. Mohrer became the liaison officer to the Central Command. I was sent to Ramat David, the IAF bomber field not far from Nazareth.

Ramat David was the home base of two bomber groups: Tayesset 103, a squadron of around half a dozen World War II Dakotas; and Tayesset 69, with three B-17 Flying Fortresses. The airfield was also home to a solitary Mosquito, plus two Rapides.

Mundane duties such as shipping equipment, as well as night milk runs, were flown by 103 Squadron, which was mainly manned by volunteer airmen from South Africa, with the occasional Brit and Canadian thrown in; they were being readied to act as carriers for the fledgling parachutists. The daytime sorties were handled by 69 Squadron. Its crew members were mostly Yanks, with the odd Canadian wireless operator or gunner. Sixty-nine Squadron never had more than two aircraft in the air whilst I was at Ramat David – the third aircraft (and it seemed the planes took turns) was forever being cannibalized for parts to keep the other two in the air.

The senior navigator at Ramat David was an Englishman by the name of John Harris, who flew with 103 Squadron – and soon, quietly, took on the role of my (much needed) strongest supporter and defender. (Years later, some months after publication of my children's book *The Princess of Tomboso*, Harris sent me a letter from Southern Rhodesia asking if I was the same Frank Newfeld who had been the FIO at Ramat David.)

The airfield was a short drive from Kibbutz Alonim.

My last week in Tel Aviv, I had met up again with Lenny Waldman, who was in town for a meeting with the Secretariat of Kibbutz Hameuchad. It seemed that Waldman, along with a number of the other Canadian volunteers in his brigade, had become interested in the idea of spending their leave on a kibbutz, with the possible aim of starting a Canadian machal kibbutz after the war. The Secretariat had welcomed the idea. They had selected Kibbutz Alonim to host the volunteers, and had appointed a member of that kibbutz, Dov Meisel, as madrich to the group.

When Lenny heard that I was being posted to Ramat David, he suggested I get in touch. As it turned out, several of the Canadians from my Grand Arenas stay – Waldman, Meyer Naturman, Jack Katz, and Al Stitz – were regular visitors to Alonim. I soon spent most of my spare time there.

Ramat David had a singularly disorderly intelligence section – starting with the war-room bunker, which was under about three inches of water. And it hadn't rained for weeks. On top of this, I appeared to be an unwelcome machal *mumche*, expert (or know-it-all!), thrust upon the airfield's Sabreh intelligence cadre – a not undeserved resentment, since anything of import at Ramat David was conducted in English, from briefings, to operation and intelligence files, to the officers' mess. The *rak anglid* (only English spoken) policy was unavoidable in some quarters, given anglophone aircrew (there were still no ranking Israeli aircrew at the base); still, there was resentment that the ops office, air control, and the intelligence office were rak anglid as well; even the files were in English, with only a few words of Hebrew.

My relationship with the aircrews of both squadrons was good. In 103 Squadron, thanks to John Harris; in 69 Squadron, thanks mainly to Jack Hurtig of Winnipeg, the senior maintenance officer. Unfortunately, relations with operations were strained.

F. N.'s Army, during Operation Ayin, 1949.

Then two incidents brought me onto a collision course with the resident Israeli powers that be.

First, the ops officer, an ex-U.S.-Army air force captain with a penchant for the fleshpots of Haifa, went to town on a two-day pass. After four days, he was brought back to the base by the military police. He peremptorily announced that he was tired of the whole business. When asked what business, he answered, 'The $400 a month that I was promised back home and never received.' When I asked him who had promised him the $400, Ben Gurion or Glubb Pasha, I received a reprimand from the CO. I argued against the decision to have the ops officer sent back to the U.S.A., and tried to have him sent to Intelligence HQ for proper interrogation, but with no success. The only outcome was my having to handle both operations and intelligence briefings for ten days straight.

The second incident involved two officers of the parachute regiment. It happened during Operation Ayin, the pivotal '48–'49 push into the southern coastal areas. The paras were sent to Ramat David in anticipation of a jump, probably around El Arish. The lead stick had been billeted in one of the parachute packing sheds. One evening, late, I had to go there to confer with the CO – the same Palgy who had bid me farewell at Sarafand.

As we talked, the two aforementioned officers decided to entertain the troops with a good old-fashioned Western shootout. The climax was to be an actual gunfight in the (packing table) corral. They both drew their six-guns. Then there was a thunderous explosion, and one of the officers collapsed in a heap, clutching his thigh. At first we all thought this was part of the stupid act. But when the shooter ran towards his fallen friend, and we saw blood all over the table, we realized that something had gone horribly wrong.

Unfortunately, there were no phones in the packing sheds. I got into my jeep and raced down to the control tower, which was supposed to have a medical orderly on duty at all times. Only to find out that the orderly was mysteriously away. Next I drove to the officers' club, where the MO was to be found most evenings of the week. Only to find him, that night, passed out at the bar. Luckily, John Harris was at the club. I told him what had happened, and we dashed over to his office, where he phoned Haifa HQ for an ambulance.

I drove back to the paras, to bring them up to date. Then I decided to wait for the ambulance at the airfield gate, so I could lead it directly to the packing shed.

I had barely gotten to the gate when a Magen David Adom ambulance, complete with a doctor, arrived there. Someone at Haifa HQ had been smart enough to phone Kibbutz Nahalal, just next door, and get them to pick up the wounded officer. (Like most kibbutzim, Nahalal had its own hospital.)

The guard at the gate promptly refused to let a civilian vehicle in without a proper pass. I remonstrated with him to no avail, since he spoke no English, and I spoke even less Hebrew. He just shrugged his shoulders and shook his head. '*Ani katzin!*' I yelled: I am an officer. Which was all the Hebrew I could muster. And then – in a manner, alas, distinctly threatening – 'Open the fucking gate!'

The guard opened the gate, displaying a sudden grasp of English.

Two days later I received orders to report directly back to Tel Aviv. I was even provided with transportation aboard a Bonanza. Which convinced me I had reached the end of my career as an air force officer – and, for that matter, as a free man.

When I arrived at HQ, I was told that everybody had left for the night. I was advised to catch some sleep on one of the planning tables in the war room.

The next morning I was sent to Tsilim, a kibbutz on the edge of the Negev. This was the northern IAF intelligence headquarters for Operation Ayin. The intelligence commander was Matt Gordon, from Toronto: a dandified, self-congratulatory graduate of Ryerson Polytechnic. He had two distinct advantages over me: one, he spoke fluent Hebrew; two, he had the perfect adjutant: a statuesque blonde, with the gift of seductive persuasion. I confess I took an instant liking to her, one that equalled my instant dislike of Katzin Gordon.

Gordon informed me that I would be the ground liaison officer to the two brigades in the Raffiach sector; in the same breath, he informed me that even if I had pulled the wool over the eyes of some people at Ramat David and Intelligence HQ, he wasn't one bit fooled. My only raison d'être, as far as he was concerned, was to liaise between him and the 8th and 10th Brigades. I was *not* to make any command decisions. And I was to avoid all rash moves, such as having ops officers arrested and threatening military policemen.

Then, he gave me two navy-blue ribbons to put on my epaulets. 'This will make the army think you're an officer.'

I was given a code sheet – a squared-off 26-by-26-box grid – which was to be replaced once a week. Next, I received a thick codes and ciphers manual, plus my own regiment of three troopers. My army consisted of a codes and ciphers clerk, a wireless and Morse-key operator, and a 'shamir,' who I decided was my very own flatfoot/lunatic attendant.

Our transportation was a jeep attached to a canvas-covered van, which was filled with something called a VHF set, and other acronym-bearing marvels. When I asked where the driver was, my army, to a man, pointed at me. When I demurred, citing scant driving experience, they informed me that none of them knew how to drive.

We set off for Beersheba, a desert town that had been taken by Israeli forces some days earlier. There I was to report to Yitzhak Sadeh, CO of the 8th Brigade.

Yitzhak Sadeh was one of the legends of the War of Independence. He greeted me with a glass of vodka and asked me my name. When I told him, he said that *sadeh* meant field in Hebrew, and that his family name had once been Feld. He added that I'd better change my name, since there was room for only one Sadeh. All this accompanied with a loud laugh.

Then I was turned over to an adjutant, who told me that the staff convoy would leave at nine o'clock that evening. I was told to take my jeep to the assembly area; we would be in the last group to set out.

After a meal, the adjutant offered to show me the town.

Beersheba was small and dusty. Every shop on the main street was shuttered. They all looked alike: single-storey stuccoed buildings with bars across their windows. As we walked by, I caught glimpses of anxious, hostile-looking youngsters. The only adults visible were numerous heavily armed Bedouins standing next to kneeling camels.

When I remarked on this, my guide smiled. 'These are our Bedouins. The Palestinians will come out tomorrow, as soon as the Bedouins have gone. The Arabs fear the Bedouins far more than they fear us. When the Bedouins are gone, the Palestinians will quickly lose their fear of us and happily come looking for baksheesh and customers.'

By then we had come to an affluent-looking neighbourhood. I had desperately needed a bathroom for some time, and finally announced my urgency. The villas all looked abandoned, and my guide suggested that I go into the nearest one and use the facilities. 'But only flush once. The water has probably been shut off, and the Arab cisterns only seem to have water for one flush.'

The bathroom was beautifully appointed. Of course there was no sit-down toilet; instead, there was a floor-to-ceiling marble cubicle with tiled foot-stands on the floor. First I let a small amount of cold water into the washbasin. Having never used a toilet without a seat, I though it best to take off both my trousers and my wind-jacket. Then I squatted down.

I left the bathroom, still carrying my pants and tunic. I came to what was obviously the dining room. The table had the remains of a meal on it, many-days rotten. There was an ornate sideboard and, sitting on it, a silver *finjohn* – a sort of small metal pot with a long handle, used to brew Turkish coffee. As I picked it up to look at it, a hand grabbed my chin from behind. Just in time I deflected a curved dagger. I have no idea how I managed to get hold of my Commando knife. But somehow I did. Instinctively, I jabbed out behind me, hit flesh and bones and twisted my knife upward – just as I had been taught in No. 6 Commando. I broke the hold around my neck.

My attacker turned out to be a smallish, older man. His apparel did not reflect the affluence of the villa. A servant? A squatter? I couldn't tell. I had obviously wounded him quite badly. The knife had gone far in. He was bleeding from a wound in his right side, halfway down his ribcage. He sank soundlessly to the floor.

I did not even notice that my left palm, cut by the deflected dagger, was steadily dripping blood. I had a bit of a blow to the side of my nose, but otherwise I seemed to be okay. I snatched a rather used linen napkin from the table and wrapped it around my hand, then pulled my clothes on and ran outside. I reported to my guide what had happened.

'We'd better go inside and look at your Arab. You say you stabbed him with your knife?'

I nodded.

'Why didn't you just shoot him?'

'It never occurred to me. There was no time to think.'

Inside, we discovered that the man had died.

We stood there for a moment. 'Well, there is nothing we can do,' said the adjutant. 'If it makes you feel better, tell yourself he died of a heart attack.'

'Shouldn't we report it?'

'I probably will. As soon as I get to Raffiach. Now take your finjohn and let's go.'

We returned to the assembly area and I found my jeep. Our group set off at 10 p.m. Ours was the third or fourth vehicle in line.

I wasn't at all happy about things. The evening's events had left me shaken. And neither the wilds of Toronto nor the tarmac at Ramat David – nor my brief stint on the Burma Road – had prepared me for driving in the desert at night.

Darkness obscured the contours of the dunes. I had never driven on sand before, and I still had not mastered the art of switching over to four-wheel drive. (It had been impressed on me that negotiating the sand dunes required judicious juggling of gears.) This was made worse by the fact that someone had stolen the knob from the jeep's gear shift – a knob on which there had been a nice diagram, showing *expert* drivers like me the location of each gear. No one in my 'regiment of three' had anything to wrap around the rather sharp, exposed end, either.

The sand got into every pore and orifice. But in spite of a few scary jolts, we managed to keep up with the convoy. And to reach our destination, a flat stretch of desert between Raffiach and the Egyptian border.

The Negev at night was freezing! All I had with me was my thin windbreaker and a sweater. My WOP declared that I would freeze in my pup tent, and suggested that I sleep inside the small trailer on top of the VHF and the other communication sets, all of which he would turn on for extra heat.

Morning came too quickly. Especially since I woke up to find myself being bodily lifted out of the trailer by a couple of medical orderlies. Of course, I had no idea who or what they were, and remonstrated vehemently. 'Where the hell do you think you're taking me?'

'To the field hospital,' one of them said, in flawless American.

'What on earth for?'

'You're covered in blood from your face and hand, down to your waist.'

Outside the trailer, I checked myself over. Everything that was supposed to move, did. I announced that my nosebleed had probably been caused by the sand. As far as my left hand was concerned, I blamed the missing gearshift. (Nobody questioned why I hadn't shifted gears with my right hand – which was, after all, on the gearshift side.)

The medics had obviously had enough. With a shrug of their shoulders, they wished me mazal tov, got into their ambulance, and drove off.

That day I went to a staff meeting attended by about two dozen senior officers. These represented both the 8th (Sadeh's tanks) and the 10th (Har-el) Brigades, as well as supporting units of anti-aircraft sections, field medical facilities, pioneer engineer corps, and liaison personnel (including me and my own 'brigade').

As far as I was concerned, the main topic of the meeting was the alacrity shown by our ack-ack guns in shooting at our own planes. Sadeh, as I later found out in translation, read aloud a long list of misidentification incidents of our planes as hostiles, sent to him by the IAF. He then said that it was lucky the ground fire's aim, so far, would have caused them to miss the Graf Zeppelin.

But just in case their aim improved, identification of enemy planes was from now on to be verified by the IAF liaison officer, before firing. Akiva *haGingi* (the ginger-haired), the young Sabreh officer in charge of the two ack-ack batteries, flushed till his face matched his locks. But even he nodded in agreement.

After a few other points of procedure had been covered, we of the support groups were dismissed. I told my small band to pack up, so that we could bivouac nearer to Akiva's anti-aircraft guns.

Akiva was a kibbutznik. (Of course! It seemed that almost every officer was a kibbutznik. How they had time to be even amateur farmers was a mystery to me.) He spoke pretty good English, and told me that he was slated to go into the Foreign Service as soon as we had won the war, if his kibbutz would let him go.

I spent the rest of the morning memorizing my personal code letters and some key code words to be used in emergency radio voice-communication. And getting to know the anti-aircraft crew. Then Akiva and I went to the field kitchen, where we had lunch. We worked out a couple of hand signals, in case we were surprised by an arrival of planes and weren't within hailing distance of one another. After that, I went back to my trailer and made contact with Katzin Gordon of Tsilim, Freddy Fredkins down at Revivim (at the time, our southernmost kibbutz), and Carmi Tscharni, back at Modiin HQ.

The following day passed uneventfully. Tanks from the 8th Brigade were obviously getting ready for some major action. But nothing else was happening. There wasn't a single plane in the sky for me to identify. Thank heavens!

I had barely returned from supper at the mess tent, however, when a jeep drove up to fetch me.

It had been sent over by Yoske Tabenkin, the commanding officer of the 10th Palmach Brigade. Apparently, a Har-el *pluga*, or company, had taken a hillock north of Gaza. They had been surrounded by a large force of Egyptian infantry and Palestinian irregulars. Tabenkin wondered if the IAF could strafe them. His troops were fast running out of ammunition, and he didn't think they could hold out once morning came, when the Arabs would likely attack.

I asked him to pinpoint the Egyptian positions. This was not easy to do. The situation was too fluid. Then I suggested two possible steps.

One: I and one of his officers could be driven to Tsilim, where Matt Gordon could contact Fighter Command. (Frankly, I didn't trust myself to transmit accurate information. Nor did I feel safe setting off any operation via VHF.)

Two: they could somehow get me within sight of the target area, wait till daybreak, and we could set up visual ground-to-air assault communication.

Nothing more could be done that same evening. Darkness had fallen, and the IAF wasn't that sophisticated. Tabenkin chose Option no. 2.

An hour later, he reappeared.

'That was fast. You don't want us to spend the whole night in the open?'

'No. You can peacefully go to sleep. The Arabs seemed to have had enough, about twenty minutes ago. We don't know why. Anyhow, the operation is off. I am on my way to a meeting. And as I was passing your area, I thought I'd let you know.'

Needless to say, I was disappointed at missing the action.

Disappointed enough to whoop with joy and dance a solo hora behind my trailer.

I slept like a log that night. Bright and early the next morning, Akiva came sauntering over. He suggested we have breakfast at his place, since his men were almost finished cleaning both of the anti-aircraft guns. I went over to the trailer to get my Narodni Podnik. I had made the trailer my permanent boudoir.

Just then, a squadron of five planes – which looked very much like Spitfires to me – appeared on the northern horizon.

'Shit! We don't have any Spits. They must be Egyptians.'

My VHF man made lightning-fast connection with HQ. A young voice, with a strong sabreh accent, answered. I asked to speak to the duty officer, only to be told he had just gone out for a while. I told the young voice that I had just been sent a bag of five lemons (our code word that week for enemy planes). And that I really needed someone to send me some oranges.

To which he replied that he couldn't understand why I thought he would have any oranges, and suggested I go to the nearest *shuk*.

The planes were getting closer by the second. Not only that, they were flying in a tight finger formation, and were bristling with twenty-millimetre cannons.

Really, all I wanted to do at that moment was to dive into one of Akiva's slit trenches. Still, all eyes were upon me. So I yelled, 'Forget the previous message! I have a flight of five enemy planes overhead.

— 154 —

Contact operations to scramble fighters over to Raffiah.'

There was total silence at the other end.

Then, a moment later, the young voice came back on and said, 'I've looked out of the window. There are NO planes overhead.'

At this point, Freddy Fredkins' South African voice roared out from the receiver: 'They're over *his* head! Not *yours!* You mentally constipated putz!' Then to me he said, 'I'll handle this, Frank. I'm already scrambling Tel Nof.'

The next thing I knew, the Spitfires were flying right over our ack-ack emplacement. I yelled to Akiva to start shooting. His guns were still in the process of reassembly after cleaning, but one began firing away, despite the fact that, half assembled, it could only fire on a fixed axis.

'A lot of good that'll do,' I thought.

Then, to my surprise, smoke appeared from the engine of one of the planes. As the pilot bailed out and lazily drifted down, I realized something horrible had happened. The wing tips of the spinning plane carried RAF insignia. I had just shot down a British plane.

No! I had shot down two British planes. Another Spitfire spouted smoke: this one shot down by an Israeli Messerschmidt, which had suddenly come on the scene.

No! I had shot down three British planes. Every rifle and machine gun in the area had opened fire. Then a fourth Spitfire started to come down, belching smoke. And another parachute opened up above us. This one had been shot down by the Ramat David Mosquito, which had somehow appeared on the scene and also joined the fray.

The fifth RAF plane flew off in the direction of Egypt, hotly pursued by the Mosquito plus another of our fighters. I jumped into my jeep and drove over to the 8th Brigade HQ.

Yitzhak Sadeh was still in a slit trench, watching the three planes flying away. 'We have just shot down four, possibly five British planes! Do you know who called on the attack?'

'I'm afraid I did.'

'On what evidence?'

'They were Mark XVIII or later Spitfires. I assumed they were Egyptian. And they were flying in tight finger formation! I assumed this was an attack.'

'This is going to cause an international incident.'

Like an idiot, I decided to enlighten a brigadier. 'I don't think London will admit that British planes were anywhere near Israeli territory, much less mention they were lost in action. Not to a bunch of Jews.'

'They'll mention it if their last plane gets shot down in Egypt.'

'I imagine it definitely will be,' I said – stupidly. 'The flier of our Mosquito is an ex-World War II RAF pilot, a George Somebody by name.'

Sadeh gave me an irate look, and without another word stomped off.

First thing next morning, I was ordered into a jeep, which took me quickly away. At Tsilim, a Piper Cub was waiting to take me back to Tel Aviv. Carmi was waiting for me at HQ.

'I'm afraid you're in trouble,' he said. 'Sadeh refuses to have you anywhere near Miftzaim Ayin. What happened?'

I told him everything I could remember about the unhappy chain of events. I added that I shouldn't have sounded off about London's position.

Carmi frowned, 'That part wasn't mentioned. What is this about you claiming to know who one of the pilots was?'

'Did I? No, wait. Maybe I did. One of our fighters was a Mosquito – the IAF's only Mosquito that I know of. The only one who flies it is a little Englishman, with a whistle hanging out of his old RAF tunic pocket. I think I may have mentioned him.'

'Let's leave it at that for the moment. I'm glad we had this talk. Nat Cohen will want to see you later. I fear that you have been elected to be the goat.'

Later that day, I was ordered to see Nat Cohen. My days as an intelligence officer were finished.

I was given a choice: I could be transferred to Jerusalem and take a course on aerial photo identification, with the rank of sergeant. Or I could become the IAF war artist, with a studio in Jaffa. This would be a new post that did not have a rank designated to it as yet.

Then Cohen added that Modiin had decided, unofficially, that I had acted correctly.

And that is how I got to be the official war artist of the IAF.

10. KISSUFIM

n late summer of 1949, after fourteen months' service, I was demobbed. The army gave me a camp bed and a mattress, my severance pay, an open travel pass, and a letter of admission to an Ulpan seminar (an intensive course in Hebrew) of my choosing. To my surprise, I also received written orders to report to the Hadassah Hospital in Jerusalem within a period of ten days for a final checkup.

My visits to the Canadian *garin*, the group of kibbutz trainees, at Alonim had convinced me to look into the idea of life on a kibbutz. Lenny Waldman was now the secretary of the fledgling machal kibbutz, and on one of my visits I mentioned to him that I would like to spend a trial period, say six months, with them. Waldman checked it out with the Secretariat of the Kibbutz Hameuchad movement, and got back to me with a favourable response.

At the time I was mustered out of the air force, the machal garin was ensconced at Ma'agan Michael. This kibbutz's original Negev location had been captured by Egyptian forces in the early days of the war. The kibbutznikim had now taken up temporary residence at a place called Cabri, in the picturesque but rugged terrain of western Galilee.

I arrived at Ma'agen Michael, armed with my demob bed and mattress, and was duly allocated a tent. This I shared with a very young American by name of Yigal, who was to become the shepherd once the garin had its own kibbutz. After only one month's stay, he was trusted enough to take Ma'agan Michael's flock out all by himself. I had the utmost respect for him, since he already had a specific profession. I was just a *pkak*, a cork. This meant I went to wherever there was a 'bottleneck', in the workings of the kibbutz, that needed 'corking': that is, a task which needed an extra pair of hands. I had to go to the dining hall each evening to check the *sidur avodah*, the next day's work list, accordingly.

After one short week at Ma'agen Michael, I had to leave for

Jerusalem for my checkup. The checkup culminated with my being told that I needed to come into the hospital once a week for therapy to my left arm. Its condition, in the ten months since my stay at the convalescent depot, seemed to have deteriorated. I told the nurse that the arm looked fine to me. To which she replied that I was supposed to be an artist, not a doctor. The next Ulpan seminar was not going to start for another month; so, after a few days, I hitchhiked (easy in Israel at that time) back to Cabri, and told the garin that I had better defer my membership.

During my trip to Jerusalem, the garin had decided to call itself Kibbutz 'Ein Kessef', which was a pun; depending on how the word 'ein' was written, it could mean either 'No Money' or 'Well of Silver'. The movement, unsurprisingly, vetoed the name. The garin proposed a new moniker – 'Kissufim', meaning 'Aspirations' or 'Yearnings' – though we continued to use 'Ein Kessef' amongst ourselves.

The group voted to refuse my offer of deferment. In spite of the kibbutz's lean budget, arrangements were made to provide me with a small living allowance, and off I hitchhiked to Jerusalem, in time for my next therapy session.

In Jerusalem, luck seemed to be in my corner. To start, the head of the Bezalel School of Art, a Mr Ardon, let me stay in one of the school's 'pachons' (small, one-room buildings made of sheet metal, and equipped with bathroom facilities) for next to nothing. Through Ardon, I met the editor of *Youth Horizon* magazine, who immediately gave me a freelance commission. The Ulpan people sent me to a private teacher, since their next course was delayed. Finally, my cousin Irene magically procured some basic bits of furniture, which included an old easel and drawing board.

My studio *(pachon)* was located in a cobbled courtyard in the back of Bezalel. There was another corrugated building next to mine. It was bigger, and was occupied by an Arab family. The husband had been a member of the Palestine Police; he was now the night superintendent at Bezalel.

That summer, Jerusalem was uncomfortably hot. I took to working evenings beneath a tree in our courtyard, since my pachon, even on a cool day, was well over a hundred degrees. There I got to know neighbour Hassim.

Both Hassim and I were heavy smokers. Where I went outside to escape the heat of my pachon, he went outside to escape the heat of his wife's strident voice; she was the only Palestinian woman I knew of who loathed the smell of tobacco.

The family soon discovered that I was even poorer than they were. One day, Mrs Hassim sent one of her four kids over with a plate of hummus and a large pita. When I sent back a sketch I had made of our courtyard, Hassim appeared with tears in his eyes and proclaimed that I was to have supper with them each Friday: 'That's the start of your Shabbat, and the end of mine.'

I was kept busy, both with commissions and with art lessons of my own. I had renewed my acquaintance with Irene's friend Ja'akov Pins, or Pinsel, the painter. He visited my studio, and after looking at my work invited me to sit in on his drawing classes, in which he had some twelve students. I protested that I could not afford to take lessons; he replied that he needed a pace-setter. So, if I would set the pace for free, he would be happy to give me a few hints, likewise for free. I learned three important things from him: 1.) honest drawing; 2.) self-discipline; and 3.) to recognize my own kitsch dependency, and avoid it like the plague.

Everything was going well – even the Hebrew lessons, which turned out not to be the ordeal I had imagined. To my surprise, I had no difficulty keeping up. After one month, my young Israeli teacher told me that I must have stored away an awful lot of the language during my military service, without knowing it. She asked if I would consider going to a higher level than that set by the normal Ulpan – then I would be able to illustrate 'in Hebrew', not just 'in English'. I was her only student. She suggested that if she could continue teaching me for the whole three months allowed by Ulpan, she would perhaps pose for me in return. I got the better of that deal in every way.

Prior to being sent to the Hadassah, I had not realized that my injured arm had started to atrophy. At the first therapy session, however, I could see that this was the case. I religiously followed the exercise regimen established by Dr Rakovchik. After six weeks I had progressed so well that I was put on a bimonthly checkup schedule. I began to have pangs of conscience. After four months, there was no longer any real reason to stay in Jerusalem. Life was comfortable, perhaps too comfortable. My pachon was a lot better than my tent at Cabri, and I liked being by myself. I decided that I needed to get back

to Ein Kessef, before I took up permanent residence as a Jerusalem plu-
tocrat.

There were two main kibbutz movements in Israel at that time:
Kibbutz Hameuchad, which was affiliated with the Mapai party, and
Kibbutz Hashomer, which was affiliated with the Mapam party.
Mapai was centre-left labour: Hameuchad was left wing, and national-
istically driven; Mapam was 'red of centre' labour: Hashomer was
communist, and ideologically driven. But the movements had similar
philosophies when it came to communal living, and both were
staunchly and self-sacrificingly Zionist. Out of these two movements
had come the overwhelming share of the Haganah's elite.

Life on a kibbutz was certainly different from middle-class life in
either Toronto or Tel Aviv. There was no such thing as a salary. The
philosophy was: 'Each member striving for the good of the community
– the community striving for the good of each member.' And the kibbutz did provide for the needs of each member, to the best of its ability: so, if *I* needed paint and paper, these were, where possible, provided – without any cries of 'what about me?' from the non-artists in
the community. Holidays of individual members were likewise
financed by the treasurer, to the best of the treasury's ability.

Adults and children ate separately, in communal dining rooms.
This obviated the children noticing any discrepancy in quantity or
quality of ration, especially in the newer and less affluent kibbutzim.
The children also slept in their own quarters; these usually afforded
more material comforts than did the adult quarters.

Laundry services were provided. At Kissufim, which was part of a
relatively moderate movement, you received back, cleaned, the same
clothes you had sent in. In more radical movements such as
Hashomer, the laundry would provide a clean change of clothes in the
proper size, but not necessarily the same set of clothes you had sent in.

Of course, there was a hierarchy among kibbutzim: some were
wealthier, some poorer. But few people seemed to join a particular settlement for pecuniary reason.

By the time I returned from Jerusalem, Ein Kessef had grown to
almost thirty people. Originally, there were ten Canadians: four from
west of the Credit River (I forget exactly where) – Jack Katz, Max
Robinson, Leib Shanas and Joe Steinberg – plus, from Ontario, Morris
Epstein, Al Stitz, Harvey Sirulnikov, and me; and, from Quebec,

Meyer Naturman and Lenny (Arieh) Waldman. (*Arieh*, Lion, was the Hebrew name Lenny had taken, in deference to his dealings with 'the powers that be', as secretary of our fledgling kibbutz. There was a fair bit of pressure for newcomers to change their names to Hebrew ones. In fact, the army would stamp: 'CHANGE YOUR NAME TO A HEBREW ONE!' on the envelopes of our mail.)

The new members of Ein Kessef came from all over the world, however, and they included both men and women. All were young people who had heard of our group; many of them had served with one or another of the 'Magnificent Ten' in the Haganah. We now had Brits (I remember one 'Wingate' in particular), Americans, French, Scots, Swiss, and one mystery man – Eskimo, the five-foot-five ex-Royal-Marine commando from Belgium.

Despite our growing numbers, Ma'agan Michael's chaverim suspected – with perhaps some justification – that we were a bunch of Canadian cowboys, who could not be seriously considered as future kibbutznikim. Their suspicions were not allayed by our work habits. We may have been sincere about our return *to* the land – but as for us ever learning how to competently work *on* the land, that was something else.

I resumed my honoured role as a pkak. Word had gotten around that I was an artist. This, with its suggestion of the effete and the elite, was tantamount to waving a red flag under the noses of a herd of stampeding kibbutznikim. My evening's visit to the dining hall to read the sidur avodah became akin to a trip to Madame Guillotine.

At the beginning, the jobs were simply messy. Ma'agan Michael had a remunerative hospital laundry contract. Although the work did not require strong muscles, it required a cast-iron stomach. You could rely on finding all sorts of unexpected goodies amidst the sheets and operating-room linens: used sponges, scalpels and needles, bullet-heads, fingers – and worse, far worse. The shift began at midnight with a 'lunch break' at 6 a.m. (I assumed this was done for the purpose of saving on food.)

After four weeks of this, I was relieved to find that I had now become a night watchman of the goat pens. When I thanked the *sadran avodah* (job allocator), he told me with a smirk that he had heard I was an important artist. He was doing his best to leave my day hours free, so that I could pursue my ART.

Life on the kibbutz was predictable and sort of orderly. Sort of, because – as we soon found – on a 'real' kibbutz, philosophy sometimes gave way to pragmatism. A good example of this was to be found in the perks enjoyed by the kibbutz *nahag*, or truck driver. Certainly, his was a rough job. Not just the fact that he usually worked all alone in an alien environment, but also the fact that he often spent days away from home, family and chaverim. Still, where we, the pkakim, smoked awful cigarettes (like the Latif, which had to be carried horizontally, or else all the tobacco would fall out) Cabri's nahag smoked Marlboros. To some of us neophytes, this seemed be carrying the dictum 'Each according to his/her ability and each according to his/her need' a bit too far. (When we raised this with our counsellor, we were told we would understand better after we had our own kibbutz.)

Once a week, we held an *assifah*, a general meeting. It was usually attended by either our madrich or some other member of Ma'agan Michael's *maskirut* (secretariat). Here, all sorts of matters were thrashed out: problems, such as being allergic to hospital laundry; complaints, such as Yigal playing his recorder at all hours of the night. (Which was considered his right as a shepherd; the only catch was that he played the thing consistently off key.) Most of the discussions revolved around trying to find *our* identity within kibbutz doctrine. What kind of farming should we ask to undertake? (There were actually strong leanings for Ein Kessef to become a fishing kibbutz.) And where would we do the most good? (Some of our members thought we should go to the Negev. Strangely enough, this group included a number of our most ardent fishing enthusiasts. When I asked how they intended to fish in the middle of the desert, I was mysteriously told, 'There are ways.') Our madrich explained that the final decision really rested more with the government than with even the secretariat of our movement.

Slowly but surely it became evident that there had developed a distinctly radical group within the garin. They were very intense and quite intimidating – and unforgivingly critical of any show of 'bourgeois tendencies' on the part of the 'unenlightened'.

The most vocal member of this group was Yoninah, a Yankee fundamentalist, who had somehow made her way to us via the Ba'hai in Haifa. She and Arieh Waldman had paired up in all things but philosophy. The most vehement member of the group was Albert, a Scot of some obscure Christian denomination. Others included Max Robinson and Joe Steinberg: our very own Canadian iconoclasts. They took exception to the Hameuchad 'no communists' policy, and were fast becoming communist sympathizers. True to Canadian custom, however, they were kind and quiet – if misguided – in their determination.

After my stints as washer and watcher, I was put on the *chazats*, or quarry detail, which usually consisted of seven men. Four would gather rocks into twenty-kilo slings and bring them to the chazats man, who fed the rocks into a machine that pulverized them. The pulverized mix would then be shovelled into fifty-kilo paper bags – with a commercial imprint in vivid red on both sides – by the two remaining men.

The job of the chazats feeder was easily the worst. The rubber slings had to be thrown up to him where he stood, on a small raised platform, in order to reach the jaws of the machine. After one day on chazats detail, I became the feeder. After one hour, the slings felt like forty kilos. After two hours, they felt like a hundred kilos. At supper, my dinner fork seemed to weigh ten kilos, itself. Luckily, nobody worked more than a month on the chazats detail. And then you got three days off.

Somehow I survived, and was moved to greater things. I now was put on *binian*, or building construction. A block of housing units was being put up to accommodate the many veterans returning to Ma'agan Michael. The new buildings were made of poured concrete. Cabri mixed its own cement. A large pile of our chazats bags had been brought up on a flatbed, for the mixture.

With typical foresight, the flatbed had been left some fifty yards from the cement mixer. All the tractors were out in the fields. We had three wheelbarrows, which had been intended for use in bringing the mixed cement to the frames. We decided to use the wheelbarrows to bring the bags of chazats close to the mixer, instead. Once enough bags were in place, mixing would be started. At that point, the wheelbarrows would be returned to proper duty. The remainder of the bags would be carried over by hand. The carting detail consisted of three Ein Kessef members: Max Robinson, Joe Stitz and me.

When it was time to switch from wheelbarrows to hand-carrying, Max said something in Hebrew to the boss of the construction group, who waved me over. 'Max says you have a wounded arm?' he asked.

'No. I'm okay. This is nothing after being on chazats.'

'How you will carry with your bad arm?'

'I can carry the bag just with my right arm. It's really okay.'

That settled the matter. I thanked Max, and off we went.

The bags were too big to sling on one's shoulder, so Max and Joe carried each bag by holding it with both hands. I had to carry mine under my right arm, since I didn't dare test my left one. It worked quite well. In fact, I was able to move much faster than either of them could, holding the heavy bags below their waists. We reached a point where I could make four trips to the others' three. 'Stop showing off,' yelled Max.

We finished in about thirty more minutes. I was promptly awarded one of the wheelbarrows filled with cement. I had just grabbed the two handlebars, when one of the Cabri chaverim stopped me and asked, in Hebrew, 'What has happened to your arm?'

'Nothing. Which arm?'

'Your right one. It is as big as a balloon. Go to the nurse.'

I left the Haifa hospital the next evening with my right hand in a cast that extended halfway up my forearm. I had pulled out the tendons at my wrist. And never even felt a thing. It was only when the nurse told me I was in trouble that my wrist started to hurt like hell.

When I got back to Cabri, the sadran avodah said that all I had to do was tell him I didn't like work. Not try to commit suicide.

After my accident, I was put on all sorts of non-demanding details, all of which entailed work that could be done with just one hand. I sat on top of the newly poured cement walls and, armed with a water hose, squirted away in the hot weather. I cleared tables at breakfast, lunch and supper, and, armed with a wet cloth, cleaned them. I emptied the mailbags, and placed the sorted letters and packages in the appropriate chaver's cubbyhole. In my spare time, I tried drawing with my left hand – and gave up in disgust after three days.

Some four weeks later, my cast was taken off and replaced by a leather harness designed to stretch the recuperating tendons. This at least gave me the use of my right hand back again.

In the meantime, Arieh Waldman had been made our *maskir chutz*, our exterior secretary. He now seemed to spend most of his time at the Hameuchad secretariat. He reported that Ein Kessef would definitely become a reality. When and where was not yet decided. It seemed that the Ministry of Defence was also involved, as was the Foreign Ministry. The Foreign Ministry mostly had the 'State of Israel Bonds in mind, and was looking to found 'Israel's one and only Canadian kibbutz' to further its fundraising efforts in Canada.

Around the time of my accident, we were joined by the first Hachalutz (a Zionist youth movement) contingent from New York. (Some time earlier, the maskirut had decided on a merger of the Kissufim garin with the New York Hachalutz Hatzair chapter. It was becoming pretty unlikely that we were going to attract too many more Canadians – though we did have two new arrivals from Canada, the Kernerman brothers.) The spiritual leader of the Brooklyn bunch was a fervent young ideologue, Yehuda Gingold by name. He and his wife were billeted in one of the newly completed buildings – ostensibly because Mrs Gingold was pregnant; actually because Kibbutz Hameuchad had big plans for Yehuda. Their quarters boasted two rooms, and it was decided that one of the rooms would be made available to me three afternoons a week, to use as a studio. The Gingolds agreed.

The next few of our weekly general meetings were taken up with discussions as to who should, at least on a temporary basis, undertake the various administrative responsibilities of Ein Kessef, and who should now receive training in specific areas. We knew, for instance, that we would most certainly need a nahag. We would need a general secretary, an outside secretary, a work coordinator, tractor drivers, a nurse, a wrangler (we already had Yigal, our shepherd), a supply supervisor, a cobbler and a nursery supervisor (the condition of a couple of our chaverot made it clear that we were going to need a nursery, soon). Of course, there were other, possible positions to be filled – such as boatswain. But since we did not know for certain that Kissufim would become a fishing kibbutz in the Negev, we deferred that one and its like.

Waldman remained our outside secretary, since negotiations with the Hameuchad secretariat, not to mention the Sochnut (Jewish Agency) and the government, would now become really serious and possibly intense. Moshe Hertzberg, one of our first non-Canadians, was chosen to become Kissufim's general secretary. Morris (Eppy) Epstein became our 'number one nahag'. Leib Shanas became our sadran, our work coordinator. I asked to be trained to be the *sandlar*, the cobbler.

At each meeting, Arieh would report that there still was no final word as to where Kissufim would be established. The adrenaline rush brought on by the thought of our imminent independence subsided, and life went on as before. I slipped back to honing my skills in both dining hall and mail room, and forgot about sandals, shoes and boots.

Life with the Gingolds had started off well, but after only two weeks things became touchy. It was obvious that they considered me a nuisance. This I could not understand, since both Gingolds were away at work during the time when I had use of the second room. I always managed to finish before they returned from work, so as to give them their privacy.

Ma'agan Michael had provided me with a large table to use as a drawing board. Once or twice, I did leave wet or unfinished work on the worktable. But I generally made sure that I left the place in a presentable state.

Then, after about three weeks, the fateful afternoon arrived. I had come in after lunch, as usual, only to find the unfinished (and still, admittedly, scratchy) masterpiece that I had left out on the table adorned with coffee-cup rings and indecorous dabs of marmalade.

I fear I lost my cool. I put my fist through the wallboard to the left of the table. To make matters worse, I wrote the word 'CHASIRIM' (PIGS) in huge Hebrew letters on a sheet of newsprint. Then I scooped up all of my art supplies, plus the soiled drawing, and stomped back to my tent.

That evening, Moshe Hertzberg came by and asked what had happened. I told him the whole story.

'Well, the Gingolds are bringing the matter up at our next assifah. I thought I'd tell you.' He sighed. 'How's your wrist?'

'Okay. I used my left fist.'

'That's good.'

At the assifah, Yehuda spoke first. He talked about respect for others' property. He talked about the hardships that Ma'agan Michael had endured, as our host – only to see its property vandalized by one of the garin members. He spoke about the abuse of privilege – and went on to question the need for the kibbutz to underwrite unproven talent. Especially when the garin did not yet have the resources to finance or support personal whims. He finished by saying that I had violated the welcome and encouragement that he and his chavera had extended to me.

At that point, Arieh got up and said that he would like to question me on some of the points Yehuda had so eloquently raised. First of all, he asked me what my last assignment had been in the Chel Avir, the air force.

'I was a war artist.'

'How many war artists did the Chel Avir have?'

'I'm not certain. Two, I think.'

'Has any of your artwork been published?'

'A few pieces.'

'Did you put your fist through the Gingolds' wall?'

'Yes.'

'Why on earth did you do that?'

'I lost my temper when I found coffee stains and marmalade on a piece of artwork which I had left on the table.'

Yehuda jumped up. 'That is not true! We never went near his artwork.'

Yigal now got up and said, 'I saw the drawing, when Frank came back with it. It was covered with stains. I can go get it.'

Arieh now asked why I would have left work lying about on their table.

'Actually, *their* table was issued to me by Ma'agan Michael. I had to leave the artwork, because it was still wet.'

After a brief discussion, the assifah made its verdict.

1.) I would provide the garin with one of my drawings. This would be framed and hung on the Gingolds' wall, over the hole I had punched, until such time as we left Cabri. The artwork would then belong to Ma'agan Michael.

2.) I would now have the use of the room *five* afternoons a week, during which times I was to be assured total privacy.

3.) The Gingolds were reminded that having one's own private store of any kind was not in the spirit of kibbutz ideology.

A month later, I was sent to Kibbutz Afek to learn to be a cobbler.

* * *

Afek, an older settlement – predominantly Polish – was located near the coast between Natanya and Acre. Its maskirah was an American, Hadassah Diener. She was a former madrich of the Brooklyn chapter of Hachalutz Hatzair, and had married the group's first Israeli *shaliach* (movement counsellor), a member of Afek.

Life at Afek was good. I had my own room. I had a steady job. Not being a pkak meant no more looking at the next day's work list. The Afek cigarette ration was much more generous than Cabri's, both in quantity and quality. And the kitchen could actually cook!

My first day in the shop, however, did not bode so well. The shoemaker, a hostile and disgruntled asthmatic called Lezer, made it very clear that I had been forced upon him. Right off, he advised me that if I thought, like the rest of the chaverim, that being a cobbler was a picnic, I was in for a rude awakening. When I pulled out a cigarette, he snarled that smoking was not allowed in his shop.

The next day, miraculously, his attitude changed completely. Both he and the 'number two shoemaker' were already hard at work at seven o'clock when I arrived. Lezer was smoking a very strange-smelling cigarette. 'These cigarettes are medicinal,' he explained. 'My new supply finally arrived yesterday evening.' Now, he said, we could all smoke to our hearts' content.

Ten years later, I found out what the unusual odour had been: Lezer's prescription was pure pot. The more he smoked, the mellower all of us became. But in spite of Lezer's 'medicine' – or possibly because of it – both men turned out to be talented artisans and excellent teachers.

I started off by preparing strands of waxed cobbler's twine. That – plus carefully watching how things were done in a sandlariah – was my only task for the first three days. Then I was given my very own knife, hammer and metal-tipped cobbler's pole. For two weeks I mended heels. To save leather, I had to insert wedges wherever possible. This was tedious work. I guessed that Afek considered leather more valuable than my time.

From patching up old heels, I went to making new heels, both leather and rubber. I learned how to smooth the insets off with thick shards of glass. Then, I was actually trusted to tack on soles: first, only toe wedges – but later, whole soles!

By now, I had been at Afek for five weeks (and it was two weeks since I had last cut my thigh, all the way through a heavy canvas apron). I was promoted to doorkeeper of the sandlariah. By the time the two shoemakers arrived, I would have the place all tidied up and have made enough twine for the day.

By the end of eight weeks, I was efficiently putting on soles using wooden pegs – which, believe me, was no mean achievement. And I made my first pair of slippers from scratch!

Then, without any warning, I was recalled to Cabri – just one day after I had delivered my slippers to Lezer. Hadassah gave me the news in the dining hall, and added that I was needed back at Ma'agan Michael that same day. When I asked her if she knew what it was all about, she said she thought it had something to do with Toronto. She had already told Lezer that I was leaving. She said that one of Afek's trucks would be departing in an hour, and could give me a lift as far as Haifa.

On the seat of the truck was a paper bag. In it, the pair of slippers I had made.

* * *

On my return to Ma'agan Michael, Arieh announced to me: 'The Zionist Organization of Canada has asked us to send someone to tour Canada for two to three months. We have decided that we should send you.'

'Why would you choose me? I don't even sound Canadian.'

'A few reasons. One: your skill as a shoemaker won't be needed until we go on *atzmaut*.' ('Atzmaut' meant 'groundbreaking'; when a kibbutz went on atzmaut, it meant it was off on its own.) He continued, 'Two: every time you do any heavy work, we finish up taking you to a hospital. Three: the Gingolds don't want another of their walls ravaged. Four: you have such a simplistic view of Zionism, that nobody in the audience will feel inferior. That was how we explained your selection to Yehuda, when he volunteered to go.'

The following week was a busy one. I had to go to Tel Aviv for a briefing at the Maskirut Hakibbutz, the main subjects of which were what I should say, in talking about 'life on the first Canadian kibbutz', and what I should request in the way of contributions, in the doubtful event that these were offered. When I mentioned that the assifah thought we needed a Massey-Harris TD9 tractor, everyone at the meeting roared with laughter.

Next, I was ordered to meet with Nat Cohen, my old commanding officer from the Chel Avir. He gave me back my British passport, along with two airline tickets, an itinerary, some Swiss francs and a used shaving-stick. It seemed that I would be travelling, by way of

Athens, to Switzerland. I would be met at the Geneva airport, and would spend two days there before flying on to Canada. When I asked how the person meeting me would know me, Cohen said that we were old acquaintances. Then he told me that I was to use the shaving-stick at the Athens airport, and to be sure to leave the top inch wet. My contact in Switzerland, he said, would take things from there.

'My contact' turned out to be the young Swiss woman who had been in charge of the *modiin* (intelligence) photo-interpretation section. She relieved me of my shaving-stick, which apparently had some microfiche concealed in it. I was told to spend a couple of days in Geneva, 'visiting my girlfriend' (?) and doing some 'sightseeing' (!), after which I would proceed on to Toronto.

In Toronto, the ZOC provided me with office space in their building on Spadina Avenue. I was given an itinerary which, besides Toronto, included Montreal, Halifax, Fredericton, Saint John and St John's. I was to stay in Montreal for about a week. I phoned Arieh's – or rather, Lenny's – parents there, as he had asked me, to say I had some photographs and mail for them. When his mother heard that I was coming to Montreal, she insisted that I stay with them.

My first talk in Toronto became the model for all but one of my subsequent presentations. I really had no idea what to say, when first I faced an audience. I lacked the knowledge to be an ideologue. I lacked the fervour to be a firebrand. I lacked the seasoning to convincingly preach to my seniors. So I decided to chat about Ein Kessef. I opted to use our jocular name, rather than the somewhat pretentious 'Kissu-fim'. I chatted about us getting used to hard work, after having grown up in the care of good – and doting – Jewish mothers. I told anecdotes, both true and made up for the cause.

Such as Meyer shooting himself while on sentry duty (true). Or the very tall Yigal taking his flock of sheep out to pasture, with the ram always trundling along between his legs (also true). Or Eppy trying to deliver a load of tomatoes to Latrun, since he could read neither Hebrew nor Arabic (false). I talked about the Negev, where we hoped to establish the kibbutz (true). I related that we had no idea how we would get hold of necessities such as tractors (very true).

To my happy surprise, the talk went over well. 'It isn't like the usual propaganda we hear,' people said.

The only time the talk threatened to run aground was on the

second occasion I spoke in Toronto. Rabbi Reuven Slonim had asked me to give a talk to the 'Friends of Israel' chapter of his synagogue. The room was packed. Every seat was taken. Rabbi Slonim introduced me in Yiddish, and I began my 'It isn't like the usual propaganda' speech. I was less than five minutes into it when Slonim leant over and whispered, 'Most of the people here don't speak that much English. Half of them don't understand you at all!'

I apologized profusely, and started again in Hebrew.

After a minute, the good rabbi leaned over once again, and in perfect Hebrew said, 'Now nobody can understand you.'

Somehow, we managed. I continued in Hebrew, and Rabbi Slonim translated into Yiddish. He must have done a passable job. The speech raised a lot of laughs, and received much more applause than had my previous one.

One morning, I received a phone call from my old friend Brigadier Ben Dunkelman of the 7th Brigade. Only now he was *Mr* Ben Dunkelman of Tip Top Tailors – could this be the same man? He said that he would like to meet me, and discuss 'a matter of mutual interest'.

We immediately recognized each other from the Gat Rimon. Dunkelman asked me if I thought the garin might consider naming the kibbutz 'Kfar Shoshanah'. *Kfar* meant village; *Shoshanah* meant rose. When I asked him why, he replied that 'Rose' had been the name of his late mother.

'Your close connection with Israel, from the beginning, would make the request not unreasonable,' I said. 'Kibbutz Hameuchad has already turned down our much too facetious suggestion of Ein Kessef. The name Kissufim is being explored, but I don't think it's been officially approved, as of yet.' I told him that the most I could do for the time being was to write Moshe Hertzberg to delay any decision regarding our name, and let me present the idea upon my return. Since this was my last week in Canada, I was sure Moshe would agree.

'That seems very fair. I am, in any case, sending your garin a small gift. It won't get there until after you'll have made a decision. So please don't think I am trying to sway you. And it is really just a small present.'

★ ★ ★

When I brought up the Dunkelman request, asking that it be presented to Kibbutz Hameuchad, there was an absolute uproar. Stitz,

Naturman, Katz and Shanas, plus Waldman and I, voted to consider it; after all, Dunkelman had distinguished himself in a number of the early Haganah operations. Our opinion was seconded by many of the later arrivals to Ein Kessef, particular the machalnikim, such as Eskimo and Eppy. Vehemently opposed, however, was the left-wing group of Albert, Max, Joe and Yoninah. They dominated the meeting, and claimed that we had been 'seduced by a capitalist plot'. Not only that, they considered the idea of naming any kibbutz after a woman who had made neither a political nor a military contribution to be a betrayal of principle.

Exhausted after three hours' harangue, the assifah voted against considering the name.

The meeting ended with Albert and Yehuda launching a motion denouncing my trip to Canada. To begin with, Yehuda stressed that we could hardly be called a Canadian group. (This argument had some logic. What with the integration of our international newcomers and the Brooklyn dogmatists, we Canadian machalnikim were very much in the minority.) Albert assailed not just my 'capitalist leanings', but also my general 'artsiness' – which he felt could only lead to a debasement of socialist ideals!

About a week after the meeting –and with characteristic tact – I decided on an appropriately 'artsy' response. I made up a 18-by 24-inch poster headed 'JOIN THE NEW CP!' Beneath the boldface heading, I painted a Heinz 57 dog, with a cork stuck in his derrière. Below the dog, in classical Venetian-style lettering, I wrote:

> The new CP!
> (or constipation party!)
> We don't give a shit!
> Pkakim only! No mumchim allowed!

Then I stuck the poster on the door of our meeting room, with a ruled sheet of paper pinned below it. Mine was the first signature. Within a week, a dozen brave souls had 'joined'. Conspicuously absent was Arieh Waldman's signature. (But then, the vocal Yoninah – with whom he was still paired off – was a good four inches taller than either of us.)

* * *

A short while later, Arieh came back from one of his trips to Tel Aviv and told me that the people at the Hameuchad Publishing House wanted me to go and see them. It seemed they had a book they wanted illustrated. Of course, this would be a commission, and the proceeds would be divided by Kissufim – our new name having been made official – and Ma'agan Michael, with Kissufim taking the lion's share.

The book was Howard Fast's *Haim Salomon: Son of Liberty,* which was going to be published in Hebrew. The book was in the process of being translated – but since could I read the English version (Canadian was much like American, wasn't it?) – I could get started right away. When I remonstrated that I had never illustrated a book before, the editor said that they had never published an American novel before. In any case, my resistance was academic; Kissufim's maskir chutz had already accepted the commission.

The story of Haim Salomon takes place during the American Revolution. Salomon was Washington's quartermaster. Finding any kind of reference material in Israel was just about impossible. But I made a fair number of doodles, to work out a style of some sort, and completed one small, finished cartouche to show the publishers, just to see if I was at all near the right track.

Then I recalled that Hadassah Diener, maskirah of Kibbutz Afek owned quite a library of Americana.

While in Toronto, I had regaled my mother and Mike with stories of my term at Afek, as apprentice to the asthmatic cobbler. A pharmacist friend of theirs, Harry Jacobs, had subsequently given me two dozen boxes of 'medicinal cigarettes' to take back to Lezer.

I decided that a trip was in order. I could kill three birds with one stone: 1.) at Afek, give friend Lezer his medicinal pot and 2.) charm Hadassah into lending me some of her books to use as reference; and 3.) in Tel Aviv, show an editor at the publishing house my finished drawing, plus my list of proposed illustrations.

Of my three assignments, number one got the best reception. Number two was finally agreed to, despite the fact that 'nobody ever brings books back!' Number three resulted in my list of illustrations being rehashed – though all present 'loved' my cartouche, and their enthusiasm allayed some of my doubts about style. I returned to Cabri with a new list of eighteen illustrations, plus an armful of brand new art supplies and a suitcase full of reference books.

The seventeen remaining illustrations took me five weeks to do.

This included three trips to the publishing house to get approval of my roughs. Back in 1951, I thought that five weeks was a really long time. But looking at the book now, in 2008, I can see that I really had *no* idea what I was doing. I must have worked on a first-come-to-mind, first-serve basis. (Two other people also thought the artwork took an unjustifiably long time, however: Chaver and Chavera Gingold.)

I delivered the last drawing. The press congratulated me, and invited me to lunch at a nearby restaurant. When we got back from lunch, a cheque was waiting for me, to hand our treasurer.

Unfortunately, even the cheque caused friction. My 'New CP' stunt had really alienated Albert, Max, Yehuda & Co. At our next assifah, the matter of the 'lengthy commission' was raised, ostensibly so as not to set any unfortunate precedent. 'How much did this illustration nonsense cost Kissufim, anyway?' someone asked.

I honestly cannot remember how much money I was paid. But I remember being pleasantly surprised by the sum. The publishing house had even added in extras for such items as travel and consultation, on top of the illustration fee. When Arieh announced the amount of the cheque, there was a long moment of silence. Then Albert asked if Arieh could repeat what he had just said.

'That is more than a nahag is supposedly worth over a four-week period,' Albert protested. 'How can we charge so much?'

'We didn't. None of us had any idea what to charge. So we left it up to Kibbutz Hameuchad Publishing to decide on the fee.'

This still did not satisfy Albert or his allies. They argued that this went against all of our principles. We had joined the kibbutz movement to be pioneers in the building of the State of Israel. Kissufim was not at the point of indulging in 'luxuries' such as art. That was best left to the established kibbutzim. Albert dismissed any argument that drawing pictures was of greater value than honest manual labour as a capitalistic stratagem. (When I protested, with my usual poor sense of comic timing, that the author, Howard Fast, was a card-carrying member of the Communist Party, Arieh whispered, 'Shut up.')

At this point, Moshe closed the meeting.

But the matter did not end there.

Changes were in the wind.

Ma'agan Michael would shortly move to its proper location, in Caesarea, on the Mediterranean coast not far from Acre. *It* was going to be the fishing kibbutz. Kissufim, unfortunately, was not. Our group was to be sent for final pre-settlement training at Kibbutz Na'an in Rechovot – the famous and well-established settlement that I had spotted on my first trip to Jerusalem.

Around this time, Ben Dunkelman's 'small gift' arrived, in two large crates. The gift consisted of 150 men's suits and 100 ladies' overcoats. One of our ideologues promptly asked what a kibbutz was supposed to do with that stuff. 'Sell it!' Arieh said. 'Just like the tomatoes at Cabri.'

* * *

Not long after, I was sent back to Kibbutz Afek, this time for good – much to my relief as well as to Albert's and the Gingolds'.

It turned out that 'the fateful assifah', at which the Howard Fast illustrations had caused such a storm, had been attended by our Ma'agan Michael counsellor. He had been sufficiently perturbed by what was said during the meeting that he discussed the matter with the movement secretariat. All agreed that I should be moved to a meshek that *was* 'at the point of indulging luxuries such as art', as Albert had so aptly put it. (Coincidentally, *Ba'kibbutz* – Hameuchad's weekly newspaper – had asked, around this same time, that I be made available to do a weekly pictorial page as well as other artwork for it.)

I went quite happily to Afek. Kissufim had come to resemble neither the original concept of a Canadian kibbutz, nor my ideal of life-long companionship. (The real clincher for me was the news that Canada had actually *sent* the TD9 tractor I had begged for; and nobody at Kissufim would even acknowledge that my trip to Canada had ever been worthwhile.)

Life at Afek was a fair bit different from life at Ein Kessef. For one thing, the assifot were without stress, rancour or urgency. In fact, they were opportunities for socializing, rather than for chastising people. Furthermore, where at Cabri people wondered why I would be drawing, at Afek people wondered why I was *not* drawing, when I turned my hand to other things. In Cabri, while I had been working on *Haim Salomon*, I'd had the sense that coming into the dining hall with clean clothes, as I did now, was somehow a cause for shame. At Afek, my clean clothes never raised any eyebrows. In fact, during a period of about a week when Lezer was sick, and I went over to the sandlariah of my own accord to help out, people anxiously asked if I had been made to work there.

It was simply taken for granted that my *tafkid* (given task) would take me out of the settlement most of the week. Still, after a couple of months, *I* no longer wanted to take it for granted. I spoke to Hadassah about being put on the sidur avodah, the work detail, for a couple of days each week.

Hadassah replied that, by coincidence, she had wanted to talk to me about that very thing. Afek had reached the stage of having to set up two (junior) high-school classes. And she wondered if I would be interested in teaching art one or two days a week. I said that I would be very interested, but there were two small problems: I had no idea how art or anything else was taught to youngsters; also, I didn't know whether my Hebrew would hold up.

Hadassah had already pondered the first of my reservations. By coincidence, a Dr Segal was presenting a one-week seminar on art education, starting in a few days. Hadassah had been in contact with the registrar, and a provisional enrolment was already arranged for me. And since Dr Segal was an American visitor, I should not find too much trouble communicating.

The seminar, which was held in Haifa's Carmel district, was most instructive theoretically. The emphasis was more on bolstering the students' self-confidence and letting them discover a personal interest in the humanities than on developing any level of orthodox studio proficiency. But the practical art projects shown and advocated for us to use seemed geared to much younger students than I was going to encounter.

Back at Afek, my first class put me in my place. I started off with an inspiring introduction to the importance of art: so inspiring, in my imperfect Hebrew, that after ten minutes, one young Sabreh got up and started for the door.

Now, I had never even heard of free-form education, and was unprepared for it, to say the least. 'Where are you off to?' I asked the young man.

'Out.'

'May I ask why you need to leave?'

'Because I am bored!'

That started a heated discussion among the students. They spoke in such rapid Hebrew that I had couldn't understand a word of it. It lasted about three or four minutes; then the deserter shrugged his shoulders and went back to his seat.

Hadassah's daughter, a member of the class, explained (in fluent English) that the student was actually *allowed* to leave, any time he wanted to, in their system. She then said that the group had agreed that, just as they had never had any art lessons, I had probably never taught any art lessons. And that my lack of Hebrew was likely more to blame for my lacklustre performance than was any lack of pedagogic skill. The class now had a proposal for me: I would teach them art, and they, in turn, would teach me Hebrew.

I didn't argue.

Thus began a good relationship that lasted my whole stay at Afek. I profited from our contract in two ways: my Hebrew improved greatly; and I discovered that I not only loved teaching, I was fairly good at it.

After I had been at Afek a few months, the kibbutz took in a group of close to thirty young refugees from Iraq. This was the time of the mass expulsion of Iraq's Jewish citizenry. They had been thrown out of the country, and all of their property had been confiscated; 135,000 people had been expelled from Baghdad alone! The penniless families had been hastily housed in a temporary tent-city near Tel Aviv. Kibbutz Hameuchad had volunteered to shelter a large number of the children, while their parents were integrated into Israeli society. Afek was one of the volunteer kibbutzim.

Two days after Afek's lot had arrived from the DP camp, Hadassah came to see me. 'You speak French, don't you?'

'A bit, but not that well. Why?'

'The Iraqi kids just know synagogue Hebrew. They speak Arabic and French, only. Among our chaverim, we have people who know Yiddish, Polish, Russian, German, English and Hebrew. But there seems to be nobody who can speak French or Arabic. The children won't eat any of the food we've brought them. And we can't figure out why. Can you talk to them, and find out what the problem is?'

The Iraqi kids were all huddled together in one room, even though Afek had made available a whole block of Swedish prefabs, recently built. At first, the children hesitated to say any more than *bonjour, Monsieur*. Then one girl plucked up courage, and asked if I was the artist she had seen sketching outside.

That broke the ice. It seemed that an artist was a safe commodity, even in Iraq.

The children had been told that they would be poisoned by the Israelis. (There were known cases of Jews being poisoned while in Iraqi prisons; perhaps it seemed to them not unlikely that their new country would treat them the same way.) When I told them this was ridiculous, they countered that there was no way for them to know I wasn't lying. Finally, one of the boys said that hard-boiled eggs – but they still had to be in their shells – would be okay. His reasoning was simple. If the eggs had been poisoned, a pinprick would be found.

But there was no way that they would leave the room. So I went to the kibbutz dining-hall. Onto a trolley, we loaded a huge bowl of boiled eggs. Then our baker came out with some five dozen or more pitas, which he had specially baked: 'They don't have bread in Arab countries,' he said. The cook loaded a cauldron of some sort of stew onto a second trolley, along with plates and eating utensils. For good measure, a big bag of Jaffa oranges was added. Oranges with peels should surely seem safe to our new guests!

The potential problem of the stew was solved by Hadassah, who had followed me with the second trolley. She simply persuaded one of the Iraqi girls to dish out the stew. Then she gave me a spoon and took one herself. And before each plate was handed out, one or the other of us would eat a spoonful of stew. Some fifteen spoonfuls later, the children were wolfing the food down with gusto.

The next thing I knew, I was madrich to the group of children, as well as being Afek's art teacher – not to mention part-time emergency cobbler. And, on top of everything, Afek's maskirut had asked me to paint a mural for the dining hall. Meanwhile, *Ba'kibbutz* had started sending me to cover major events, such as seminars or new industries, at least twice a month; these trips would keep me out of Afek three or more days at a time. When not on trips, I was expected to provide the newspaper with at least a couple of drawings each week.

The trips had variety, and took me all over Israel. I sketched fishing in the Mediterranean on a new fishing trawler owned by Ma'agan Michael. I sketched delegates at three seminars. I sketched work at an automotive plant in the Negev. I sketched at a new kibbutz in the Jerusalem corridor.

On my Jerusalem corridor trip, I took a bus up to Jerusalem and visited Pinsel. I showed him my portfolio, which he studied for a good twenty minutes. He told me that I had raw talent and that I was obviously leaning toward illustration. But he thought that I needed professional guidance and direction.

As it happened, I had felt a growing unease at Afek, despite the fact that my life there was good in many ways. Afek's members were all at least twenty years older than I was. Their children were at least eight years younger. If there *were* any kulturniks on Afek, I had not found them – though all were most supportive of my art. And therein lay the problem: even though they, personally, seldom had any need for either painter or illustrator, the chaverim of Afek claimed me as their very own artist – no matter how bad the art. (The dining-hall mural, when finished, confirmed my suspicions that I had a long way to go.) I felt the need for critical dialogue. And I badly needed to form some relationships with people my own age.

Finally, I wrote a letter to my cousin Erika in London, asking her to check if my Ministry of Labour and National Service grant was still valid. I hadn't used it for the full term before leaving for Canada. In the letter, I enclosed an application for enrolment in the Central School of Arts and Crafts, should the grant still be available.

Six weeks later, I received a letter from Erika saying that I had been accepted by Central, and had two years remaining on my grant. I went to the Kibbutz Hameuchad Secretariat and explained my position to the Tabenkins, who were the 'high priests' of the movement. The only question they asked was whether I intended to return to the kibbutz. When I replied that I fully intended to return, they agreed that I should go to England, and said that I would be given a one-way airline ticket to London.

I made my farewells to Afek some three weeks later. Lezer gave me a beautiful pair of half boots, which he had made for me. The Iraqis gave me a Russian shirt, which the girl who had spied me sketching had painstakingly and beautifully embroidered. And Hadassah gave me a kiss goodbye, and said, 'Mind that you come back.'

But as fate would have it, I never did.

The art school lino-cut that defined
my visual direction.

11. GOD SAVE THE QUEEN

ive years had made quite a difference to art school life!
Central School of Art in 1952 did not bear much resemblance to the place I had left in 1947. The building still
looked the same – grimy and Victorian – but where, in 1947,
both students and faculty had matched the architecture, by
1952 the spirit of both had been recast.

In '47, we were all of us most serious. The average age of the students was not that much less than the average age of the instructors.
Many of the students were ex-servicemen. All they wanted was an
education in as short a time as possible; their impatience with 'silly
buggers' was infectious.

Sex, for the Central of 1947, was a hush-hush affair – and anything
other than heterosexual commitment was quite simply not discussed.
Passionate political commitments, however, were an integral part of
one's personal curriculum.

By 1952, Central was back to being the typical (which is to say,
outrageous) British art school. Its students looked like art students. Its
students behaved like art students. Its students even smelled like art
students. Politics and artistic productivity had *both* become sec-
ondary to artistically exhibited navel-gazing.

On my first day at Central, I reported, complete with portfolio, to
Jesse Collins, head of design and illustration. He allowed that I could
draw (at least), and added that I might possibly have learned a thing or
two, back in 1947. I was put into second year. Then he sat down with
me and 'worked out our timetable'.

'Our' timetable was excellent. It gave me one full day each with
Paul Hogarth and John Farleigh, two of England's best illustrators. I
also had one day of life drawing with Anthony Gross. (I had discovered
Gross through his illustrations in a copy of the *Forsyte Saga*, which I
had recently bought just for the superb artwork.) Each of these artists
had his own very distinctive illustration style. I also had one day in
the graphics – etching and lithography – studio, plus one day in the

printing department. Collins suggested an evening class in jewellery: 'It will put you in contact with another visual discipline,' he said, 'one that you would probably not have dreamt of investigating on your own.'

In 1947 I had rented a large room in a condemned house on Ladbroke Grove, with fetid floors and frenetic fleas – not to mention a frumpish, fifty-something landlady by the unusual name of Mrs Brown. In 1952 I found a clean, furnished room with private bath and entrance, in a flat owned by a refined, seventy-something landlady by the name of Else von Portheim. The flat was located in a ritzy apartment building on Rivermead Court in Putney.

The school year flew by. Fortunately, I formed a good student/teacher relationship with Anthony Gross. In the studio, he refused me any attempt at slickness or copycatting. ('Mr Newfeld, it isn't even good enough to be called plagiarism! In fact, it is pure rubbish!') He pushed me mercilessly. Yet he always seemed eager to hear my stories about Israel. He was very British, and in spite of his name, it simply never occurred to me that he might be Jewish.

One day, as the end of the spring term drew near, he asked me whether I would be interested in a working holiday at William Hayter's 'Atelier dix-sept' in Paris. Hayter had told him that he was looking for 'a menial to help out with the crappy end of things'. It would, of course, be non-paying. But I would probably learn a great deal.

Of course, I agreed. Gross selected about a dozen of my etchings to send to Paris, warning me not to be overly confident.

Atelier 17 was at 17 Rue Boissonade on the Left Bank of the Seine. Hayter was completely uninterested in anybody's work other than that of the artists who employed his skills as an expert printmaker. But this was not surprising, considering that artists like Lurçat, Chagall and Picasso – to name just a few – used Atelier 17.

I acquired a good grasp of some invaluable techniques at the atelier – how to make multiple-colour refinements, or control an aquatint. I also learned some tricks of the trade that had never occurred to me before. (Most of this I learned not from Hayter but from one of his assistants, a young printmaker who had taken me under her wing – among other places.) And being in an environment that exulted in creativity was both rewarding and contagious. It was then that I made up my mind that whatever artwork I was going to do, from here on in I would not compromise artistic principle for political or commercial purpose. (I didn't realize, then, how very easy it is to compromise one's principles without even knowing it!)

In my last year at Central I enrolled in two new studios. Laurence Scarfe had come on faculty. He was one of England's hottest illustrators. I somehow managed to get into his studio. The other studio was a design one. Anthony Gross had suggested to me that since I seemed to be heading for book illustration, I really needed at least some knowledge of type design. A new course was starting in that area. It was to be run by Anthony Froshaugh, an up-and-coming typographer with a reputation for challenging experimentation.

I immediately felt at home in Froshaugh's studio. Typography was a discipline that I hadn't even known existed, but the 'minute differences' between typefaces – Venetian, Old Face, Transitional – stuck out a mile for me.

At Froshaugh's suggestion, I visited the Monotype Corporation offices at Queens House in Lincoln's Inn Fields. At the time I arrived, the only person there was a very small lady. I requested a few type-specimen sheets. She asked me which typefaces I wanted, and I rattled off the names of the few faces I knew. We chatted a while, and I showed her a couple of the exercises I was working on. She then said that she could indeed give me a goodly number of specimen sheets; she disappeared into the back and, after a few minutes, returned with two hefty pale-blue Monotype binders filled with type specimens.

'I have added some of our better faces to the list, and left some off from your list. You might show me more of your work after you've been at it a bit longer. What you have shown me seems to suggest promise. Perhaps you would come and show me what you've been doing in a month or so – but telephone first, since I do have to travel around a bit. Here is my card.'

The petite lady was the famous Beatrice Warde, the High Priestess of the Monotype Corporation, with an international reputation in just about all areas of type design.

(Some years later, Ms Warde visited Toronto on company business, and I had a chance to hear her speak to the Typographic Designers of Canada. At the end of her talk, she *raged* about two insidious practices being popularized in contemporary typographic design. One was the excessive use of lower case – too often just to draw attention to a mediocre piece of work – and the other was the indiscriminate use of sans serif for just about any kind of communication, whether it was a letterhead for an architect or a novena card for a shrine. 'I defy anyone to set "God Save the Queen" in lower case sans serif!' she concluded, to thunderous applause.

That night, Sam Smart, who worked for MonoLino Typesetting, went up to her room at the King Edward Hotel, and slipped a large sheet of paper under her door. On it, set in large san serif type, was the following:

god save the queen / there, i've done it, and i don't care! sam smart

About four weeks into my last year at Central, Jesse Collins called me into his office and asked if I had any plans for the evening. When I shook my head, he said that one of the evening-school instructors had called in sick. It was for a life-drawing class. Mr Kestleman, who was in charge of the life-drawing section, needed someone to fill in, and since I was one of the older students – and also had an imposing moustache – Collins had naturally thought of me. He told me that I would be paid the regular evening-school rate.

The class appeared to be made up exclusively of businessmen, ranging in age from forty to sixty years. They were a silent lot, who sat on their seats, each with his drawing board pushed grimly against his groin. Not a single one of them made use of the school easel that had been provided. Actually, not too many of them seemed willing to draw at all, when I posed the model. Only as I came by to see what they were doing did each in his turn commit line to paper. I decided to model the class after the traditional life-drawing studios, which used one or two long poses for all but the last thirty minutes. The last thirty minutes would be given over to quick poses, ranging from three to five minutes each.

At the end of class, each businessman thanked me profusely.

The model for the class was a pretty Scottish girl called Bonnie. She also modelled for the day courses, so we knew one another. After the evening class, we went for a drink at the local, where she asked me how I had enjoyed teaching. I replied that actually I was a bit worried. For some reason, the students hadn't seemed to like the poses I'd set. Only a few of them drew much of anything during the long poses; and none of them even touched paper during the quick ones. 'I obviously did nothing to motivate them,' I said. 'All they did was sit there, holding on to their drawing boards for dear life. Waiting for someone to tell them what to do, I guess. I have no idea why they thanked me. I suppose they were being sarcastic.'

'I can explain that to you very easily,' she said. 'They loved your poses! The Windmill Theatre now charges one guinea to see a show. There they get a number of distant tableaux, with a few naked – but-you-can't-really-see-any-of-the-best-bits – lassies. Here, they pay less than three guineas for twelve nudie shows. Plus, tonight you had me darting around for thirty minutes exposing my best bits, like manna from heaven. They clutch their boards because they have to, for decency's sake. They only thanked you because the regular instructors know better. And *that* piece of enlightenment will cost you another gin-and-tonic!'

Despite this dubious start, my career as a fill-in instructor continued. Mr Kestleman seemed to have problems with absentee teachers at least three times a month – and the illustration program usually provided me with another two days' work on top of this. Suddenly, I found myself singularly wealthy!

Solvent enough that I took a weekend trip to Rochester (not the Rochester of Kodak fame in New York, but the Rochester of Pickwick fame near London), with Tzilah Nehab.

Tzilah was one of two youth counsellors who were in charge of the London Kibbutz–Hameuchad Youth Movement. I had met her after being conscripted to run some of the activities for the members. Our casual friendship had, by this point, grown into something much more serious.

Tzilah was a member of the southernmost kibbutz in the Negev. The kibbutz was regularly attacked, both during and after the war. Tzilah's husband had been mortally shot one evening, just eight months before I met her, by Arab infiltrators. He had been crossing over the quadrangle from the dining hall to their home. His death was probably the main reason that Tzilah had been sent to London by the secretariat. (By coincidence, her late husband's sister was studying at Central at the same time as I was there.)

Though we were close, I had never talked much to Tzilah about my work. This was probably a hangover from my days of eating supper in the Ma'agen Michael dining hall with only one or two paint stains to show for my day's work, while the other chaverim had changed from honest sweat- and dirt-stained clothes.

Still, Tzilah knew that I was teaching part-time. She also knew that I had been elected president of the student union at Central (without even running!). And she had been told that I was one of the 'bright lights' of the new course in typographic design. All this made her broach the subject of my plans post-graduation.

She brought the matter up on our last day in Rochester. 'I am not convinced that you should go back to Afek,' she said.

'Which kibbutz would you suggest, if not Afek?'

'To tell the truth, none.'

'Are you going back to your kibbutz?'

'Of course. It is my home.'

'And Afek, or some other meshek, is not my home?'

'I am not so certain any more.'

* * *

On being accepted into Laurence Scarfe's class, at the beginning of the year, I had dropped Farleigh's studio. That gave me Scarfe and Hogarth (illustration) plus Gross (life-drawing) and Froshaugh (typography) as my studio bulwark. To this I added etching and mural painting – the last because there was a rumour that Ben Nicholson would give a three-week workshop.

Scarfe and I started out badly, however. In truth, we started out horribly. He looked over my portfolio and stated that I seemed to have turned out a lot of rather cute and faddish work.

At Central School, you proposed projects to your studio head. I had had no problems over my choices with anyone before, but with Scarfe, each of my project choices turned into a long argument.

After a month, we were at daggers drawn. It reached the point that one day I asked him if by any chance he was pro-Palestinian. To which he answered, 'If that means anti-Newfeld, then – as far as illustration is concerned – the answer is most definitely "YES".' At that point, I said that the best thing seemed to be for me to withdraw from his class. I packed up my things and started down the stairs to the registrar's office.

To my surprise, Mr Scarfe caught up with me. He said that leaving his studio was not the solution.

'What is the solution, then?' I asked.

'A commission that will preclude any possibility of your producing cute work might do the trick. Try it. If that doesn't work, then we should probably give up.'

I came home to Rivermead Court, furious.

Paul Hogarth had given me a copy of the *Apocrypha* the week before. I had rather liked the story of Susannah and the elders. And I had thought of including it in my submission for the NDD (the National Design Diploma). With gritted teeth, I got to work. I started doing a rough for the figure of Daniel. I grabbed a paint brush, dipped the wooden end into my ink bottle, and attacked so furiously that the brush completely tore up the paper halfway through my drawing.

But there was something new here.

I happened to have some sheets of battleship linoleum, so I drew the Daniel figure directly onto the lino, still using the wooden end of the brush-handle. Then I started cutting. I figured that nothing would come of it, but at least I would expend my anger. By seven the next morning, I had finished.

I printed the linocut on the Columbia Press in the school print shop and hung the sheet up to dry. John Farleigh happened to be there, and took a long look at the illustration. Then he turned to me and said, 'That isn't at all bad. Who is it for?'

'Probably just me.' This was a silly thing to say, as actually I rather liked the illustration – even though it did not look, to me, at all like 'my work'.

I went on to develop some roughs for the lead illustration for the story. This would become a double spread of Susannah in her bath, with the two dirty old men spying on her.

When Scarfe saw the printed linocut, he said something to the effect that he had seen my Bawden illustrations; he had seen my Ben Shahn illustrations; he had seen my Ardizzone illustrations and my Trier illustrations. But this was the first time that he had seen my own illustrations. Finally, and about time.

Halfway through the last term, Jesse Collins notified me that I was approved to exhibit for the school diploma. I now had to get enough work together for two portfolios, due just two months apart: one for the NDD and another for the Central School diploma.

There was one small problem. In a rash moment, I had thrown out most of the illustrative work I had 'amessed' prior to my discovery of *Susannah and the Elders*. The only way I would get enough portfolio pieces would be to duplicate. But both diplomas specified that entries had to be original art. The only way I was going to get a sufficient number of examples of 'original work' would be to use a large number of prints.

I think that I must have turned out the greatest number of etchings, aquatints and linocuts, in the shortest time, of anyone ever at the Central School of Arts and Crafts. I monopolized both etching presses, as well as the Columbia printing press. Mr Robinson, the print-room technician, closed his eyes to my coming in at all hours. He placated any part-time students who protested, by telling them that all my work had been burned in a house fire.

The NDD was no big deal. We had to spend three days at the London School of Economics, where we were given a number of faux commissions, for which we had to submit finished roughs. (To this day, I still don't understand why the School of *Economics* was picked!) Like all applicants, I had been given four months to prepare a thesis, as well. The thesis, and a portfolio of no fewer than twelve pieces of art, had to be handed in along with our 'finished roughs' at the conclusion of the test.

The school diploma was something else! In my year, only eight illustration students were allowed to set up a show of their work. The jury was composed of a panel of three adjudicators. Each was at the top of his/her profession, and without any current connection to the school. Three assessment levels were available to them: fail; pass; pass with distinction. A member of the technical staff remained with the adjudicators throughout their deliberations, in case they should need anything. No one else was permitted access to the exhibition area during the assessments.

The judges took four hours to come to their decisions. Out of the eight of us who had been allowed to mount our work, two failed, four passed, and two passed with distinction. Mr Collins told us the results in private. I had passed – with distinction.

Then the total exhibition was opened to the public. No grades were posted, so that visitors saw an exhibition of eight illustrators' work, and not an unveiling of eight students' work, marked for success or failure. All of this seemed most fair and proper.

Anthony Gross attended the show, knowing the results of the assessments. He went over the artwork in my display, finding more positive than negative things to say about it. Then he asked me what I was going to do now. I told him that I would return to Israel and stay at Afek initially, until I found a kibbutz with people closer to my age.

'I usually make it a practice not to give advice in matters of *Lebenschmerz*,' he said, 'but I really need to say something. I think that you must delay going straight away back to the kibbutz. There is a chance that you might become better than just good at your work. You should really try to find that out. I believe that you should spend at least a year close to your peers. I don't know that kibbutz philosophy can provide an arts barometer. It sounds too much like trying to create in a vacuum. Give yourself a year to find out whether you can make a worthwhile contribution *within* our field. That is, if you want to. If not, then I agree that you have a role to play back on the kibbutz.'

I, myself, had been in a quandary for some time about the direction my life, post-Central, should take. Tzilah's observations in Rochester kept coming back to me. And now, Anthony Gross's advice not only gave me somewhat of a swollen head, but made me finally accept that my love affair with typography depended on an intimacy with both the language and the typeform of the alphabet. Not only was I barely literate in Hebrew – I still could not write with facility – I honestly had neither visual nor semantic fluency for its letterform.

I decided to go back to Toronto.

★ ★ ★

I arrived back in Canada in the summer of 1954. After three weeks of my being the guest of my mother and Mike, we all agreed that I needed a studio – and my own place to sleep. No one realized this with greater conviction than my stepfather. And to think that I had always thought of Mike as somewhat lacking in what the Japanese call 'kimouchi'!

With Mike's help – and to his undisguised relief – I found the two essential ingredients for la vie bohème: a car, in the form of a 1937 Chevrolet, and a top-floor studio, above a sewing machine factory. The car cost $50, and the rent was $40 a month.

The studio was on Spadina just south of Dundas, on the east side of the street. (The building was next door to a charming, small, white-painted house belonging to Irving Grossman, a well-established and very talented young architect.) There was a fully appointed washroom on my floor, with two pissoirs, a toilet, two washbasins, one of those roll-on-forever towel appliances, and, of all things, a working shower stall. And though there were a number of other doors, both on my side of the hall and facing me, I was the only tenant on the third floor when I moved in.

The one-year lease was very simple: I could use my premises for any legitimate business purpose, including the pursuit of painting, commercial art, or printing. I could not, of course, establish a private residence or use the premises as living quarters; this would constitute a breach of contract, resulting in immediate eviction! However, the landlord agreed to properly heat the premises twenty-four hours a day, commencing no later than the fifteenth of November. The twenty-four-hour clause had been inserted because I had mentioned that I would do a lot of my work at night, since I needed absolute quiet – being a typical, eccentric artist, as my stepfather hastened to add.

Among the Macphersons' friends ('the Macphersons' being my mother and Mike – a convenient sobriquet), was a Barney Kronis, who owned a second-hand furniture store, and who was an ardent Zionist, to boot. My mother suggested I go to his shop, since he apparently had all sorts of drawing tables and other studio equipment, which he had recently picked up for next to nothing.

I followed her suggestion and, and for a ridiculously small amount of money – I only remember that it was less than $45 – my studio was fully equipped! In addition to the fold-up easel and Adana tabletop printing press that I had brought over from London, I now owned lots of furniture: a forty-eight-inch drawing table; a beautiful swivel-stool with a cane seat; a venerable paper cabinet, with three shallow and two deep drawers (this antique must have weighed over a hundred pounds); an almost new camp bed (every bit as good as the one I had slept on for over four years as a kibbutznik); plus a spare mattress, a deep red vinyl art-deco armchair, a coffee table and a taboret.

Delivery was included. And when the Kronis brothers brought my new furniture up to my studio, Barney looked around, and said that they just happened to have some bamboo curtains that would fit beautifully across my four windows. If I could pick them up I'd be doing the Kronis brothers a favour, as they didn't seem to be able to sell them.

I bought a dozen glass bricks and some nice eight-foot maple shelving boards. That made up my bookcase. Hardly yet a library, since I owned exactly twelve books: Gombrich's *Story of Art*, Dunlop's *Anatomy for the Artist*, Max Doerner's *Materials of the Artist*, Winston Churchill's six-volume history series, Laurence Scarfe's *Alphabets* (autographed somewhat reluctantly by the author), *Lady Chatterley's Lover*, and *The Seven Pillars of Wisdom*.

Other friends of the Macphersons suddenly found all sorts of pillows, sheets, blankets, cushions, bedcovers and other domestic bits and pieces, which were simply taking up much too much space in their own houses. Within a week the place looked as though it had been my home for many years.

Setting up the studio turned out to be fairly simple; putting it to good use was another matter. Not that people did not try to help me get started. Before I had left London, Janet Clothier, a Canadian student at Central, had given me a letter of introduction to a Will Ogilvie, warning me that he was a fine artist, and probably would not know the commercial art scene that well. Janet was right. Still, Ogilvie had me over for supper, at which time he made me an invaluable list of people and places to contact.

From that list ensued an interview with Jim Williamson at the Art Gallery of Toronto, which resulted in my teaching a Saturday morning painting class for children. Which in turn resulted in my being offered an evening painting course for kindly ladies at the R.H. King Collegiate, and also a similar evening course (without kindly ladies) at Central Technical School. The Saturday classes started immediately; the other two would begin in September.

One of the names on Ogilvie's list was Mr A.J. Casson, art director of the printing house Sampson, Matthews. Mr Casson looked at my portfolio and remarked that my work was 'rather British'; though he liked many of my things, he felt that the local magazine art directors would be unaccustomed to this kind of illustration. He added that there was not much in the way of book design or book illustration being done in Canada – though this was coming quite soon, and he had a feeling that I would find lots of work once it did. He added that he didn't think I would be happy doing advertising stuff.

Then he picked up the phone and made a couple of calls, which opened doors that had hitherto been closed – and very daunting.

Casson arranged an interview for me with Bud Thrasher, art director of *Farmers' Magazine,* one of many publications in the Consolidated Press conglomerate, which had recently been acquired by Jack Kent Cooke.

Among other samples, I showed Thrasher a number of illustrations done in lino, including some of my illustrations for the *Apocrypha.* Thrasher looked at these for several minutes. Then he said, 'I've got just the right commission for you. We are starting on our Christmas issue, and the major bit of holiday culture is a piece titled "Each Heart an Inn". Very biblical. And we've been breaking our heads trying to find a different style in which to do it. I think your linocuts might just be it.'

He gave me the manuscript and asked me to come up with a rough within a couple of weeks. He added that I could have a double spread, as long as I left enough room for a hundred or so words. Next he gave me half a dozen back issues of *Farmers',* and ushered me out.

I got back to the studio at about three o'clock. I promptly prepared my virgin drawing table for its heroic role in my conquest of Canadian magazines. I lined up six exquisitely sharpened pencils, plus two penholders armed with my last two Oriental nibs – all this placed to the right of a brand new layout pad. I took one bottle of black India ink plus another of grey India ink, and placed them in their containers, which I had carefully pinned to the table by way of accident prevention. Next, I ruled up a dozen thumbnails – exactly to scale. Finally, I took the telephone off the hook, put a sign on the door – BACK IN ONE HOUR – and sat down.

And sat. And sat. Finally, I gave up and looked at my watch. No wonder I had not been inspired! It was almost seven o'clock. Time to eat at the corner drugstore diner-counter. I was convinced that inspiration would arrive with the main course.

But the meal wasn't up to par. No wonder the muses sulked. Perhaps a nice glass of slivovitz, back in the studio, was needed.

I stayed in a complete mental freeze for two days.

It looked as though my first Canadian commission was going to be my last.

"Each Heart an Inn", of course, was the story of the Nativity. I could just see Thrasher phoning all his art-director confreres and advising them never, ever to entrust an illustration for a New

Testament article – especially a Christmas-issue commission – to an ex-kibbutznik pretending to be an illustrator.

In desperation, I looked through my portfolio. Anything to get an idea. And there it was! My own *Susannah and the Elders*. Of course, it could only be a jumping-off point. After all, Susannah was taking a bath – *presque au naturel.* But the style and feeling were appropriate. And both ladies were Jewish – and both were virtuous and chaste.

From then on, the illustration seemed to find its own way. I had the finished rough done in just over two days. Something told me not to take the rough in before the two weeks were up. So I decided to buy some battleship lino and do a bit of experimental cutting. This, I told myself, was merely the responsible way for an illustrator to tackle a major commission; it had nothing to do with the fact that it was the only job in the studio at the time!

Before I realized it, I had finished the whole linocut – on precisely the day I was to phone Mr Thrasher. I had even spooned a trial print and felt fairly satisfied. I made the appointment and arrived with my pencil rough plus a small detail of the print, which I had cut out and pasted on a piece of black board.

'I think I like it. No, I'm *sure* this'll fit the bill! How long will it take you to finish the linocut?' Thrasher asked.

'About a week.'

'That's fine. But I don't want you to rush. So if you need more time, give me a call. Do you need anything?'

'Well, there's the problem of taking a pull of the engraving. I think I should mount the lino: it'll be pretty big, and may otherwise break off. The wood might be a bit expensive.'

'We'll pay for it. Just charge extra. Anything else?'

'You don't happen to know where I could find either a Columbia or a Washington press?'

'I think we've got a Washington at our plant. I'll let you know.'

Ten days later I arrived at the Consolidated Press plant, with the mounted linocut under my arm, as per Bud's (I was slowly getting used to calling people by their first names) instructions.

The Consolidated Press turned out be an impressively sizable and modern printing shop. I was met by the shift foreman, who took me over to a Washington press, which, he said, was only used once in a blue moon, for the production of outsize repro proofs. There we were joined by a pimply-faced young man of about sixteen years of age. The foreman explained that this was a union shop, and only a union member could operate the equipment. But he was certain that the young man would do a good job.

Twenty minutes later, after scrapping several pulls, I began to fear for my lino. The young man had rejected a number of my suggestions. He insisted on piling more and more ink on the plate, and increased the packing to the point that he had to brace both legs against the press and lean his two-hundred-plus pounds back, trying – unsuccessfully – to bring the lever over.

Finally, I could not stand it any longer. I went over to the press and took my linocut off, in order to try some simple make-ready on the back of the wooden mount. I had barely stuck a first piece of paper on the block, when all work in the plant stopped.

The shift foreman came running over. I explained that I had not touched the press. The only thing I had done was retrieve my linocut – and I wouldn't have had to do even that if the young man hadn't been 'so bloody obstinate'. I said this rather loudly.

'Careful!' the foreman whispered to me. 'He's a cook.'

'I can believe that. But if he wants to be a chef, what's he buggering up my artwork for?' I didn't exactly whisper.

'No. He's Jack Kent Cooke's son!' the foreman whispered.

Miraculously, it all turned out. The union representative had made his way over, and he tsk, tsk'd sympathetically to my explanation. Even young Mr Cooke volunteered that I obviously knew the idiosyncrasies of the Washington better than he did. The union man concurred, and thought that an exception could be made, seeing that I was an ex-student of the London School of Printing.

The next day, I took two prints over to *Farmers' Magazine.* Bud was delighted and introduced me to the AD of *Canadian Home Journal,* John Richmond – who, in turn, called Frank Davies, the AD of *Liberty Magazine,* to come over and meet me. That day, I left Consolidated with two new commissions.

A week later, Bud phoned me to say that another story had been unexpectedly yanked from the issue supposedly going to bed in a few days. Could I do a fast linocut for the new, substitute story? I remember it entailed drawing an older woman sitting with a purse on her lap.

Suddenly I had actual samples to put into my portfolio. I made a

number of appointments with new confidence. With my evening classes, as well as a steadyish stream of work from Thrasher & Co., as well as from *Maclean's*, I was able to breathe a little more opulently.

One morning in the spring of 1955, just as the doldrums were setting back in, I received a phone call from a thrilled Bud Thrasher. He announced that he had sent *Each Heart an Inn* to the Toronto Art Directors Show, and had just been informed that it had won the award for best black-and-white illustration. What did I think about that? My first AD award for my first illustration in Canada!

'That's great,' I replied. 'But it would be even better if you could find some work for me. Things are getting a bit slow.'

'Everywhere. But you're right. I've got a couple of stories. I'll give you one of them; but I'm not sure which.'

We arranged a date and I duly turned up at his office. When I entered, Thrasher put a hand to his brow and showed me a memo:

> To: Bud Thrasher.
> Re: Art Directors of Toronto Award
>
> Congratulations on your Art Directors Award! Do not use Newfeld again! Any illustrator whose work merits an AD award could not possibly produce art that farmers would understand.
>
> – JKC

NEVER A DAY
SO BRIGHT

Part-title for Kate Aitken's *Never a Day so Bright*. Longmans Green, 1956.

12. MR ROBERTSON

My first Canadian teaching job was the Saturday morning class for children at the Art Gallery of Toronto (which would later become the AGO, the Art Gallery of Ontario); this led to my being offered a number of evening classes elsewhere, as I said. But it was Dudley Gaitskell, director of art education for Ontario, who became my first influential promoter in the field of art education.

I was put in touch with Dr Gaitskell by Mr Baldwin, director of the Toronto Art Gallery. After a long interview, in which Dr Gaitskell first looked at my portfolio, and then chatted with me for over an hour, he offered me a position on the staff of the summer course for public and high school teachers that he ran at the Ontario College of Art (OCA). Though this would be only the third time the course was offered, its reputation guaranteed an overflowing enrolment. The course would start the week after school was out for the summer.

The course was intensive and hectic. The student teachers worked from eight in the morning until five in the afternoon, six days of the week. They were expected to take some five or six different subjects, ranging from 'Directions of Contemporary Art' (whatever those were!), to 'Introduction to Puppetry' (both creating and performing), to 'New Methods of Art Education', to 'The Crafts in Canada'. There was also a rich menu of hands-on studio courses from which to choose. Enthusiasm was the key requisite for success – and, somewhat to my surprise, every student had an abundant supply of this 'key requisite'.

I was engaged to give the six-session course in 'Directions of Contemporary Art'. This popular lecture series was Aba Bayefsky's brainchild. Bayefsky was a prominent figure in Canadian art, and a tenured member of the faculty at OCA. The course was now oversubscribed – hence the school's decision to recruit me to teach a second section.

Not knowing that I was, in fact, an interloper (nor being either astute or seasoned enough to consider the possibility) I prepared a slide presentation for my premiere lecture – without consulting anyone.

To start, I compared depictions of particular subjects through the ages. Animals, for instance: I would show an Egyptian statuette of a ceremonial cat, then go on to show a Greek marble sculpture of a horse, then Dürer's *Rhinoceros* and Kokoschka's *Mandrill*. Or the Last Supper: I would start with a Gothic painting of the subject, then a Renaissance painting, then an Expressionist painting, and finish off with Stanley Spencer's controversial masterpiece.

Essentially, this was a provincial condensation of Gombrich. I accompanied it with some discussion of sociologically influenced developments in art, in works by Matisse, Seurat, Léger, Picasso, Mondrian, Klee, Magritte, Nicholson, Borduas (the only Canadian non-objective painter I had as yet discovered), and so on.

The lecture went over well, and I continued 'my' series with talks in a similar vein. Gaitskell, pleased, invited me back for the next year.

Unfortunately, two weeks into the course, Bayefsky objected that I had introduced elements 'contradictory to his original intent' – and very different from what he was doing in *his* section of the course. This, he said, could only stand to confuse 'our' students.

Since we were, by then, well into the program, I could see no solution but to continue to 'confuse' them.

At the planning meeting for the following year, Gaitskell announced that the summer course, successful though it was, needed to address new markets. He asked me to teach a new course in graphic design, with emphasis on poster design. This announcement was heartily endorsed by Bayefsky.

Much to my surprise, early registration indicated that my new course would have a full slate of victims. Many of the students' names were familiar, and I looked forward to the coming summer.

The summer courses were open to Ontario's separate schools; as a result, I always had between three and five nuns in my studio. They could be counted on to be the hardest-working students, and the most enthusiastic. Their only fault was their tendency to be far too critical of their own work. I often had to remind them that their art wasn't *supposed* to be better than mine!

On one occasion, during my rounds, I had gone over to one of our most senior nuns. A kindly person, she was the sort of teacher who spelled out exactly what she wanted from a student – and expected to be taught in exactly the same way.

As I sat down, she purred, 'Oh, Mr Newfeld! Last night I prayed that you would come and help me!'

'Oh, Sister! Last night you should have prayed that I would not *need* to come and help you.'

'You are a naughty man, Mr Newfeld. But I fear you are right!'

From day one, she had been more than frustrated by the fact that, in my class, no two students worked on exactly the same project. 'One requires a direct method of comparison, in order to evaluate a work,' she opined. 'How is one to compare a poster for *The Hunchback of Notre Dame* with the likes of a poster for *Damn Yankees?'*

'Why does one *need* to compare one piece of art with another, Sister,' I asked – 'except, perhaps, for size?'

She looked bemused.

Dr Gaitskell had gathered quite an array of talent for his faculty. The group included, in addition to Aba Bayefsky, George Merton, a well-known puppeteer and author, and William Withrow, who went on to become director of the AGO. Each season, a visiting lecturer would also arrive, from as near as New York or as far away as Trinidad.

Easily the most flamboyant member of the faculty was Bill Broome, a Scottish sculptor. Mr Broome was a hirsute bull of a man. He stomped through life, bellowing at student and academician alike. Snots and snobs quickly learned to head in a different direction, rather than meet Bill head-on. He invariably wore a kilt, and left nought to the imagination as far as Scottish tradition was concerned.

One day, he offered to show me some of his 'worrrk'. I expected an Epsteinian form of New Scottish Brutalism. Imagine my surprise when I found that it consisted exclusively of gentle nudes. Female nudes, that is. Evincing, on the part of their sculptor, a passion for hair. Broome's figures were lovingly handled in an intense Expressionist/Realist manner – as were the tresses on each lady's head. But as one's eye reached the nadir of his ladies' torsos, realism gave way to fanatical, stylized eroticism. Any critical comments were vigorously brushed aside with a snorted '*You* have a dirrrty mind!'

Bill had a thundering Morgan sports car. He drove it fiercely, completely oblivious to speed limit and traffic – vehicular or pedestrian. He also had a wife called June – a virago, three inches taller than he was. She drove Bill mercilessly. June taught at one of Toronto's ritzier private schools. And even though I never heard of Bill having a show or selling any of his sculptures, he and June always seemed affluent enough to enjoy all sorts of little luxuries.

In the summer program, Broome taught a course titled – in something of a misnomer – 'Sculpture'. It might better have been named 'Wood Whittling'.

The course was wildly popular. Nine out of ten of his students were women. Half of these women were invariably nuns. The course was offered in both one- and two-week sessions. The final assignment was always to make an 'abstract form': carved in wood, mounted on a wooden plaque, and hand-polished to a lustrous finish. Invariably, the women came up with divers variations of an undulating mini-obelisk. The men invariably produced a rather suggestive central perforation, placed between two interlaced 'limbs'.

On the last day of each session, it was a well-known tradition for Bill to go round looking at all the pieces in their final stage of completion. Each student would be feverishly polishing away, to give his or her masterpiece its last, deserving chance at fame. Bill would stop at the desk of one of the nuns and loudly ask, in a Scottish accent still more pronounced than usual, 'What will you call that thing you are rubbing so hard, Sister?'

'I think I might call it *Dancing Form*, Mr Broome.'

'Och, it's nay a dancing form. It's a very nice rampant penis.'

Whereupon all the other nuns would giggle, and most of the men would swiftly wrap up their well-rubbed masterpieces!

Bill's other passion in life – alongside wood-whittling – was the noise and smell of car racing. Through our summers teaching together, he and I became friends, and the Broomes introduced me to Mosport and Edenvale. It did not take Bill long to persuade me to buy a decent car – one to replace the 'bourgeois monstrrrrosity' I was currently driving. That being an eight-month-old fire-red Ford Fairlane (quite an improvement, I'd thought, from my $50 Chevrolet!) I duly traded it in for a slightly used 1957 TR3.

It did not take me long to roll the TR3, however. The damage to the car was minor – the damage to my neck slightly less so. Luckily, I was friendly at that time with a physiotherapist named Goldie, who put my neck in traction and more or less fixed it up.

Toward the end of 1957, Goldie threw a party. There were about twenty guests. One was a young woman who looked very familiar – most attractive – but I couldn't place her. Later in the evening, I noticed her sitting by herself on a radiator in the corner, quietly nursing a drink. I sat down next to her, and remarked that I was sure I knew her, but could not remember from where.

'I expect that you saw me in Mr Broome's class, last summer.'

Her name was Joan Hart, and she was in just her second year of teaching public school. We chatted for quite a while. When she got up to join her friends, who were getting ready to leave, I asked whether she would be coming back for the next summer course.

'I thought I might.'

'Well, I'll see you then. Please don't take my course,' I said.

I volunteered to help at pre-registration for the summer course, that year – something I had never done before. By sheer coincidence, Miss Hart appeared in my queue. After I signed her up for all sorts of courses – carefully excluding mine – from Bayefsky's 'History' to Bill's 'Sculpture', I realized it just happened to be my lunchtime. We spent our lunch together. And we continued to spend our lunches together, and our evenings, throughout that summer.

Joan, at the time, was a boarder at Georgina House, a residence for single young women, on Beverley Street in Toronto. The house had a strict curfew and an even stricter set of visiting rules. Both of which, I fear, we broke with impunity. Before the end of the course, it was clear to me that I was miserable when not with Joan. A few days before the summer's closing faculty dinner, I asked Joan to marry me.

Coincidentally, Dr Gaitskell had begun to drop numerous hints regarding the prudence of faculty members waiting until after *his* summer course was concluded, before engaging in 'extracurricular activities'. So when I brought Joan to the closing faculty bash, I deliberately deflected any further 'hints' by introducing her as the future Mrs Newfeld.

This announcement unleashed a series of worried phone calls from both public and private doyens: the head of the Ontario College of Education; Mrs Gaitskell; several members of the summer school's faculty; and even the chaperone at Georgina House. (The only party not heard from was Bill Broome; he had vanished the day the summer course had finished, bound, apparently, for some university in Jamaica.) The shared conviction of these callers was that my proposal of marriage was an irresponsible whim – that such a hurried liaison had all the earmarks of failure. More than forty-five years have passed, but there is always still that chance.

* * *

Through my acquaintance with Dr Gaitskell, several doors were opened for me. One of them was at Central Technical School, where I was offered an evening class in 1955. A few days before the evening class ended, I had a phone call from Charles Goldhammer, head of the Department of Art and Design. He offered me a regular, full-time position with the art program, starting that fall.

My duties were quite diverse. I was to instruct third-year students in typography, book illustration and graphic design; and second-year students in typography, illustration and anatomy. In addition to these art department classes, I was assigned a typographic design course for final-year students in the printing arts program. To round things off, I was to teach art to a 'special' group of students from 'Interior Decoration'. (I wondered why the department wasn't called 'Interior Design', but decided 'decoration' must be an Americanism.) When I explained to Mr Goldhammer that I was, to say the least, unfamiliar with (not to mention apathetic about) interior design, he suggested that I work out a course of study and bring it along to one of the staff meetings that were to take place in the week preceding the start of the school year.

The summer passed quickly and I came to the first faculty meeting with humility and guarded enthusiasm. The first session was mainly an opportunity for the faculty members to reminisce about their summer achievements and adventures, and to meet the 'new man', namely me. And vice versa.

The department consisted of about half a dozen instructors, plus one technician, and, of course, Charlie Goldhammer. I met Miss Doris McCarthy, an already well-known, soon-to-be-famous painter, who was treated with a great deal of respect by everybody at the meeting. Another teacher was the appropriately named Miss Virginia Luz, a kindly woman who darted about like a nervous sparrow. Then there was Don Neddeau, a taciturn gentleman with a decidedly red nose, who held forth at the meeting on the problems of discipline at Central Tech – though he turned out to be one of the more liberal thinkers in the department. As was 'Mr Murphy', a pipe-smoking little man in nautical attire, whom everyone called Rolly or Rowley. I was told that I would not see much of Mr Murphy, since he secluded himself in his aerie, and preferred not to have his privacy invaded.

There were two other instructors, my memory of whom has faded. But the ones I have named, I remember as though it was yesterday – possibly because I did not realize how much they deserved to be loved until after I had left.

After the second meeting, which was an orientation session, Goldhammer showed me my classroom, and the other facilities in the department. I was actually given my own keys to the staff toilet, my supply room, the Xerox room, my desk and the so-called faculty lounge. Then we went to Charlie's office, where he asked if I had worked out a course for the 'interior decorators'. I told him that I had put together a course on colour. He replied that it sounded as though it might work, as long as it wasn't too advanced. Next, he asked what I intended to cover on my anatomy course. I replied that I wanted to do the human skeleton and then go on to some of the human body's muscles. I hoped that I would at least be able to cover the surface muscles of the arms and torso.

The mood changed.

'I taught anatomy until this year,' pronounced Mr Goldhammer, 'and I can tell you from experience that you will never be able to cover all that. I always gave them just the skeleton and the face muscles. You'll find that quite sufficient, I should think.'

'Is this the only dose of anatomy the students will get?'

'Yes.'

'Then wouldn't it be better to give them some insight into what the more unfamiliar bits of the body are made of? They've all drawn faces left, right and centre. But I wonder if they can draw the human figure with any great facility. Would it be not be helpful if they were given some sort of road map?'

'What did you do before you went to art school?' Mr Goldhammer asked.

'Actually, I was on a kibbutz in Israel.'

'Good Lord! How did you get there?'

'Well, I served in the Haganah during the Israeli War of Independence, and on being demobbed I decided to join a group of Canadian volunteers who were going to start a kibbutz.'

'And why did you leave the kibbutz?'

'They didn't really need artists on the kibbutz.'

Mr Goldhammer considered for a moment. 'Well,' he said, 'all right. We'll try your anatomy course. But let's review it at the winter break. Since you've spent time in the army, I hope you'll understand when I say "I am the CO here." We try to run the most liberal department. But remember that we have a fair bit of experience in the running of a Canadian art school. I'm sure that you will fit in very well, once you get used to things. And if you should encounter any difficulties, I hope you won't hesitate to come to me: we've all had to go into something new at some time in our lives.'

Well, that told me! Not the best of starts, I decided.

Central Tech's architectural style – penal-system Gothic – matched its institutional atmosphere to a T. This I discovered on my very first day. The morning had gone really well, and at lunchtime I repaired to the basement, where I had been told I would find the faculty cafeteria, with bouncing foot and lighthearted air. With my usual unerring sense of direction, I became a bit confused; still, I resolutely turned left upon emerging from the staff elevator, as I had been advised – and found myself in a dead-end corridor, at the far end of which two tough young gentlemen were beating up another, distinctly pacific, young gentleman, in a most businesslike fashion.

Without thinking, I intervened – by rushing over and kicking the nearest of the two assailants rather sharply in the area of the family jewels. The other fled.

The pacific person and I bodily marched the Central Terrorist to the vice-principal's office, and left him there, over the protestations of the secretary. The pacific person repaired to the nurse's office.

That, I thought, ended the episode quite neatly.

But it led to a meeting with a Mr Gore. *He,* it turned out, was CO to Charlie Goldhammer – and to everybody else at Central Tech.

He began by thanking me for my somewhat misguided attempts at assistance. Then he suggested that in the future I would be well advised to call Security, rather than bodily assaulting a student and taking the law into my own hands.

I soon realized that the art department was in fact an oasis of trust and enthusiasm in that desert of doubt and hostility which was the rest of Central Tech.

I was starting to get my work published, around this time. *Maclean's* had commissioned me to do a series of illustrations for something called *Canadianecdotes*, and Gene Aliman, the art director, had let me sign the drawings. The students found them. The first two books that I had done for Nelson Canada had also been published, and the students found these, too. I was new. I was closer to their age than anyone else on the faculty. I was actually working in art. The art students looked up to me, accordingly, to an extent that was quite out of proportion to my pedagogic 'expertise'. (And looking back, I can see that I made any number of pedagogic mistakes in that year!)

When the printing department students arrived, they were surprised that I knew at least as much as they did about printing (this thanks to a night course at the London School of Printing; not to mention Atelier 17). This gave my course a (misleading) aura of solidity and professionalism. Still more helpful was the fact that I remembered my own first typography class – which I had gone to convinced there was no subject more boring. In the hands of Anthony Froshaugh, typography had taken on new meaning: it involved purpose, and experimentation. Not only was my own 'conversion' still fresh in my mind, so were some of the tricks of the trade that Froshaugh had used to captivate his audience.

I wouldn't say I ever *captivated* my printers, but we did work fairly well together. (As one of them said to me, 'It isn't as artsy-craftsy as I expected.')

The first week, then – meeting with Mr Gore aside – went much better than I'd dared to hope.

And then, along came Friday.

At one o'clock I was to have my first class with the 'interior decorators'.

At five past one, about thirty wasted-looking wretches shuffled into my room. They appeared to range in age from fourteen to seventeen, and were led – or rather dominated – by two particularly disagreeable-looking young men. Without as much as a by-your-leave, these two allocated desks, without any arguments from their vassals, and then seated themselves in the back row of the classroom. The general hubbub had by this point crescendoed, in spite of my repeated shouts of 'Settle down, settle down.'

Finally, one of the Gauleiters snarled, 'Shut up!'

Silence.

I started in: 'My name is Newfeld. I think we should get to know each other. Let me start by taking a roll call.' The first name on the list was Thomas Bint. When I called it out, one of the two dominators responded with a mumbled 'yo'. The roll call went smoothly until I came to 'Robertson'. At this point the second dominator snarled, 'Fuck off.'

I looked up. 'Don't even think about saying that to me again. You'll just be inviting me to give you a week's worth of detentions.'

'No you won't. I'm all booked up!'

'Oh, believe me, I can wait. How long are you booked up for?'

'The rest of the year. There's fuck-all you can do about it. You can phone the office to check.'

Which I did, and he was!

Apart from his colourful vocabulary, the only evidence of artistry Mr Robertson displayed was his full name, in letters about an inch high, carved into his left forearm and allowed to suppurate. The resulting colour scheme was as stomach-turning as was his sense of letterform.

It turned out that the 'interior decorators' were 'sort of' learning different trades – house-painting, plastering, bricklaying, roofing and such. 'Sort of', because this was a so-called 'terminal class': the Department of Education was just waiting for the inmates to turn sixteen, at which age they could legally be let loose upon the public – at least for the short period they would spend in society prior to taking up permanent residence in the Don Jail. There were, of course, only boys in the class. This was not a co-educational assemblage.

Three o'clock finally came around, and I was gratefully alone. I pulled my (Goldhammer-approved) course outline out of my new briefcase and ceremoniously tore it into small pieces.

So ended my first full week at Central Technical School.

The second week went more or less the same as the first.

I did learn one thing rather quickly about 'Canadian art school': Toronto students expected much more entertainment and hand-holding than did the students at either Brighton or London. When I casually mentioned this to Mr Goldhammer, he looked at me in a surprised manner. 'Well, they do pay us to teach,' he said.

Obviously, the Socratic method, as employed in British Art

Colleges, was as yet a bit foreign to Central Tech.

When I handed out my first illustration assignments – no two students receiving the same topic – there was a fair bit of consternation among the students. Finally, one of the braver ones asked me how they were supposed to judge their work, with nothing to compare it to.

'This may come as a shock to you, but very few working art directors hand out the same commission to more than one illustrator. As far as judging goes, rest assured that I'll let you know if you have produced crap or gold.'

Once they got to work, morale improved, however. 'This *almost* feels like working in a studio,' one student said.

To my surprise, even the anatomy class went well!

But the interior decorators remained unresponsive. Certainly, the back row – firmly in the thrall of Mr Robertson – remained averse to any and all of my approaches.

Robertson, with distressing consistency, arrived for my weekly torment armed with pornographic magazines that would have made Larry Flynt blush. When asked to put away his literary accoutrements, he finally would, but only after vehemently protesting, 'This is worse than the Don Fucking Jail!'

Four weeks of Friday-the-thirteenths had beaten me into the ground.

By Wednesday night I would be unable to sleep. Lying in bed, I would conjure up any number of graphic images, from incineration to dismemberment, discarding each in turn as far too impractical – or not painful enough!

Among my friends at that time was a former evening-drawing-class student, Loy Noronha. Loy, who originally hailed from Bombay, was now a medical resident at Toronto General. We were both avid table tennis players, and a couple of nights a week I would repair to the hospital when Loy had night duty. The staff lounge boasted a professional ping-pong table, which nobody really used. There we competed and cut calories.

On one of Loy's visits to my studio, he brought a friend (I'll call him Dr Smith, since I neither remember his name, nor think it advisable to make too public his advice) who afterwards became a regular visitor at Spadina Avenue. Dr Smith was a psychiatrist. He worked at 999 Queen, Toronto's psychiatric hospital. One day, when he happened to be the only visitor at the studio, he mentioned that I looked a bit peaked, and asked if there was something the matter. I mentioned the Interior Decorators problem, and described my friend Robertson.

'What would you ideally want to do?' asked Dr Smith.

'Ideally, I'd like to punch the bastard in the mouth!'

'Then, I suspect that you should do just that.'

'I can't do that.'

'Why not?'

'I'd be fired on the spot. You simply can't do that sort of thing at Central Tech! I tried something similar on my first day, and got one hell of a tongue-lashing from the Beak.'

'Still, what have you got to lose?' Smith asked. 'The situation is making you quite sick. Think it over. But if you decide to do it, for heaven's sake don't say I was the person who encouraged you. Then we'll *both* be fired.' He paused. 'Come to think of it, do tell 'em. I'm tired of 999 Queen.'

On the next Friday, a major change took place. Tommy Bint unceremoniously kicked one of the meeker students out of the front row and took possession of his desk. Before I had a chance to intervene, Bint turned to me and said, 'I've moved to the front row. I can't get no work done in the back. There's too much tension. And maybe I won't become no bricklayer. I've been thinking of becoming a artist.'

That seemed to be that.

I had noticed in the last class or two that a small minority of the interior decorators actually seemed anxious to get some work done. Which was difficult, in light of the intimidation methods employed by Mr Robertson. Still, where his calls to civil disobedience had been happily followed in the first few classes, they now had to be enforced by snarled threat. Tommy Bint's conversion, I prayed, might signal a tipping of the scales.

Mr Robertson disagreed, with fervour and innovation.

After seven weeks of terror, I decided I could not stand the pressure any longer. Life simply was not worth living with Robertson. I would have to force some sort of a confrontation.

I spent the next few days persuading myself of the ethics of my decision, and working out a plan. I even prepared a letter of resignation, which I drafted on Bill Sur's typewriter – Bill was my Korean neighbour on the third floor of the Spadina Avenue building – and put into my briefcase on the morning of the Fateful Showdown.

I could barely wait for that last afternoon class to begin!

I gave out a new assignment. When Robertson voiced his usual profanity-riddled objections, I was surprised to hear Tommy Bint growl, 'For Christ's sake, shut up!' This was new.

To my still greater surprise, most of the class got out the proper accoutrements and went to work. And even though a few half-hearted threats bounced back and forth between B and R, nothing really developed. In fact, I was about ready to reconsider my planned showdown.

Then, one of the meeker students, sitting to the left of Mr Robertson, asked me if I could look at something he had done. Quite innocently, I sat down at the boy's desk with my back turned to Robertson.

Not two minutes had passed before my resident miscreant slammed his fist down on his desk and proclaimed, 'Now those are tits! That's art! Not the crap we do here!' I heard the rustle of magazine pages being turned.

'Robertson, put that rag away. Get on with your work.' I did not bother to look round.

'Fuck off!'

I still did not look round. But my left hand flew towards Mr Robertson – and connected, to judge from the pain in my fist and and the traces of red on my knuckles. I turned to the – now rather faint-looking boy I was teaching and asked, 'Now, where were we?'

At this point, Tommy Bint's voice rang out: 'Look out, Mr N!' His shout was followed by a mass exodus from the back of the class.

I spun around only to be confronted by Robertson, who sported a bloody nose and brandished an open switchblade, at least four inches in length. 'I'm going to cut your fucking heart out!' he said.

The fact that he had threatened me verbally, rather than simply proceeding to 'cut my effing heart out', was reassuring. That, I had learnt back in Marseilles. Obviously Robertson was not all that sure of himself. (Neither was I, for that matter!)

I suspected that the best way to prevent the confrontation from escalating was to get Robertson alone, and thereby avoid any public loss of face. Whose face I wished to save, was not exactly clear to me.

The situation was being exacerbated by the minute; there were shouts of 'Kill him, Robertson!' and 'You can take him, Mr N!'

'I think we should settle this man to man,' I said, 'in private. Let's go to my supply room before we scare anyone. Unless, that is, you need help, or an audience.'

I would never have gone into the supply room, had I been the student. I surmised that the word 'help' had done the trick.

Once we were in there, I locked the door and took off my jacket, which I rolled round my left forearm. I pronounced, 'You really can't win, no matter what happens. If you should happen to hurt me – which outcome is not at all certain – you'll have to get out of here and hide. The cops will be more than happy to look for you. The upshot will most certainly be imprisonment, which will be quite unpleasant for someone as young as you.'

'Why for someone as young as me?'

'Lags love fresh meat, my friend. But next: say that you don't manage to cut me so badly that I can't retaliate. Then I will break both your arms – and some other bits, just for sport – and it will be in self-defence. Know that you won't be the first yahoo I've had to practise my self-defence on. Also remember, you pulled the shiv in public. Your best bet is to go home, and we'll forget this ever happened. I think you should put the knife away, before anyone else sees it.'

We went on like this for over twenty minutes. I cajoled; he threatened. I reasoned; he railed. I encouraged; he anguished. Where I looked to better times, Robertson saw only hopelessness. Finally, he muttered something about my not being the real enemy and, to my great relief, put the knife away. Whereupon I unlocked the door and he left the premises.

He never came back.

After winter break, I was entrusted with a new group of interior decorators. This time I was prepared. Before the first class, I doctored the spine of a Toronto telephone book with an exacto knife. I let them go into the classroom ahead of me, and gave them five minutes to vent their spleen. Then I entered the room and threw the book on the floor. As the noise died, I said – quietly – 'Shut up, and watch.'

Then I picked up the Toronto phone book – which was quite hefty, even in those bygone days – and tore it in half with barely a grunt.

'My name is Mr Newfeld. And I not only like peace and quiet, I get peace and quiet. Find a desk and sit down.'

* * *

I returned to teaching in the illustration program at Sheridan College in 1979.

It didn't take me long to discover that the vast majority of first-year students come to a commercial art course without any idea of what the profession is all about. And this led me to discover that a fair number of the new inmates had sponsors no better informed about our profession than the students were.

More than a few of our students had been encouraged to go to art school simply because 'he/she could draw a bit' (and not much else). As well, too many high school art teachers seemed unaware of the . high level of ability expected by the profession. In fact, both the students and their former teachers seemed to have approached illustration as a fun, but lesser trade, rather than a profession. Few new art students thought of visual communicators as being capable of wielding compelling influence through the content or style of their work. Even fewer saw any social significance in what the illustrator does, or considered the illustrator to have any larger responsibility, beyond skillful execution of the work at hand.

At the final '79 full faculty meeting of the illustration program, this whole issue came up. I suggested that the Year One program offer a course which would not only introduce the students to the tenets of our profession, but would also attempt to foster philosophy and conceptual approach. The idea would be not for the students to glean what we expected from them, but rather for the students to find and explore their own individual design sensibilities.

Students would encounter a whole plethora of social and visual dilemmas, some familiar to them, some quite alien:

Illustration was not just a product, it had purpose.

Illustration was not just an article of purpose, it could also be an article of persuasion.

Illustration was not just a solitary entity, it usually was needed to enhance or expand another's intelligence.

Illustration was not just an arbitrary service, it was an article of personal philosophy.

Illustration was not just a trade, it was also a profession.

My first magazine cover. Art directed by Keith Scott.

13. CONCEPTUAL MATHEMATICS

n the spring of 1955 – my portfolio now augmented with some half-dozen just-printed Canadian samples – I decided it was time to take a shot at the world of book publishing. (I would opt not to go back to Central the following year: the studio was starting to get very busy, and I'd already had some inquiries regarding the possibility of my teaching a day or two a week at OCA.)

First, I designed myself a visiting card, which I printed on my Adana press – in two colours yet – to show that I wasn't some Johnny-come-lately! Then, I went through the 'Book Publishers' section of the Yellow Pages.

Only four names struck a chord: Longmans, Green; Macmillan; Thomas Nelson; and Oxford University Press. Macmillan and OUP I dismissed as being too grand to approach. The decision was between Longmans and Nelson. I knew that Nelson was a Scottish company, and decided that my mother's name, Rose Macpherson, might stand me in better stead with Scots than with Brits.

I told the receptionist that I was a book designer and wanted to show my portfolio to – now, I had absolutely no idea who to ask for – 'the director'. With a grand flourish, I handed her my card.

After a few minutes, I was ushered into the director's office, where the gentleman sat, with his back toward me.

This I thought was a rather peculiar way to conduct an interview.

'Why should I look at your portfolio?' he asked.

Now, years of British schooling had impressed upon me that a decent chap didn't blow his own horn. Finally, I stammered, 'I was hoping you might find it interesting.'

'Tell me,' he said, 'did you ever live at 34 Waterloo Street in Hove, Sussex?'

He turned his chair around.

The director of Thomas Nelson, Bernard Neary, turned out to be the former Colonel Neary of the British Columbia Regiment, Fourth

Canadian Division – and regular patron of Forces Day at my mother's Waterloo-Street card club.

I left Neary's office with my first Canadian book-design commission, *Canadian Stories of Action and Humour I.*

It was just a small textbook, and really did not require all that much care. It was to have a two-colour case, and had a very simple text. More by good luck than by logic, I treated the design in an appropriately simple manner. It enjoyed unexpected success, and even got into the 1956 Art Directors Club Show, to which Neary had submitted it. In hindsight, I can see it was a 'welcome package', courtesy of Colonel Neary and Thomas Nelson. Neary, more than anybody else, got my career started.

When I first hit Canada's publishing scene, I wore an Edwardian five-button suit, complete with turned-up sleeves and stovepipe pants. I was the epitome of starving artsiness. Neary gave me an advance on my second Nelson commission, advising me to use the money to buy as normal a suit as I could find.

He also advised me on how to conduct myself at meetings; and told me to park my car – that 1937 Chevrolet – at least two blocks from whomever I was calling on, until such time as I could afford a car less than eighteen years old. He explained to me that most Canadian publishers were just a little suspicious of artists, and viewed all illustrators and designers as cut from that same unreliable canvas.

More important, even, than Neary's good advice was the steady supply of commissions he secured for me from Nelson. I designed their catalogues for three years. I designed my first trade book, *Adventures with God*, by Jane Scott, for them, and also persuaded them to let me illustrate an adult trade book, *Pageant of B.C.* Neary's giving me this job was a piece of pure favouritism – but it luckily proved justified. Sales were good, and the book was featured in *Canadian Art* magazine.

Other books followed, including a book of photographs by the Harringtons – *B.C. in Pictures* – which was my first coffee-table design. Nelson even commissioned me to design a 'how-to' book on puppets and marionettes by my summer-course colleague George Merton.

Neary then introduced me to Bob Kilpatrick of Longmans, Green, who started me off with Kate Aitken's *Never a Day So Bright*, which required both design and illustration.

Upon publication, *Canadian Stories of Action and Humour* had caught the attention of a Colonel Watson of the Ministry of Education. Watson apparently had already known my name from Dudley Gaitskell. He phoned me up one day, and asked if I would bring my portfolio and meet with him.

We had an interesting meeting. It quickly became clear that Watson was unhappy with the general lack of design-sense and visual identity in our indigenous textbooks. On the strength of *Canadian Stories of Action and Humour,* he had gone to the trouble of mentioning my name to a Hugh Kane, executive vice-president at McClelland & Stewart. He suggested that I give Kane a call.

Kane was somewhat stout, somewhat short and somewhat Irish – not in accent, but in sense of humour. Of course, what endeared him to me immediately was the fact that he liked my portfolio! But this later grew into the closest and most trusting of friendships.

I learned that there was method to Colonel Watson's referral and Kane's willingness to meet with me. Apparently, M&S had recently published an English literature textbook, *Word Magic: An Anthology of Poems,* for grades nine and ten, that had been rejected by the Ontario Department of Education. Both Kane and Watson felt that the main reasons for the book's failure were its underwhelming appearance and poor legibility. Kane told me that a revised edition with a decent design could well achieve the success M&S had hoped for.

The editorial department had already effected some minor revisions to the text. Sam Totten, head of the educational textbook division, agreed with Kane that the book should be republished. Kane asked if I would be willing to take on the redesign. He suggested that my fee be divided into two parts – the first for a preliminary proposal, with me retaining full copyright in the unlikely event that it was rejected; and the second for completion of the work, with me providing production supervision if my proposal was a go. I agreed.

The original book was a mess! But one really could not blame the publisher. It was accepted practice in Canada, at the time, to entrust the printer with all aspects of the inside design of just about any publication that wasn't a coffee-table book or a *belle livre.* And there really weren't many coffee-table books or belles livres being produced in Canada in the early 1950s! (The closest thing was M&S's *Indian File* series, a rather limited collection of case-bound poetry books, which had been seen more as the publisher's obligation to the nurturing of Canadian poetry than as a money-making venture. The books were handsome; they had been lovingly designed by Paul Arthur, just before he went off to Switzerland. By the time I came to M&S, however, they mostly lay forgotten.)

Word Magic had been set by the printer in Linotype Garamond, an intimidating choice for the book's prospective (young) readers. It was set to a measure that produced more hyphenated words than one could keep count of. The lines were under-leaded and the text was accordingly hard to read. There was a hodgepodge of display faces. The end-matter was forbidding, to say the least.

The book was divided into two parts, which might have helped to ease the reader's experience – if it weren't for the fact that the separate identities of the two parts only became clear after lengthy perusal of the (hefty) tome.

Luckily, I was enough of typographic neophyte that I was undaunted by the problem Hugh Kane had thrown into my lap. Also, I had no other commissions at the time, so I could devote myself to this one. I laboriously did an accurate word count. The fact that the book had already been set once helped in the cast-off. And I now had a sufficient number of books under my belt that I understood about things like 'formes and widows and orphans, oh my!'

I decided that I needed to somehow clearly distinguish the two parts of the book for the reader. It occurred to me to use two different colours of paper, one white and one light India stock. The idea seemed so obvious that I almost rejected it. Luckily, I could come up with nothing 'better'.

I abandoned Garamond as being too fussy, and unfamiliar to the students, and selected Times Roman instead. The word count suggested that I could easily fit the prelims and Part One so that they finished on a printing forme – same for Part Two, combined with the extensive end matter.

As for the cover, the bountiful budget allowed for two colours on Linson (a mock-linen paper product). I decided on an abstract design, based on a number of different-sized groups of hourglass triangles. Two inverted triangles formed the 'W' in *Word*; these sat on the two upright triangles of the 'M' in magic.

'Are you sure that your text-length estimate is accurate?' Kane asked me.

'Oh yes,' I said. 'My conceptual mathematics are never wrong!'

'That's a wonderful line,' Kane said, laughing. 'You must copyright it.'

For a change, my length estimate *wasn't* wrong. And the book became a runaway success. It was the start of a most rewarding relationship.

What with the work from Nelson and McClelland & Stewart, Spadina Avenue started to get busy. Added to the publishing houses' commissions was a sporadic bit of magazine work for *Maclean's* and *Mayfair*. I got to know a number of Toronto's art directors and senior editors. Two are still good friends of mine, more than fifty years later: Keith Scott, then the art director of *Mayfair Magazine*, and Bill Toye, then the senior editor and production manager of Oxford University Press.

One day, Bill Toye asked if I had ever considered 'doing a children's book'. Out of that grew my first picture book, *The Princess of Tomboso*. It was a charming, traditional folk tale, with terrific visual potential. And Bill Toye – one of our best kid-lit publishers – was a joy to work with. He could steer you on a proper course, without appearing to have interfered or taken over.

Toye agreed to let me experiment with type ornaments as texture within the drawings, combined with a (for then) pretty extreme style of illustration.

Luckily it all worked out. *The Princess* went on to be co-published in England, and somehow found its way to Africa, Australia and even the U.S.A. Eventually she received the 'Runner-up Award of the Hans Christian Andersen International Exhibition'.

The Oxford *Princess*, along with a series of covers I'd done for Keith Scott at *Mayfair*, were career catalysts for me.

★ ★ ★

In 1956, Jack McClelland decided to start Canada's first major paperback series. The New Canadian Library, as it was to be called – a series of republications of Canadian 'classics' – was primarily intended to serve the university market, and each title originally sold for one dollar. Jack also expected a wide trade market, however. In the editorial briefing, he asked for a look that had just a touch of 'snob appeal' – without scaring off 'a wider market'.

By this time, I was on retainer to M&S, and spent one day a week at Hollinger House. (The rest of my M&S work was done on a free-lance basis from my Spadina Avenue studio.)

Hugh Kane had some very definite ideas regarding the merchandising of this new and potentially risky series. He suggested that it might be a good idea if we went over my proposal for the look of the series at my studio, in private.

I was more than happy to agree. I had observed that, only too often, when I presented my thoughts at editorial meetings, people would rush to weigh in – more to show off their own 'visual expertise', than for reasons of honest criticism. On a one-to-one basis, opinion was invariably more honest (unless, of course, the one-to-one happened to be an art director asking a junior designer's opinion!)

Not only did Kane and I work well together, he was confident in both his opinion and position. And he seldom voiced a criticism that lacked merit. In addition, I guessed that a pre-presentation consensus with the company's senior vice-president would provide me with an invaluable advantage when it came time to present my proposal to the editorial group.

'I really admire the Washington Square Library,' Hugh said, in our first meeting at my studio, 'and I think that the Penguin books look superb. André Deutsch puts pieces of art on its paperback covers. Atheneum's NAL, I'm certain, will get all kinds of awards at the next AIGA show. You are familiar with these designs?'

I nodded.

'Good. Then ignore them. Do your own thing. I'm convinced that you have to produce a new type of cover.'

One thing could be counted upon at M&S. Though the treatment of the book jacket was the subject of everyone's opinion – from warehouse personnel to editor-in-chief – the only person, apart from Claire Pratt, ever curious about my plans for the mise-en-page of a book was Hugh Kane.

This phenomenon was certainly not restricted to M&S. In the 1950s, a concern with the look of the book jacket to the exclusion of all else appeared to be the practice in all but three Toronto publishing houses (along with M&S – thanks to Hugh and to Claire Pratt – the exceptions were U of T Press and OUP).

Hugh finally persuaded me of the logic of the 'many cooks' approach to jacket design. One: award-winning jacket designs invariably confined their titles to esoteric status; these books would never be bought in the thousands. The mass market simply preferred jackets that were less visually challenging. Two: if the marketing group was at all uncomfortable with a design, that discomfort might temper the group's enthusiasm to promote the title; for this reason alone, the design was often rejected. (At each year's publishing meeting, Jack would jestingly say that he would send me a list of those titles which he felt could become bestsellers. 'Please try *not* to win an award for 'em.')

I eventually realized that my occasional defeat in the area of book-jacket proposals was a small price to pay for being left to my own devices as far the rest of the book was concerned.

I had never designed a paperback when the New Canadian Library came along, let alone a paperback series. And though I had a number of paperbacks on my bookshelf, none was particularly current. So I spent several days haunting the stacks of Britnell's, where Barry Britnell gave me a short, invaluable course on the mystique of the paperback. I also visited Classic Books, whenever the indomitable Louis Melzack, monsieur le directeur, was out of the shop and back in Montreal.

After much deliberation, I decided that the series needed a pictorial approach – rather than a purely typographic one, like that used for the Penguin paperbacks of the time – though the look would have to be miles away, of course, from Mickey Spillane. I felt that each jacket must visually reflect the author rather than the subject matter – yet somehow evoke the spirit of the book. The problem was in how to translate these ideas into a piece of appealing communication: a design that looked neither pretentious nor contrived. The solution stubbornly refused to come.

I had not been in Canada long enough to be familiar with more than two of the titles to be republished. I knew even less about the deans of Canadian literature. I was soon at a complete stalemate.

On one of my aimless searches, I went to see Steve Rankin, M&S's publicity manager, and asked if she could let me have some authors' bios. Together with these, Ms Rankin handed me a file of authors' photographs. The photographs turned out to be a treasure trove. They screamed out to be drawn, painted, engraved, lino-cut, scraper-boarded, classically treated, appropriately abstracted, caricatured – each (author) to his own (depiction). Here, finally, was my solution!

The rest of the design idea flowed easily. It seemed logical to me that just as the author's image would appear in the same place on each cover, so would the author's name. And just as the style of illustration would vary, according to the spirit of the book, so would the style of lettering, or the typeface.

I roughed up covers for two of the coming titles. The styles of illustration and typography were quite different, from one cover to the other; however, the rest of the design elements followed a strict grid, front, back and spine. I thought that the jackets worked well, and showed them to Hugh Kane.

'They are certainly different. I can't think of any paperback series that they remind me of.'

'Is that a bad sign?'

'As far as I am concerned, no. On top of that, I think they work and are exactly what we should use.' Then he added. 'But you'll have to mock up another one. As lousy a cliché as you can manage. That's what we'll show first. Leave the rest to me.'

'What about the design philosophy regarding the inside? Should I prepare a mock-up?'

'Forget that. Just leave the selling of what you will finally do, also to me.'

The first four NCL titles were published in 1957. They were printed in England. The introductory group consisted of Frederick Grove's *Over Prairie Trails*, Morley Callaghan's *Such Is My Beloved*, Sinclair Ross's *As for Me and My House*, and Stephen Leacock's *Literary Lapses*.

Of the four authors, the only one I'd had a chance to meet was Morley Callaghan. Jack McClelland had taken me over to Callaghan's apartment to meet him and I had managed to make some pencil notes as we talked. These sketches, combined with photos from Steve's file, served as research for my illustration. I was never going to meet the other three authors, all of whom were deceased, so I had to work from Steve's files alone.

The Grove and the Leacock were the most successful. For Grove, I

produced a linocut. It looked pretty good on the linoleum. Since I no longer had access to Jack Kent Cooke's Washington press, I laboriously spoon-printed the lino cut at my Spadina Avenue studio.

For the Leacock, I did a simple pen-and-ink line drawing. I had found just one photo in the file. It was excellent. I literally worked for hours, trying to get the illustration as far away as possible from looking as though it had been drawn from a photograph. And I thought that I had succeeded.

Everyone – even critics besides Pearl McCarthy of the *Globe and Mail*, who always seemed to champion my work – liked it.

One morning, however, I received a phone call from Jack McClelland.

'What are we paying you for the NCL cover illustrations?'

'Forty dollars.'

'Hm. Well, we'll have to pay you more than that. Tell Hugh that I said you are to get $80 per drawing from now on.'

'Thank you very much. I appreciate that. May I ask why?'

'I will tell you next time you're here.'

I had to be at Hollinger House a couple of days later, in any case. I went to Marge's office (Marge Hodgeman was Jack's secretary and protector), and asked if she would make an appointment for me to see McClelland. From behind his closed door, Jack hollered for me to come in.

'I suppose you want to know why I've doubled your fee?'

'I assume that the paltry amount you're now paying is giving you a guilty conscience. But you said you would tell me, the next time I was in.'

'Right. I did,' said Jack, and brought out a letter. 'Read this.'

The letter wasn't a letter at all. It was an invoice from Yousuf Karsh. It ran something like this:

Fee for second rights _____ $250.00
Modified Karsh photograph of Stephen B. Leacock,
used as cover illustration for the paperback edition
of the book *Literary Lapses*

I was astonished. 'My drawing doesn't look remotely like a photograph,' I protested. 'In any case, Karsh sold the photograph to M&S, to use on Leacock jackets.'

'I agree,' Jack replied. 'But both Bob Martin' – McClelland & Stewart's lawyer – 'and Hugh felt it would be easier to pay the man. Also, Steve Rankin said that she might be able to use the story as a fun bit in her publicity campaign. *I* figured that if we were willing to pay Karsh $250 for one of *your* drawings, you would bitch about getting only $40 yourself. In any case, I am much too tired of the whole business to argue the point.'

And that was that.

The wedding party, from left to right: Frank Davies, usher; Maureen Sze, bridesmaid; Joan and Frank N.; A.D. 'Mike' Macpherson, bestman; Leslie 'Sam' Smart, usher.

14. THE MOST GAINFUL COMMISSION

n 1961, Keith Scott and I decided to open a new design studio. *Mayfair* magazine had folded – David Crombie saying that he had made sufficient donations to Canadian culture – and Keith was pondering his future.

Keith Scott was probably the most innovative and sensitive magazine art director of the time in Canada. Years before the much-acclaimed American designer Otto Storch took the U.S. magazine world by storm, Keith rolled out a succession of visual feats of derring-do at *Mayfair*, with the fervent support of his editor-in-chief, Robert Fulford.

Nevertheless, Keith averred that he wanted away from the magazine world, and back to the drawing board.

As for me, I had four motives for opting for the partnership:

One: Since 1956 or 1957, I'd been working from a studio-apartment (specially designed for the ex-kibbutznik-in-residence) in the Macphersons' new house on Hi Mount Drive. The house had been designed by my friend and erstwhile neighbour, Irving Grossman. Though the location was beautiful, I felt this 'home-studio' gave me the look of a designer trying to establish himself; I felt that I was past that point.

Two: There was enough work coming in that I felt it time to add a bit more manpower – but didn't think that I could keep a 'gofer' in remuneration by myself; two hotshot designers, however, might just bring in enough money between them.

Three: I hated going to clients, and felt that I was an absolutely distressing salesman. On top of that, I resented the time away from my drawing board. Keith and I had talked about this, and agreed that he would be the more logical outside man.

Four: I was weary of working alone. I liked Keith. And I needed a target – and counterbalance! – for my 'artistic' temper(ament).

We had been scanning the papers for about a fortnight, when Keith saw an advertisement for office space to rent on Grenville

Street, in the heart of Toronto. It was just thirty seconds from Yonge Street, across the intersection from the Westbury Hotel.

'This will cost a fortune!'

'Let's at least go and look at the place. We don't have to rent it.'

The office space was on the ground floor of a very presentable building. The landlord, Harry Felton, was himself a tenant, who wanted to sublet excess space to which he had over-ambitiously committed himself. His own enterprise – the Homeservice Club – simply didn't require or pay for the amount of space he found himself stuck with. To our joy and relief, he agreed to let us have a one-year lease for around $90 a month. On top of that, he was prepared to build a partition, complete with door, which would give us a reception area for visitors – whom we did not want coming into the studio proper!

Keith immediately took over the keeping of books and the maintenance of studio provisions and time sheets. (Not that we really needed the latter, since we had no new accounts for which to open files in the first four months.) And he kept both me and my side of the studio from appearing our customary chaotic-looking selves. Also, his talent and experience as an art director stood us in very good stead as we prepared work, together, for clients.

Luckily, I still had the M&S retainer as consultant art director, which brought in a steady supply of work for both of us – M&S had a substantial list by now – as well as a monthly cheque. On top of that, I was now teaching those two days a week at the Ontario College of Art, which brought me a fair personal income.

It soon became obvious that Keith disliked calling on clients as much as, if not more than, I did. A number of small jobs did materialize, however, and slowly but surely we built up a fairly impressive portfolio of 'non-book publishing' samples. The Here & Now Gallery became one of our clients, and guaranteed us a year's worth of invitations and small posters. In addition to this, we had a fairly steady supply of work from the ROM. Then the Art Gallery of Toronto came to us, and also became a frequent client. These impressive accounts brought us lots of prestige – if little profit.

Even though we had decorated sparingly (I must have retained, from my Central Tech days, my distaste for 'interior decoration'), the studio looked pretty good. It soon became a meeting place for a growing number of members of Toronto's design community, and was frequently visited by many of 'my' authors. Most importantly, I was having fun and getting the type of work one only dreams about.

The downside was that I began to sense that Keith was languishing. He disappeared for hours into the YMCA across the street, with greater and greater frequency.

In the midst of all this, there arrived at the studio our first major commission.

It was brought to us by Ted Hughes. Ted was the most successful and respected salesman of bookbinding materials in Canada at that time. One day, he asked me if I might be interested in developing a pyroxylin book-cloth range for a 'large Canadian company' – a range that would compete with that of Columbia Mills, a major American book-cloth manufacturer that had a virtual stranglehold on the Canadian publishing-house market. The 'large Canadian company' turned out to be CIL. Keith and I were suitably awed.

There were any number of reasons for us to try to get this commission. We were assured that CIL would give us full credit (though, to my chagrin, they ultimately used my name alone, eager to capitalize on my publishing reputation). On top of this, Ted prophesied an aggressive advertising campaign for the range, which would propel our studio's name into the lexicon of just about every Canadian publisher.

Our main quandary was the fee. What should we charge for a job like this? I had no idea, Keith had no idea. How long would a job like this take us? I had no idea, Keith had no idea.

Ted had impressed on us that this was all very hush-hush: we were not to discuss it with anybody in or outside of 'the field', since it would be a disastrous if any established competitor got an inkling that the new line was in the works. So we didn't dare ask anyone for advice.

Ted and I went to meet with the CIL brass. The meeting seemed to go well and ended with them saying that they would be in touch very shortly. Two days later, a messenger service brought a letter from CIL, inviting me to tender on the design of their forthcoming PX77 book-cloth range. I phoned Hughes and said that we were both happy and honoured to accept the commission, and promised to get back to him with a quote within forty-eight hours. (Ted had mentioned that he would be happy to act as a go-between for us, and had stressed that he would take no fee.)

That evening, I told Joan that we had just been offered what could be our biggest contract to date. I told her the client was CIL, and what the job was all about. 'The only problem is, I have no idea what to quote them. As far as my experience stretches with this kind of a problem, we could quote $1,000 or we could quote $10,000. Keith doesn't know, either. And I'm certainly not going to ask Ted about it!'

'So, it is between those two numbers?' Joan asked.

'I guess. But, who knows?'

'I suggest that you compromise.'

'Well, that's a great help. Thank you so very much. If I knew a good compromise, I wouldn't be in this quandary. Pray, what is your idea of a good compromise?'

'If it's between one and ten thousand dollars, compromise: ask for $11,000.'

The next day I informed Keith that Joan had amazing acumen in the area of pricing cloth-range design commissions. I explained to him her 'conceptual mathematics.'

'Well, that sounds rational to me,' Keith said. 'Let's go with Joan's $11,000. It's as good as any figure we've been able to come up with.'

CIL expressed some qualms, serious qualms, about our calculations, however. We weren't sure what to do.

Ted suggested that we sit tight and let them come back to us with a counter-offer. 'They'll make the next move. They really do want you.'

CIL did come back with a counter-offer, about ten days later. They offered $4,000, to be payable as an immediate deposit of $2,000, and a second, equal payment upon completion of the design work. In addition to this, they proposed a royalty of 1.5 cents per yard of the cloth sold, for a period of three years. There were a number of the usual clauses committing both parties to the usual gobbledegook. All of which sounded to us like manna from heaven and tasted like the peal of victory bells. We danced with joy.

Then we sat down on the couch in our antechamber and said, in unison, 'Now what do we do?'

When the first CIL cheque arrived, I went out and bought the Color Harmony Manual put out by the Container Corporation of America. It cost $250, an absolute fortune in those days: more than two and a half months' rent! But it was worth every penny. The manual's main feature was a collection of thirty hue-cards, each containing twenty-eight chips of the particular colour. The hues were gradated, from the darkest to the lightest value of the colour, and each chip showed both a matte and a coated side. Everything was coded, to facilitate an assembly of different colours that would retain a family harmony.

Next, I phoned Aaron Burns. I had met Aaron through Alfred Knopf, in New York, whilst working on a Pierre Berton book that they were co-publishing with M&S. Because of changes to the jacket copy, I'd had to make a visit to the Composing Room, Inc., New York's leading typesetting house, where Aaron was at that time art director. We had become good friends. Now, Burns was in the process of starting his own company – what would become the International Typeface Corporation. He put me in touch with the art director of a major U.S. automotive magazine. His rationale was that the car industry not only brought a huge influence to bear on colour trends, it also worked years in advance.

The art director suggested that I might profitably come to New York.

By coincidence – and somewhat to my puzzlement – I had just received a letter from the Columbia Broadcast System Corporation, expressing the hope that I might be coming to New York in the next while, as they would very much like to meet with me regarding a 'potentially mutually beneficial' matter.

I phoned CBS, who said that they would book me a room at the St. Moritz, at their expense, if I could spend an afternoon with them.

When I returned to Grenville Street four days later, I had obtained a reliable forecast of the probable colour direction to be taken by the American automobile industry in the next two to three years. I had also turned down an offer to become the art director of CBS's Print Publications Division – mainly since this would have meant moving to Texas, which I simply could not envision (even though I loved cowboy boots).

Within two weeks, I had a pretty good idea of how I wanted to handle the cloth line and how many different colours should be called for. The Container Corporation Manual, combined with my (hopefully well-founded) lowdown on the American market, had saved us weeks of work. Luckily, there was the familiar backlack of work in the studio, so Keith put himself onto the PX77 Swatch Detail pretty well full time. We covered the walls of the Newfeld & Scott Studio with hundreds of decoy swatches.

The CIL gang certainly kept an eye on their investment. They were very polite, very enthusiastic, very receptive – and very attentive. Before each visit (which they always pre-arranged, so that we were never caught unawares) Keith and I would put up a number of 'newly proposed colour swatches', and move the 'rejected colour swatches' to the end of the wall.

After about four weeks of this, Ted phoned and asked if I was getting any closer to being able to make some final decisions. He explained that CIL was really pleased with what they had seen, and didn't want to interrupt us – but that the laboratory was itching to get involved. CIL had asked him to feel us out.

I told Ted that we could easily give them a few of our finalized colours for their lab to test; and that we had a pretty good idea what the range should comprise. Ted thought serving them one course at a time would be better for everybody's digestion, and suggested not to stuff them with too many goodies all at once.

That afternoon, as I was fiddling with an M&S jacket and getting nowhere, I turned to Keith and said, 'I've just had an idea that I'd better try out on you, in case it is too corny. How about giving the colours Canadian names? We have some great place names: Athabaska, Blackhead Bay, Chicoutimi, Drumheller. Or am I nuts?'

'No. I think the idea is great. But you're really just a newcomer to Canada. I think I could put together a more appropriate list, and work out logical colour associations. If you wouldn't mind?'

'That would be absolutely super!'

The whole project was completed within two more months, and the product appeared in 1961. It was well packaged. It was very well advertised. It was very Canadian. And it was more than well received by the Canadian publishing industry.

And that is the story of PX77. CIL did us the greatest favour by deciding that our proposed fee of $11,000 was just plain greedy. They cost themselves well over 400 percent more by proposing a 1.5 cent royalty per yard! But they never whined, and ultimately seemed happy to have been partners in the whole adventure. The Canadian publishing industry was soon using PX77, almost to the exclusion of any other cloth, whenever linen rather than a paper product was called for.

Jacket, front and back, for *The Princess of Tomboso*, OUP.

The Newfeld & Scott Studio continued to land blue-chip commissions, though the majority of these fell onto my plate. *The Princess of Tomboso*, which Oxford University Press had published, was doing well. Around this time, the Royal Ontario Museum embarked on a merchandising drive, which involved my designing a series of hasty-notes. The hasty-notes were looked after by the ROM women's committee, which was headed by a Mrs Ayala Zacks. When we were introduced, I thought she looked familiar. But I wasn't able to place her.

'I have a feeling that we have met before. Am I correct?' she asked, a few minutes into our meeting.

It suddenly came to me.

'We have. It was way back in 1948.'

'That must have been in Israel.'

'In Tel Aviv, actually. You sent me to the Chel Avir Agam.'

'Now I remember. You had been hurt in Jerusalem, and Palgy couldn't use anybody who wasn't "zug aleph", or a sabreh. This really is a small world!'

The Zackses became loyal patrons, and Newfeld & Scott were the beneficiaries of a couple of small but lucrative corporate image programs at their behest. Also, the ROM decided to do another series of hasty-notes.

In 1960, the Art Directors Club of Toronto picked us to design their *Annual*, to be published by M&S in 1961 (it would contain an ad for PX77).

All of this was good, and kept us busy. But by then we were dying for another 'gainful commission'. And then Keith brought in what promised to be the Most Gainful Commission of All. It was an advertising series for the British Overseas Airways Corporation and British European Airways. The commissioning agency was F. W. Hayhurst, and the art director was Ray Cattell, a very proper English gentleman: proper in manners and decent in professional conduct, as well. The job, as we worked it out with Cattell, would entail the execution of over twenty illustrations, plus the design of a series of newspaper ads, plus the possible design of two to four billboards.

Keith and I rubbed our hands in anticipation of not just balancing the books, but taking long-hoped-for holidays, and finally adding a bit of cash to all this kudos.

Cattell had given us the space specifications for the newspaper campaign, as well as a rough draft of the copy for the first group of ads. It looked as though BOAC and BEA were buying a fair bit of space.

The campaign was a sort of trailblazer. The airways had come up with what was then a novel idea: an arranged holiday tour. It offered a number of different itineraries, embracing a variety of options. BOAC would fly you over to London, and BEA would take it from there, flying you to an impressive choice of European cities. The 'variety of options' included pre-arranged hotels, day-trips, guided tours, and even a form of 'American plan'. Sound familiar? Well, it was new in 1961.

Keith and I discussed the possible direction and style of the job for the better part of the day. 'Why haven't they taken a whole page,' I asked Keith, 'rather than a bunch of quarter-page ads? I think you should check it out with Cattell.'

Keith reported back that the aim was to have the reader encounter the ads on more than one page.

Finally, we came up with the idea of designing a series of ads that were only one column wide, but took up the full depth of the newspaper page: the best of both worlds, we figured. We mocked up a sample ad, one that zigzagged down a column width, and had a mock-up of a newspaper page photostatted, with our ad in position. It looked good.

Keith took it over to Hayhurst, where Cattell asked him to leave it.

When Keith came back, he sat down at his drawing board. After a long five minutes, I could stand it no longer and asked for some sort of a report. 'Well, what did he say?'

'Nothing too much.'

'He must have said something.'

'He did allow that our submission was different from what he had expected. And he said that he would probably get back to me within a week or two.'

'What does that suggest to you?'

Keith looked pained. 'The only time *I* used that line at the magazine, was when I hated what had been brought in to me. It was easier to phone the illustrator back a couple of days later and say we couldn't use it. That way I could simply hang up if a "creative genius" got abusive.'

'Charming! Well, at least we can charge for the roughs.'

Much to our relief – and, I confess, to my surprise – Ray Cattell telephoned us a week later and said our plan was a go. They would need finished art for the first group of ads within three to four weeks. And the client had agreed to spring for the billboard campaign we'd proposed as well, to tie in and coincide with the ads. And had chosen us to design the billboards.

We split the work up, with me taking care of the design and handling over half of the illustrations. The final design still zigzagged down the column. The advertising agency had modified and reduced its copy to fit the narrow format. Keith took over the development of the billboard, which proved harder to do than the newspaper ads. Still, we had time, since the first billboard was scheduled to coincide with the second lot of ads.

We were getting closer and closer to the deadline for the illustrations, however. By the Friday before Keith's delivery deadline, we had all but one finished. Naturally, the holdout was one of mine. I had it in pencil form, however, and promised Keith that I would have it finished for him by Monday.

Saturday morning, I arrived at the studio around nine o'clock. I opened the door, and found Keith fast asleep on the couch in our antechamber, with his face turned toward the wall. This had happened before on the odd occasion, and each time that I had woken Keith up, he was absolutely startled and most apologetic. The poor man had obviously put in an all-nighter. I decided to let him sleep. I closed the outer door as quietly as possible, opened the connecting door and crept into the studio.

The sight that greeted me was beyond belief! The studio had been trashed. It resembled a war zone! Our typewriter had been flung across the room so hard it had put a hole in the wall. The machine itself lay shattered on the floor. Ink bottles had been opened and thrown around. Roughs had been torn off our long pin-board and littered the floor like wounded poems. One piece of finished artwork was indeed finished artwork: not just mortally wounded, but disfigured and dispatched. And what really turned the vandalism into an affront, for me, was the fact that there wasn't a single example of Keith's finished work to be found among the debris.

I tore into the outer office, grabbed Keith by the scruff of his neck and the seat of his pants, and sent him careening to the floor, face down. 'What the fuck have you done? Are you mad? Is this your idea of a form of buggered-up suicide? Answer me!'

A startled Keith turned around, and I found myself looking a complete stranger in the face. He was the same size as Keith, and his clothes were of the colours Keith favoured. But that is where the resemblance ended. The bleary-eyed invader looked to be in his mid-twenties. He was totally disoriented.

He gave me one dismayed look, jumped up and staggered into the studio. There he let out a tremendous moan, and promptly came tearing out again. Thrusting me aside, he ran out of the building with me in hot pursuit. In the meantime, alerted by the noise, Harry Felton had appeared in the hallway. As I chased after Attila the Hun, he shouted that he would call the police.

The young man, in spite of his hungover and dishevelled condition, was making remarkably good time. He had gotten as far as the College and Yonge subway station before I brought him down in a – most surprising, to me – flying tackle. I'd had him in a hastily applied hammerlock for less than a few seconds when a squad car screeched to a stop and two cops jumped out. After I explained what was going on, the older of the two said, 'We'll take it from here, sir. Would you mind coming with us to our division? We'll drive you back to your office after we're through: it shouldn't take long. This matter looks pretty much cut and dried.'

It turned out to be anything but!

The young invader was quickly identified as an Imperial Oil management trainee, who had just passed his apprenticeship. To celebrate his 'commission', he and some other Imperial Oil officer cadets had attended a graduation bash held in an (unpublicized) downtown office of Imperial Oil. Which just happened to be on the second floor of our building.

In a somewhat inebriated state, he had wandered downstairs in order to use the building's public washroom. By chance, our cleaners – we had a cleaning service, courtesy of the Homeowners' Association – had left our front door open, while moving their equipment to the next office on their list. Our night visitor wandered through into the studio area just before the cleaners returned to switch off the lights, our light-switch panel being located by the front door. They closed up for the night without realizing that somebody had entered the premises.

When the lights suddenly went out, Attila the Imperial Oil Hun panicked. In the dark, he banged into walls, drawing tables, work tables, filing tables, taborets. Everything but a door! In utter frustration, he changed from Attila to Don Quixote. There being no windmills at hand with which to joust, he attacked anything that came within reach. Finally, he accidentally collided with the door, which he managed to open, and – to his horror – found himself in another labyrinth, our nine-by-fourteen-foot outer office.

By chance, he fell against Keith's couch, and passed out.

That was what the duty-sergeant had managed to piece together. There was one other bit of disconcerting data: the young man's papa was one of Imperial Oil's senior people. Did I think I really wanted to lay a charge against the 'irresponsible young gentleman', the officer asked. 'Why don't you think it over and let me know Monday morning. Laying a charge may not be the best solution for anyone concerned. We'll hold the young man for twenty-four hours. That alone should teach him an invaluable lesson.'

Waiting for me, when the police and I returned to Grenville Street, were Keith and Joan. The studio really didn't look all that bad. At first I thought my mind had wildly exaggerated the whole thing. But then I saw half a dozen large garbage bags, full, and realized that the two of them had sanitized the place as best as they could. But the hole in the ink-spattered wall, the wrecked furniture, and the crumpled-up artwork spoke volumes.

I was about to tell them about the sergeant's parting words, when the phone rang. It was Gerry Moses, the art director of Imperial Oil's well-respected magazine, *The Imperial Oil Review.* Both Keith and I knew Gerry, who was a member of the TDC (Typographic Designers of Canada), and also a prominent figure within the Toronto art community.

'I've just heard what one of our young idiots has been up to. I don't know what you intend to do about him, and it is none of my business. And frankly, I really don't want to know. I am only calling to tell you that we have already made arrangements for a crew to come to your place on Tuesday. Can you have a list of any damages, no matter how slight, for me to come over and collect tomorrow? I am appalled and really sorry this happened.'

We did not charge the young man.

Imperial Oil had the wall repaired, and the whole studio repainted. A brand new and better typewriter arrived, as did some other studio furniture, to replace stuff that had even the slightest damage. We had made a list of the art supplies that had been ruined. Imperial Oil replaced everything with double the quantity listed. And they paid in full for any damaged artwork.

On Monday, Keith phoned Cattell, only to be told that BOAC had already been in touch with the agency. We were to be given whatever extension we required.

And so ends the story of the Most Gainful Commission.

From *Words like Arrows*, U of T Press.

15. EARLY DAYS ON SIMCOE STREET

n 1964, McClelland & Stewart went into partnership with the *Weekend Magazine* group from Montreal. The object-ive: to launch a Canadian mail-order series for Canada's 1967 centennial. It was to be called the Canadian Centen-nial Library (CCL); and would initially consist of eight books. The books were to range widely in subject matter and in tone – from the weighty (*The Making of the Nation*) to the witty (*The Canadian Look*).

Pierre Berton agreed to be editor-in-chief – this, after assurances from Jack that Berton would have a top-notch publishing group, plus the finest personal secretary, so that he would be able to concentrate on his own work most of the time. He would lend his creative genius, but basically the place would 'run itself'.

I was informed that I would be the only M&S staff member to join the creative group of CCL; at the same time, I was to be made a member of the board of directors of the CCL's parent company, which was to be called the Canadian Illustrated Library. The new position would mean a 50 percent salary increase, effective immediately.

Just a year or so before, Hugh Kane had asked me to join M&S, with the incentive of a seat on the board of directors within three to four months; I had become director of design and production and felt that I had only now gotten these departments running as smoothly as I liked. I had also managed, at last, to establish an excellent rapport with the editorial group, which had initially been none too happy about having an *art director* on the board. (My appointment had set a precedent for publishing in Canada.) I confess that I really didn't want to move to CCL.

I spoke to Kane about my misgivings.

Kane thought that I would not have to spend all that much time at CCL initially. 'Hell, we haven't even decided on a list of books yet. Let alone received a manuscript to work with. Let's see how things work out in the interim.' He pointed out that I would be keeping my position as M&S's director of design and production, in any case: it wasn't as if I was 'leaving'.

So I agreed, and said we'd talk no more about it.

That was on a Friday. On the Monday following, just as I was getting ready to go home, I received a telephone call from Gene Aliman, the former art director of *Maclean's*, with whom I had worked on *Canadianecdotes*. 'I had lunch with George Gilmour today. He tells me that you are going to be the art director of some new publishing house, with Pierre Berton as editor-in-chief. That isn't true, is it?'

'Well, it isn't official as yet. But, yes, it looks that way.'

'Look, Frank, it's none of my business. But we've always worked well together, and I simply must tell you this: Berton will drive you nuts, if not kill you. He's the main reason I quit *Maclean's*. He is notorious for meddling, and has undermined each and every art director he's worked with. Please, don't do it!'

That evening, at home – just as we were finishing supper – I received another telephone call, from Allan Fleming, a vice-president at Maclean-Hunter. 'I had a call from Gene Aliman today. He tells me that you intend to accept the position of art director of a new publishing house, which is going to have Pierre Berton as editor-in-chief. That isn't true, is it?'

'Well, it isn't official as yet. But, yes, it looks that way.'

'Frank, it's none of my business. But we've been good friends for a long time, and I know how you work. Berton will drive you nuts, if not kill you. He is notorious for meddling, and has undermined each and every art director he's worked with. Please, don't do it!'

First thing Tuesday morning, I went to see Hugh Kane.

'I've had two phone calls from people, neither with any connection to M&S,' I started. 'Both have worked with Pierre, and neither had anything pleasant to say about the experience. In fact, each had the same advice: "Don't take the fucking job!"'

'And?'

'I suspect that it is probably very sound counsel.'

'I've got a bunch of things I have to do this morning,' said Hugh. 'Let's talk about it over lunch. My treat.'

Lunch was at the Walper Hotel in Kitchener, Hugh's favourite eating establishment and Frank-inveigling place. (Twice before, when I was at the end of my tether with Jack, Hugh had treated me to a wiener-schnitzel lunch here, and persuaded me to reconsider quitting, or worse.)

We got through the salad in silence. While we were waiting for the main course to appear, Hugh lit his customary cigarette, and said, 'I've thought about your misgivings regarding Pierre. I really don't think that you need be concerned.'

'But I am. Gene Aliman, I don't take that seriously. But Allan Fleming, I do. It's not just that he's a good friend of mine. It's that he doesn't have an axe to grind. Besides: say I were to take the position, and then find it impossible. I would set up an entire art department, and then, three weeks later, saddle some other poor shnook with a fait accompli, as far as the group of designers was concerned. It's far better for an art director to find his or her own people.'

'You're right, of course. But I don't know why you've already decided that you and Pierre won't be able to work together. You've done all of his books since you arrived at M&S. Pierre specifically asked for you, because, according to him, you work well together.'

'Yeah. But so far, it has always been at arm's length. I know lots of lovers who came to hate each other once they were married!'

'May I make a suggestion?'

'What?'

'I recommend, as a friend, that you take the job. And at the first opportunity establish the type of relationship that *you* insist on.'

'How am I supposed to do that?'

'Easy. The first time Berton steps out of line, let him have it with both barrels. And remind him that you are on the board of directors, just as he is.'

'I can imagine how far that'll get me. Straight out the door!'

Kane took a different tack. 'Frankly, if you don't take the job, I doubt that Jack will let you stay at M&S. I doubt he would forgive you for making him lose face with the *Weekend Magazine* group.'

'Okay,' I grumbled. 'I'll try it. But the wiener schnitzel had better be good!'

This was the usual finale of Kane's 'Kitchener routines'.

The CCL premises on Simcoe Street, in downtown Toronto, consisted of two floors over a Speedy Auto Glass shop; they were accessible via a steep set of stairs – presumably to accommodate the high ceilings required by the glass shop below.

Each floor contained several rooms, and had complete bathroom facilities, as well as a decent kitchen set-up, with fridge. The top floor had two smaller rooms plus a large room (about twenty by thirty feet square). This large room faced east, and boasted five huge windows on the street side.

I had quietly gone down to take a look at the building, prior to meeting with Pierre for the allocation of space. I knew exactly what I was going to lay claim to. The top floor would make the perfect art department. Just let Pierre start throwing his weight around, I thought, and I would let him have it with both of Hugh Kane's barrels.

'Well, what do you think of the place?'

'Pretty good.'

'I think so, too. How many rooms do you want?'

'The top floor would be best for the art department. It already has a large room, ideal for the bullpen. The windows just need some gauzy curtains to diffuse the light. The bathroom is just across the corridor, which gives us our water. And, to be honest, the climb will discourage most visitors. Would you like to go back up for another look at the area?'

We went back up, and after five minutes Pierre nodded: 'I agree. There's just one thing.' (Here we go, I thought.) 'I think I'll take one of the other rooms on this floor as my office. Your mention of the "visitor's climb" has convinced me.'

Well, I couldn't make a fuss over that. It would make me look like a real prick. I had mentally kept the larger of the two rooms as my own. It was just the right size to reserve one end for my design paraphernalia, and use the rest as my production office. Still, the smaller room was quite adequate. It was just as big as my Hollinger House office, which was the second biggest office *there*. 'That seems logical,' I said. 'Where will our secretaries sit?'

'We'll make a secretarial pool on the editorial floor. The Bell can provide them with a shared line to us.'

'I imagine you will need the bigger office,' I said. 'The other room is fine with me.'

'No,' he said. 'I want the smaller office. I'm not going to be here all that much, once things get rolling.'

So much for Hugh Kane's 'both barrels'!

The next six weeks were spent getting 'Canada's newest

publishing house' into shape. Pierre and I met in my office at Hollinger House, and in one lengthy meeting we – or rather Pierre – established the range of titles for CCL, and all areas of responsibility. He evidently believed in a double-quick-time decision-making process!

Apart from procuring furniture and other office essentials – which simply meant phoning Owen Wilson at M&S – it was my job to set up manufacturing specs for the series. At this point I got my first pleasant surprise: Pierre not only expected me to establish extents, and the proportion of colour to black-and-white visuals for each book – which more than suited me – he asked me to establish a projected visual-to-verbal relationship for each book. This was something new to me. In the past, with any coffee-table book I'd worked on, I had been presented with the text as a fait accompli from editorial; often, even the caption text was preordained, without any concern for the problems length might pose for the designer looking to establish an effective visual/verbal statement.

Though Pierre had a tentative list of titles he intended to publish, the only one with a detailed outline was the first book of the series, *The Making of the Nation*, which William Kilbourn had been commissioned to write.

I told Pierre that I would be able to establish (tentative) publishing specs on the basis of Kilbourn's outline, including suggested number of illustrations, maximum text lengths and so forth. As far as the other titles were concerned, however, all I would be able to provide would be guidelines– at least until I got some working estimates from editorial.

I reminded Pierre that Jack had given me a pretty tight budget – one that would probably force me to go in unconventional manufacturing directions.

'How long will it take you to make sort-of-final decisions, provided you get the estimates before too long?'

'Just about six weeks. I'll draw up specs in such a way that I can interpolate the estimates, to best fit my budget, when I get them.'

'That makes sense. Can you let me have something for Kilbourn within two weeks?'

This sounded reasonable enough. So much for Hugh Kane's 'both barrels', once again.

I had to admit that Berton was impressive. He made decisions only after consultation, but then he made them quickly. He was blessed with an amazing memory (something I always found remarkable, if at times a bit embarrassing; I came to dread the words, 'But at our last meeting you distinctly said....')

Four weeks in, however, Pierre had never once tried to be either designer or art director.

Of course, I told myself, we hadn't as yet gotten into any design specifics. He would probably show his true colours once we got going, and once we had an art department for him to grandstand before. *Then* I would let him have it with both of Hugh Kane's barrels.

The editorial group was coming together rapidly. Ken Lefolii appeared on the scene as senior editor, followed by Peter Gzowski as managing editor. Prue Hemelrijk arrived as picture editor and editorial researcher. Add to this the two secretaries, and the second floor was soon a hubbub of mysterious activity.

In contrast, I reigned in peaceful solitude on the third floor. The silence was only occasionally broken, by printing house reps coming in with revised estimates – and complaints about the impossibility of my extravagant demands for quantity and quality at bargain-basement prices.

After word-of-mouth drew a blank, I ran an ad for designers and illustrators in all three Toronto papers. The first person to answer the ad was a young Englishman, newly arrived in Canada, by the name of Nick Milton. He had an impressive portfolio, mostly in the area of magazine design. What caught my eye were a number of beautiful and sensitive experimental typography projects that screamed 'book designer'. In one of the best hiring decisions of my career, I signed him on.

We now had the start of an art department. Since I was still handling the design of all of the M&S list, I decided I needed reinforcements. I proceeded to hire the main body of the visual group, regardless of the fact that we only had in hand two completed manuscripts for CCL.

To the design side, I added Don Fernley and David Shaw; Hedda Scharke and Vlasta van Kampen made up a very talented and capable nucleus for the illustration group. (Hedda was married to Doug Johnson, a former OCA illustration student of mine; he went on to become a successful and sought-after illustrator in the States.)

Eventually, the art department would grow to eight people. But at this early stage of the Canadian Centennial Library, there were four – and they worked more on the M&S list than on their own.

The design work for CCL initially consisted in finding a distinctive cover treatment, and establishing a 'house look' that would accommodate the variety of subject matters planned, yet still maintain a series identity.

Prue Hemelrijk by now had an impressive set of files of photographs and slides, and we had begun to get some estimates from editorial. This meant we were able to put together some realistic specimen pages.

These were the pre-computer days, when everything had to be pasted up and laboriously put together, by hand. The editorial group was quite adept at reading 'pretend' pages – but even our editors needed at least a glimpse of type and picture in action. The mock-ups were also needed by Jack McClelland, who was receiving impatient and insistent demands for 'something to look at' from his Montreal partners.

Now the art department became the Canadian Centennial Library's preeminent beehive of activity. And since editorial was not yet firmly in the throes of polishing potential bestsellers, we received more than our share of visitors from the lower floor. (We also happened to make better coffee than did editorial, which regularly encouraged Gzowski to make the climb.)

One late morning, after taking something or other over to Jack McClelland, I arrived at Simcoe Street to find Pierre ensconced at our light table, poring over slides. With him, armed with my best loupe, stood Nick Milton, looking like a bemused barrow boy.

'What is going on here?' I snarled.

'We're just looking at some of Prue's new slides.' Nick replied.

'Selecting, you mean! Pierre, could we go to my office!'

I stomped off, not at all certain that Berton was following me, but determined not to spoil the act by turning round. To my relief, he came in close behind. Here, at long last, was my chance to let Mr Berton have it with both of Hugh Kane's barrels!

'Don't you ever give my people any orders or tasks on your own initiative! In fact, don't even bother to come into the art department when I'm not there. Do I make myself clear?'

'Quite. But I had absolutely no intention of interfering. Nor have I. The visual end is totally your decision, and responsibility,' he said. And left.

An hour later, I began to wonder what the blazes had possessed me. Pierre had given me absolutely no occasion to complain about loss of control. In fact, he had gone to extreme lengths to leave me and mine to our own devices.

In fact, thus far, I'd really enjoyed working with Pierre – more so than with any other 'bookie.'

So much, once more, for Kane's both barrels.

* * *

The topics of the books planned for CCL were so various that I soon decided a 'family look' for the mise-en-page would be restrictive from both designer's and reader's point of view. I drafted a memo in which I set out my visual philosophy, accordingly. Though I proposed the establishing of a clearly recognizable series look for the covers, I recommended that the flavour and content of each title determine the design approach to the interior.

What sort of 'series look' the jackets might have was another question. The group included a solemn historic chronicle, a sublime art anthology, a tongue-in-cheek curiosity volume.... I had no idea how to find a common thread. But I certainly had no intention of telling Berton or Lefolii that!

I decided the easiest way to buy myself time – and breathing room – to muddle through this problem was to convince editorial that the personality of each volume's author had to be served and properly protected in the cover treatment, 'even at the cost of the visual'.

Nick thought this a brilliant bit of conniving. 'Believe me, they'll go for it. In any case, they're scared of your luv'ly temper.'

One of the things that had often bothered me about 'cheapie' coffee-table books was the frequency with which pages were left half empty at chapter ends. The avoidance of needless blank space was one of the most forceful points that I made in my design-philosophy memo. I argued that, given our direct-mail audience, it was essential to avoid giving our readers the impression that they were paying for empty pages.

To my surprise, Pierre agreed. 'This is just like usual magazine policy,' he said. He added that design would be responsible for settling the length of captions and the size of pictures. And that editorial would give design proper notice, whenever there was 'a lot' to say about any visual piece.

At this point, some production issues arose. There was the issue of preparatory versus constant costs. These were the days before computerized preparatory, so plant costs could be high; normally, given the short runs of most M&S books, they outweighed running costs. With CCL, however, I would be printing a minimum of 80,000, first run. The mathematics changed completely.

In the sixties, the average Canadian run was 1,500 to 3,000 copies. Here, the 'constant costs' of materials – paper, binding cloth, et cetera – did not play as decisive a role in the total cost of the book as did the amortization of the high but one-time plant costs– colour separation, four-colour plates and printing, commissioned illustrations, et cetera. For instance: if one commissioned ten illustrations at a cost of $30 each, the amortized cost over 3,000 books would be ten cents per book; the amortized cost over 30,000 copies would be only one cent per book. On the other hand, if better paper cost, say, ten cents a copy, that would add just $300 to the budget for a run of 3,000; but with a long-run book, the extra ten cents per copy would become much more significant – adding $3,000 to the 30,000-copy run.

I had gotten an inordinate number of quotes for CCL production, and had explored both sheet and web printing. Web printing – though inappropriate for an art book like the planned *Great Canadian Painting*, which would require high-quality colour reproduction – could work for many of the volumes in the series, and would allow us to afford more four-colour work, in general. The unique configurations of a web forme established a number of permutations of 'full-colour' availability, however, quite different from those of a sheet-fed press. This required a different way of thinking.

My solution was to propose a policy of 'minimal visual interruption' of an author's treatise. To compensate for the lack of mid-text visuals, and to sustain a high level of visual attraction, I recommended the inclusion of a number of luxurious albums in each book, which would work as breaks, or bridges. (To be honest, I wasn't sure whether the CCL would be sold as literature, or more as furniture – but I thought my proposal allowed for both possibilities. And it

The public figure   becomes the anonymous tourist

The Making of the Nation by William Kilbourn was the first mail-order book published in Canada by M&S.

accommodated itself to web printing.) To my relief, and surprise, both our editors and the American direct-mail expert endorsed the idea.

The first book, Kilbourn's *The Making of a Nation,* set the pace. Kilbourn was a kulturnik, and also an enthusiastic supporter of TDC, of which I had been a founding member. (Early meetings had been held in my Spadina Avenue studio, and I had served as president of the society in 1959, the year it received its Ontario charter.)

Early on, Kilbourn asked me if I'd decided on a typeface for his book. I told him that I had just about decided on Pilgrim. He had never heard of it. I showed him the sample setting I had procured.

'It looks a lot like Perpetua,' he ventured. 'I like it.'

'You're absolutely right. As a matter of fact, Eric Gill designed both faces. He cut Pilgrim for a deluxe, limited edition of *The Pilgrim's Progress* published in the United States.'

The Making of a Nation turned out well. And the picture-album solution, which I'd proposed as an identifiable part of the 'CCL look', turned out to be not just practical, but visually effective – and liberating for the designer, too. (In fact, I would go on to incorporate this solution in the design of just about all of my future coffee-table books.)

★ ★ ★

In 1965, people valued the book as a traditional instrument of entertainment and edification; books belonged with the theatre and the concert hall, rather than with the cinema, the television, the newspaper. Designers actually worried about interpreting an author's message, and finding the typeface that might best accord with the tone and tempo of the text. Some of us even sought to give 'sight-sound' to an author's far-too-often muted voice.

Some years later, at a symposium sponsored by the AIGA in Boston, a young Canadian maven would vehemently denounce the ('antiquated') practices of such ('aged') typographic designers. He ridiculed the professed expertise of people like Williamson and Meynell. He termed obsolete and redundant any obsession with word spacing, or the selection of one typeface over another for any reason other than personal fancy. He laughed at the idea of 'the psychology of type', as theorized by 'relics' such as Fry or Dwiggins.

'I am not sure that Allen & Unwin would agree with you,' I said. 'Not after the misadventure with Perpetua.' (Allen & Unwin had made Perpetua their house typeface, only to discover that this mannered face made texts difficult for readers to take in and retain.)

Then I foolishly added, 'As a fellow Canadian, I hate to admit that I'm not familiar with your name. Perhaps you could tell me the titles of one or two of the books you have designed?'

'I find *that* belligerent and offensive,' the young man sniffed. 'And I will not dignify your attempt at character assassination with a reply!'

What I didn't realize was that the young man's proclamation, though absurd, would prove prophetic: many of our preeminent publications would subscribe to his 'philosophy', as soon as they had cast their lot in with computer typesetting.

But in those naive days of metal typesetting, at CCL, we still anguished over typefaces as though it really mattered. I even prepared a short list of preferred 'house fonts':

LINOTYPE:
Baskerville, Caledonia, Electra (with sloped roman), Palatino, Pilgrim, Times New Roman

MONOTYPE: (when affordable)
Bembo, Bodoni, Ehrhardt, Monotype Plantin

TABOOS:
Caslon, Estienne, Garamond, and any sans serif

The argument I gave regarding sans serif was that the CCL audience would most likely include a high percentage of newcomers to the bibliophile world, who would expect to receive something that had the time-honoured 'bookish' look about it. (In truth, design treatment of sans serif faces required a mastery I wasn't certain our design department could provide at that time.)

* * *

In 1964, in the midst of my time with CCL, I was presented with a diversion: the design and production of a history of the Bank of Montreal. Merrill Denison was the author. Editorial had finally handed over the finished, though unedited, manuscript. With that, an enormous box of photocopies of the bank's archival material also arrived in my office.

Neither the directors' meeting nor an editorial meeting about the book, several months earlier, had furnished me with anything beyond the barest description of the project. I therefore phoned Hugh and asked him directly about publishing intent, size of run, and budget. Hugh referred me to Jack, who told me that he wanted a lavish book, which gave the impression that no expense had been spared. 'You can spend all the money you need,' he said. 'But don't go overboard!'

Given this somewhat ambiguous decree, it took me a whole week to put a visual proposal together. I costed out all sorts of normally impossible embellishments. Fold-out full-colour illustrations. Special endpapers. Chapter-head illustrations. Two-colour text (which would require six-colour printing, given the colour reproductions that would also be included). I came up with a list of potential artists I wanted to commission for both the fold-outs and the chapter heads.

I then commissioned Laurence Hyde to produce a sample chapter opening. I had a number of specimen pages set and printed up, with the two-colour text. Then I put John Elphick, a former OCA student I'd recently hired, to work, matting everything up for a hopefully dazzling super-presentation.

All this, plus the analyzing of the numerous estimates, took the better part of a month.

As I remember, it was a Tuesday that I took everything to Hugh Kane, and asked him what he thought.

'I think it's exactly the right solution. And it has the unmistakable look of an M&S book. Jack is looking after this project himself. So you'll have to take it to him. I'm sure he will like it.'

'I'm sure he won't.'

When I tried to see Jack, he was, as usual, out of the office. I told Marge that I had everything together, and needed a meeting with him. Whereupon she asked whether I had booked my flight yet.

'What flight?'

'Next Monday.'

'Where am I going?'

'Montreal. You've got a meeting with him *and* the Bank of Montreal. Jack said that he would tell you himself.'

'Well, he didn't. What's Jack's flight number? I'll get Lorene to book me on it.' (Lorene Wilson was my secretary at the time.)

'I'll do it for you. It'll be easier to arrange seats and so on.'

In the meantime, for just about a month I had barely touched any of the next season's books (for M&S, never mind CCL). And time was running short. Even though I was now spending ten or twelve hours a day at work, it seemed the more I did, the more piled up. On the Wednesday, I went back to our neglected publishing list.

On Friday, when Jack still had not reappeared, I decided to put together some sort of presentation folder for the Bank of Montreal. Just in case. It included a brief outline of the publishing philosophy, as regarded both manufacturing standards (excellent, of course) and visual enhancement (bountiful, without needless ostentation). Next, I gave a description of the major illustrations – the fold-out paintings – to be specially commissioned for the book. This included a short list of the artists whom we had by this time approached, and who had expressed a firm interest in the (hypothetical) project. Then I described the other visual components of the book – and added a reaffirmation of the publishing philosophy as concerned quality and artistic merit.

In a final section, I gave a list of the different materials to be used in the physical production of the book; this included specimens of the cloth, the papers, the boards, and so on. It also included full specifications for all materials.

I described our requirements for proofings, from one-colour

through to full-colour separations, and I set out the approval stages for roughs of all commissioned artwork (really much more clearly than I needed to).

I put together a manufacturing cost analysis, and a cost guesstimate for artwork, as well. These I kept out of the presentation package, since neither Hugh Kane nor I had any idea what Jack had in mind – or of what he had promised the bank. Though both of us assumed that this was a piece of vanity publishing, neither of us could remember whether Denison was our author, or the bank's. And Jack had the editorial file.

Back at the shop, John Elphick had to put this paper charade together in triplicate. And to matte up the sample pages and a large colour photo of the sample painting. There was nothing for it but for both of us to go to Hollinger House both Saturday and Sunday.

On Sunday, Jack phoned around four in the afternoon. And said that he had been looking all over for me. And asked what I was doing at M&S.

When I explained what we were doing on our Sunday (this in what Elphick said was none too pleasant a manner) Jack beat a hasty retreat: 'Let's go over everything on the flight to Montreal. I don't want to disturb you now.'

We – or rather Elphick – finished just in time for a midnight snack.

On the flight to Montreal the next day, Jack skimmed quickly over both the presentation folder and the page spreads. He spent much more time going over the production estimates. When he came to my suggested art and illustration budgets, he donned his signature look of determined disgust. 'You're asking for *ten thousand dollars* for the paintings you want to commission?'

'I was sure that you'd want me to only use top artists like Franklyn Arbuckle, Jimmy Hill and Gerry Sevier. I've felt out most of the people I hope to use, and the least I can possibly offer them is $800 per painting. I know that's more than we are used to paying. But these are all well-known, established illustrators, who are used to getting four figures for their work. The only reason that they are willing to do it for eight hundred dollars is the prestige and publicity I've assured them will be associated with the project.'

I thought my argument sounded pretty damn good.

'No, no,' said Jack. 'You can't ask for ten thousand. The bank will think that they are just getting trash. You've got to ask for more.'

'How about $20,000?' I suggested, hoping Jack would notice the sarcastic tone.

'That's a bit better, okay. The rest of your presentation reads well, and looks even better. In fact, I think you might as well make the design-and-production presentation at the meeting. Just don't touch on any of the established costs, other than the painting budget. I'll look after the rest.'

The meeting took place in one of the bank's private dining rooms, the bank being represented by Mr R.D. Mulholland, the senior vice-president and general manager, Mr J.E. Totten, the bank's treasurer, and a Mr C.W. Harris. Mr Arnold Hart, the bank's president and chairman came to the luncheon, as did some half-dozen other gentlemen, all boasting subdued sartorial splendour. But they, with Mr Hart, left as soon as lunch was over.

Lunch was tasteful and beautifully served. The *History* was not even mentioned during the meal. Jack sat between Messrs Hart and Mulholland, and I was seated next to Mr Totten. Mr Totten turned out to be the perfect dinner companion. With dessert, the subject of bank accounts was somehow brought up. I mentioned that I, alas, did not have an account with the Bank of Montreal. 'So I noticed. You deal with Toronto-Dominion, don't you?' Totten asked.

This observation was impressive, in a scary sort of way.

'Yes. I hope that that's okay?'

'Of course,' Totten laughed. 'We were just making the usual enquiries about people we intend to work with. Mind you, we weren't able to find out too much about you.'

'Well, I am happy to say that I've never had to take out a loan for anything. And I don't believe I've ever had an overdraft.'

'Ah. That is admirable! But a bit short-sighted. Allow me to give you a bit of good advice. When you get home, borrow something like $4,000 from your local bank. I guarantee that you'll get the loan. Say it's for finishing your basement, or something. Then pay it back after one month. The whole exercise won't cost you more than about $24. A small amount as far as establishing a credit rating is concerned, which is something you lack, at this time. And stay with the TD, they are good people.'

After lunch we were joined by Mr Munro Brown, a rather fawning, tweedy English gentleman. He was introduced as the bank's project officer for the *History*. Brown nodded vigorously to everything that either Mr Mulholland or Mr Totten had to say; he frowned suspiciously at anything that I had to say. Jack came off only a little better, his remarks punctuated by pained, audible *hmmms* from Brown.

Then the serious work began.

Jack made persuasive publishing noises for about five minutes. Then he indicated that I would kick off the presentation. This proved much easier than I had imagined it would be. Mr Totten's positive reception to almost every one of my proposals subtly but successfully subdued Mr Brown's attempts at criticism.

Jack was masterful. He painted a glorious future for the book; convincingly extolled the talents of the creative team brought together for the project; praised the Merrill Denison manuscript – which, it turned out, had been commissioned by the Bank of Montreal – and slipped in the advantage of the bank's having the help of 'M&S's best editor' in the 'final polishing' thereof. He even had a perfect title for the book, up his sleeve: *Canada's First Bank*. Jack never even mentioned money.

He left with a verbal contractual commitment from the bank.

And I left with a new title, also: M&S Project Officer/ CANADA'S FIRST BANK.

By the end of the second week following our meeting in Montreal, I had accumulated a dozen memoranda from friend Munro Brown. Of these, only three made sense. To the rest, all I could reply was that we had not yet reached that stage, but I would furnish him with all details the moment I knew them myself. Brown dutifully replied to each of my replies, putting on record that he had received my reply and had now replied to it.

After four weeks of this, Lorene threatened to either quit or send him an envelope bomb the next time she had to waste time answering the deluge.

But things got worse. Each mail delivery saw one or more pieces of waste paper from Munro. Before two months had gone by, Lorene was up to Memorandum No. 136 – less than a dozen of the 136 comprising legitimate queries. At No. 137, I drew the line. I told Lorene not to bother me with anything less than the financial collapse of the Bank of Montreal. And not to bother answering Munro's mumbo-jumbo herself, either. 'Let the Brown matter fall where it may!'

Once we had reached a consensus with editorial regarding the selection and presentation of the twenty illustrations, I sent a final list of proposed artists and subjects to Munro. The list was duly approved by Messrs Mulholland & Company. By week ten, I had taken delivery of eight finished paintings.

Jack decided that now would be a good time to invite the bank to come to a progress session at Hollinger House. Unfortunately, 'Merrill Denison's editor' was quite a bit behind schedule in getting the manuscript in shape for typesetting. This news we decided to keep to ourselves. The eight paintings, plus Laurence Hyde's roughs, would make for excellent window dressing in the mean time.

Munro promptly replied, for the bank, stating that he, personally, would be coming down – alone.

The presentation was set up in our boardroom.

There was one minor problem. When Jack became president of M&S, he had appropriated his father's office. Mr McClelland Sr, who still came in to 'work' two days a week, had been moved to the board-room, our only spare space. Normally, Jack drove his father to and from Hollinger House. That morning, however, Mr Mac Senior had caught a ride in without notifying anybody and had arrived at M&S quite unexpectedly.

Mr McClelland Sr appeared in the boardroom about twenty minutes after my meeting with Munro had begun. (Jack had begged off at the last moment, pleading, as usual, that 'an emergency' had just cropped up.) I introduced Mr McClelland Sr. to Munro, and explained that I was just about to show Mr Brown some of the illustrations for the bank's book. I invited Mr McClelland Sr to also stay and view the pieces.

'No, thank you. I have a number of important matters to attend to. Will you be needing my office for very much longer?'

I remonstrated very gently that Jack had initiated the meeting, and that we were expecting him at any moment. To which Mr McClelland Sr grunted that Jack was *always* 'expected at any moment' – and that he hoped we'd be through with his office *very soon.* He disappeared.

Excusing myself, I left Munro alone in the boardroom. I went to see Marge and begged her to locate Jack. 'Tell him that his father wants his office back. And wants it back in no uncertain terms!'

'He's on his way. I phoned him as soon as Mr Mac Sr arrived.'

I hurried back to the boardroom, only to find Munro cowering in one corner. Confronting him was Mr John McClelland Sr, brandishing a pitcher full of water. 'This is *my* office! I want it back right now! If you aren't out of here by the time I count to ten, I will throw this water over both you and your silly pictures. 'ONE ... TWO ... THREE ... FOUR ...'

At this point, Jack came running in at full speed, bodily picked up his father and, as he carried him out, called, 'Nice to see you, Munro. Carry on. I'll be with you in just a minute.'

For the rest of the meeting, Munro was unusually subdued. His visit elicited three very formal memos, however, wherein he registered some qualms about 'our attitude towards the project'. These arrived by special delivery two days later.

And a few days after that, I got a phone call from Jack.

'I'm just reading a most perturbing letter from Mulholland. I think we'd better get together. Can you come to my office?'

When I arrived, Jack looked up from his desk. 'Munro Brown has complained that you haven't answered a number of his memos,' he said.

'Absolutely true.'

'In fact, this letter says that 'most of the memos from number 136 to number 180 remain unanswered.'

'Not true.'

'You mean you have answered them?'

'No. I mean that I've only answered three of his memos, out of a total that now exceeds 240! Either Mulholland is way behind, or Brown doesn't have the nerve to admit that he has a memo addiction. I don't have the time to *read* the things. Ninety-nine per cent of them are totally fatuous. Lorene has threatened to quit because of the wretched man. Munro may have nothing else to do. But I do. Apart from the bank book, I have your bloody list to bring out.'

'Well, you've got to tell him something. Make some excuse.'

'I honestly don't know what to say to him.'

'Well, at least give him an evasive answer.'

'Like what?'

'Think of something. Goodbye.'

Ten minutes later, my phone rang. It was Jack again.

'I've thought of an evasive answer for Munro Brown.'

'Yes?'

'Tell him to fuck off!'

The next morning, Marge Hodgeman brought me a copy of a letter to Mr Mulholland. In it, Jack agreed with the spirit of Munro's grievances, but added that they placed him in a quandary, inasmuch as I was an officer of McClelland & Stewart and also the company's director of design and production. And though *Canada's First Bank* was my primary concern – and I was handling it, he assured Mr Mulholland, most proficiently – I still had certain other company responsibilities. In fact, had I answered all of Munro's 240-plus memos, he (Jack) would have had no choice but to ask for my resignation. He suggested that Mr Brown write fewer memos.

Obviously, the bank concurred. And though the memos kept coming, their numbers decreased dramatically from that point. The book came out on schedule, and looked good. The bank loved it!

* * *

By 1966, I was back at work at CCL, on *Great Canadian Painting*, a title that would bring with it the greatest trials, tribulations and – eventually – triumphs of any of the Canadian Centennial Library volumes.

Elizabeth (Betsy) Kilbourn – William Kilbourn's wife – had been commissioned to write the book. The first editorial meeting was encouraging. Betsy provided us with an excellent outline of her book, and promised to quickly prepare a complete list of the transparencies needed. Prue Hemelrijk and Marjorie Harris, our researchers, would be able to obtain the transparencies from divers Canadian galleries, in good time.

The second editorial meeting was less encouraging. Betsy managed to bring only a partial list of transparencies. We were beginning to run behind schedule, and Pierre explained the need for the timely meeting of deadlines, where direct mail publishing was concerned. Betsy promised the rest of the list within a week.

Two weeks later, Pierre came in to see me and announced that Betsy would not be able to complete the work.

'Why? What has happened?'

'Confidentially, she has had a breakdown of some sort.'

'So do you intend to postpone the book?'

Pierre shook his head. 'No. I've thought about it. But *Great Canadian Painting* fits the series' rhythm much too well, to replace it with *The Canadian Look*. We're going to do it in house.'

We had a full editorial meeting that afternoon.

Ken Lefolii was elected to write the book.

He protested, 'I know next to nothing about Canadian art.'

'Well,' said Berton, 'you'll have almost two months to learn. Someone else will select the art pieces for the book; and I have in mind a researcher to provide you with details about the pieces chosen. I'm sure you'll produce an excellent text.'

Pierre then announced that I would select the paintings and other visual components, as well as designing the book.

'I know even less than Ken does about Canadian art,' I said.

'Well, you too can learn on the job.' He smiled magnanimously.

Said Marjorie Harris, 'I'm scared to ask who is to do the research.'

Pierre looked through his notes, 'Ah, here it is. You are.'

Berton must have burnt the midnight oil. He presented us with a proposed table of contents, suggesting an introduction followed by a number of albums: 'Landscape', 'The Cities', 'Daily Life', 'The Canadian Figure', 'The Abstractionists', and so on – with further categories to be determined as we went along.

My connections with the Art Gallery of Ontario came in handy. Betsy Kilbourn's list had been fairly comprehensive up to the end of the 1940s, but from then on things were scant. All we had was her outline, which was pretty general. I shamelessly picked the brains of the people at the AGO, and wound up with more 'artists who simply had to be in *Great Canadian Painting*' than I could handle.

It took me a solid week of looking through catalogues and gallery lists of available transparencies to put together the file of potential paintings. These more than augmented the stack of transparencies we already had in hand. Pierre and Ken suggested the addition of one more album – 'The Loners' – to those already on our list, and changed a couple of the existing album names ('The Canadian Figure' became 'Faces and Figures'; 'The Abstractionists' became 'Feelings and Ideas').

Pierre suggested that I produce a number of specimen spreads, plus a thumbnail layout of the whole book. When I said that we would first have to select the pieces to be shown, Pierre said we were too far behind schedule to have a meeting. I would have to make the initial selection alone.

My design proposal was approved and my layout okayed with just a few minor changes. I had allotted some twenty-four pages for Lefolii's main text, including pertinent illustrations, which I would size to fit. I had also allotted two pages for prefatory text to each album, plus six pages for end matter.

We must have set a record time for putting an art book together. The design of the albums was completed in just over one week. The main text arrived promptly on my desk three weeks after Lefolii had received a 'maximum word-count'. The complete manuscript was ready for typesetting in only six weeks. And that included captions to accompany the plates – all written exactly to count! (Of all the writers I worked with, Berton, Lefolii and Gzowski were exceptional – not only in writing to count, but in understanding and accepting the complexity of the design intent.) Just two weeks later, we had corrected repros of the typesetting.

While this was happening, the last of the transparency reproductions arrived in final proof. Nick Milton and I completed a dummy paste-up. I gave one copy to Pierre, and cabbed another to Jack. Camera-ready paste-up was likewise completed in record time.

Ken liked the book. Marjorie liked the book. Jack liked the book. Our direct-mail expert liked the book. The art department liked the book. Pierre made one change. The title page now read:

EDITORIAL CONTRIBUTORS
Paintings: Elizabeth Kilbourn, Frank Newfeld
Text: Ken Lefolii
Research: William Kilbourn, Marjorie Harris, Sandra Scott

A few days later, Pierre asked me to come to his office.

'How would you feel about the *Weekend* plant printing *Great Canadian Painting?*'

'That's a web plant. You can't print an art book on any of Canada's web presses. Not even on the best coated stock. It just can't be done. Both Canadian Centennial Library and *Weekend* would lose their shirts.'

'I thought as much. Well, they definitely want to print the book. McConnell is pushing hard. There's a meeting at Hollinger House tomorrow. I think you'd better come. I'll tell McClelland.'

The meeting was heated. In attendance were Jack, Pierre, and I, from M&S; plus, from Montreal, the director of the *Weekend* printing plant, his plant manager and an unidentified VIP. We argued back and forth. Pierre and I stressed that an art book had to have fidelity reproduction; the plant director insisted that his printers would have no problems producing *our* art book.

In spite of our warnings, the meeting finished up with Jack capitulating to the Montreal VIP, with just one condition: CCL would have the final and sole say as to the acceptability of the printed sheet. The VIP accepted this. The plant director then suggested that the decision be made by an officer of CCL – and not, as he put it, by some disgruntled artist.

Jack again agreed. 'That seems reasonable. Frank Newfeld is a director of McClelland & Stewart and of CCL, and also creative director of both companies. He will fit the bill perfectly.'

There, the meeting ended.

The printing plant was located in the outskirts of Montreal. I was put up in a small motel, and told that a car would fetch me once the plant had finished the prep. This meant not only that I was prisoner in a seedy room, but that both the plant and I were going to waste a lot of time waiting for taxis.

Finally, I was taken to the plant and shown to a boardroom. The first two sheets were laid out on the table. The separation proofs which our art department had provided were nowhere in sight. When I requested them, I was told that they seemed to be missing. As were the ozalids, the blues, which the plant had already sent to me, and which I had okayed. Both were essential to the checking of the sheets. By sheer chance I had photocopied the ozalids, and packed a second set of the colour proofs.

The sheets were awful. They looked like the cheap magazine images that they were. Their definition was poor. The colour was worse. The director of the *Weekend* plant said that all that was needed was some ink adjustment. The Montreal VIP, who was also there, nodded sagely. Sheet after sheet was brought in to us. This went on for well over two hours, and the plant came no closer to producing an acceptable sheet.

I suggested that we did not appear to be winning. To my surprise, the plant manager came over to my side. After asking me a couple of questions about printing, he turned to the director, and said, 'Frank knows his printing, and he's right. We're not going to manage to print the job properly. And I will very soon need this press to print your magazine. We're wasting more and more time and money. I think we have to call it quits.'

The meeting in Toronto followed two days later.

The Montreal VIP again represented *Weekend Magazine.* On the M&S side were Jack and Pierre; I could only suppose that I'd been asked along as the proverbial sacrificial lamb.

Jack opened the meeting by lamenting the course of events. The Montreal VIP opined that the quality of the printing had been quite acceptable, and that I had made unreasonable and spiteful demands. At this point Jack picked up the phone, and called Marge Hodgeman. 'Check if those printed sheets of the art book are still in my wastepaper basket,' he said. 'If they are, would you bring them to the boardroom?'

When Marge brought in the sheets, Jack turned back to the *Weekend* VIP. 'These sheets are pure shit. We tried to warn you. Frank did not do anything that I wouldn't have done hours earlier. Had we published as is, it would have been a huge financial disaster for M&S and *Weekend.* And for the whole CCL series.'

At this point the VIP turned to me: 'Print wherever you want! But you'd better produce a perfect book. Or you can look for another job.'

I replied that I could leave right away.

Whereupon, Pierre said, 'If he goes, you can also start looking for a new editor-in-chief.'

Some weeks earlier, I had received a visit from an Enzo Angelucci, head of the North American division of Mondadori Editore, Italy. Mondadori, one of the biggest publisher/printers in Europe, had recently entered the U.S. printing market. Their impressive array of customers and samples of beautifully produced coffee-table books had convinced me they would be miles beyond our price range.

But Angelucci stressed that Mondadori was anxious to explore the Canadian publishing market. So I had let him have the specs for *Great Canadian Painting,* with the admonition that I was surely wasting his time. I didn't think there was any chance of Italy's being able to compete with the local suppliers. If nothing else, I felt the cost of shipping would prove insurmountable.

'We may surprise you,' Angelucci replied.

And surprise me they did.

I phoned New York and told Enzo that I could give him the book, if his estimate held true. Not surprisingly, he called back the next day and said that the rate of exchange had altered since the time of the original quote.

Here we go, I thought. 'So how much more is the job going to cost now?'

Enzo laughed, 'We Italians must have a bad reputation. As it happens, the lira has gone down, and you should save about $2,000.'

I trotted back to Hollinger House, and told Jack that I wanted to have our *Weekend* provocateur printed by Mondadori in Italy. I told him that the costs had worked out, and showed him the work sheets. Not only would the book come in on budget, we would probably get a better printing job than we had on any of the previous CCL books. And we would meet our deadline.

'I suppose that you yourself would need to put the book on press?' asked Jack.

'It would be advisable if I did. This is our first time working with Mondadori. Luckily, the Italian lira has just saved us some $2,000. So I'm still under budget.'

'Whereabouts in Italy is the Mondadori plant?'

'In Verona.'

'Naturally.'

Great Canadian Painting turned out to be a beautifully printed volume. The colour work – for the book's $2.95 price – was beyond anything else on the market. Ken Lefolii's text was well received. Even *Weekend Magazine* admitted that Mondadori's production could not have been equalled on their web presses.

We never did hear from the VIP, however.

The good relationship established between McClelland & Stewart and Mondadori Editore bore fruit in other projects. And my own acquaintance with Enzo Angelucci grew into a close friendship, and later into an excellent business association: I became Mondadori's representative – which necessitated further trips to Verona, at least twice a year. Naturally.

16. MANY FACES

t seems to be an inalterable rule in the turbulent world of graphic design, as in music, theatre and the like, that one commission leads to another – until the inevitable moment that your 'flight of fancy' transforms into the 'flight of the once fancied'. Certainly, this was my experience with art catalogue design – always one of my favourite challenges.

My first taste of catalogue design came with two small leaflets, which barely qualified as catalogues, for the Royal Ontario Museum. One was for an exhibition called *British Silver*, and the other for a show of international posters called *Impact*. I found both experiences right up my alley.

I designed my first major catalogue in 1959. It, too, was commissioned by the ROM. It was the museum's first major publishing venture – aside from learned papers – and had been suggested in my recently completed 'image program' for the museum (which had included the design of their logo). The catalogue was for an ambitious and spectacular show of masks from around the world, entitled *Masks: the many faces of man*. I was delighted to be asked to design the volume.

After much consideration, I decided that I would propose a landscape format, even though this was not the easiest shape for a gallery-goer to carry around with him or her, through a throng of people. I would argue that the show would surely be well labelled; thus the catalogue should probably function more as a souvenir or an addition to the viewer's library, than as a tour guide.

The masks were superb! The cover proved difficult to design, however. I looked time and again through the pile of photographs of the pieces in the exhibition. I felt that the cover needed to signal expressly that this was a show of many images from many cultures. Each time I made a selection, I became painfully aware of the serious omissions – both of images and of cultures – that resulted.

I could no longer delay the presentation, however. I had fallen in love with one particular photograph: a profile shot of a marvellous African mask. I finally had it Photostatted in over a dozen different sizes. These I pasted up in an informal design, and went off to see Duncan Cameron, the ROM's public relations officer. I liked the result, but suspected I was taking too much designer's licence. I decided to tell the ROM that I needed to consult with them about which masks to show on the cover. Luckily, before I had a chance to make my excuses, Ted Heinrich, the museum's director, dropped by. He looked at my rough and congratulated me on finding the perfect allegory, in the form of my 'universal spokesman'.

Both show and catalogue were well received, by critics and public alike. The Art Directors Club of Toronto gave it an award. Even the curator Walter Kenyon – who had once expressed to me a belief that good design was merely a cover for bad writing – liked the catalogue. The whole experience served to convince me to concentrate on designing books and museum/art-gallery ephemera. Though the world of publishing and gallery graphic-design paid a pittance compared to the world of industrial advertising, the attractive nature of both product and purveyor more than compensated for any financial shortfall.

Looking back at *Many Faces* today, it is obvious to me that this was my first catalogue. I made more than my fair share of questionable design decisions. Dr Heinrich and Duncan Cameron at the ROM clearly indulged me, while patiently steering me away from still worse blunders! Still, the catalogue doesn't look bad. The text pages read well in the Aldine Bembo, and the pages on the coloured (yellow) stock marry well with their function, and with the theme of the exhibition. The illustration sections were a delight to lay out. Even today, almost fifty years later, the catalogue manages to capture both the spirit of the show and its diversity. But as a truly functional exhibition catalogue, it is a bit flawed!

The next catalogue I designed was really a book – in fact, my first coffee-table book. This was the commission from M&S to design the twelfth *Annual* of the Art Directors Club of Toronto. (Not that M&S had much choice in the matter, since the Art Directors Club had selected 'Newfeld & Scott' to design the publication. And Keith and I were on the ADC's exhibition committee. And I was, at this time, consulting art director of M&S!)

And then Bill Withrow unexpectedly became director of the Art

Gallery of Toronto. Suddenly, the institution showed a much greater – and more informed – interest in its graphic image. I was one of the lucky beneficiaries of this new direction. My just-about-forgotten relationship with the gallery was revived: this time as a designer, rather than as a Saturday-morning painting instructor for children.

The art gallery embarked on a much more ambitious program of exhibitions at this time, as well. The chief curator, Dr Jean Sutherland Boggs, who was soon to become director of the National Gallery of Canada, established the Toronto Art Gallery as one on the international circuit of major exhibitions. The first big show was the Canaletto exhibition, in 1964. The gallery entrusted the catalogue-design to me.

This was my first experience working with Dr Boggs. I found her to be design-savvy, design-sympathetic and above all, open-minded. She recognized the creative freedom of the graphic designer; in return, she expected the designer to have a responsible understanding of the timeline and tenor of the project at hand. She had a knack for imparting the do's and don'ts of curation, without making one feel like a neophyte. We both felt that we worked well together. I even enjoyed our rare disagreements.

The next major catalogue I designed for the gallery was for their second international exhibition, *Picasso and Man*. This proved to be a landmark commission for me in a number of ways. First, a portfolio of my work had to be sent for approval to Picasso's agent – which did give me a bit of a swelled head when I was given the job! Then, the catalogue received international recognition in the design field, winning awards in both Europe and Canada. It set an all-time sales record for a Canadian art catalogue, and established me as a 'safe bet' in the field of art and coffee-table books. Finally, it confirmed that my studio could provide a reliable production supervision service, in addition to furnishing high-quality illustration and graphic design. This last came about in a curious manner.

Arthur Kembar, the gallery's secretary-treasurer, approached me with the proposal that I provide the finished product – the catalogue itself – rather than just the design. He explained that he didn't feel qualified to deal with 'the trade', on what appeared to be major purchases. And since the Art Gallery of Toronto had not yet established a print production department, there was really no one with the proper

The *Picasso and Man* catalogue sold a Canadian record of over 39,000 copies for the Art Gallery of Toronto.

expertise to determine matters of supplier, production or price.

I asked to think about it. Frankly, I was in no position, financially, to take on the risk of something going wrong, despite the potential of much greater monetary gains. I went back to Mr Kembar and said that I was really in the design business, and didn't want to set up an empire that might force me off the drawing-board. I also admitted that his proposal was too much of a financial burden and risk for me to undertake at that time.

Kembar pondered the question for a couple of minutes, and then suggested that I might consider providing a production-supervision service. I would provide the gallery with cost analyses, advise on supplier selection, negotiate with the supplier selected and assume responsibility, for the AGO, in areas of quality and cost control.

'How on earth would I establish a fee for that?' I asked. 'There are all sorts of intangibles, from the start of the commission through to the completion of manufacturing.'

He proposed that the fee be a percentage of the total cost, plus an out-of-pocket expenses add-on. He suggested 6 percent, and I agreed.

Picasso and Man went through several small printings, due to Kembar's conservatism and the norms set by the sales records of previous catalogues. After the gallery had sold 19,000 copies, a rush order arrived for a further 3,000. Guy Upjohn, of the Hunter-Rose Printing Company, and I decided to take a chance and printed 10,000 sheets, but only bound up the 3,000 copies ordered. By the time the exhibition closed, the Art Gallery of Toronto had sold well over 39,000 copies. With no remainders.

Other catalogues followed, under the same sort of agreement (6 percent of the billing total, plus out-of-pocket expenses). With my assignment to CCL in 1964–65, however, I had to drastically curtail my freelance activities. (When I first joined M&S, the agreement had been that I would continue teaching one or two days a week at the Ontario College of Art, but restrict my freelance design to the odd 'cultural' catalogue.) The Art Gallery of Toronto – now the AGO – was the client I most hated to give up.

Some fifteen years intervened for one good reason or another.

But in 1981, the AGO brought me back to design the print material for its blockbuster exhibition *Vincent van Gogh and the Birth of Cloisonism*. The commission went well, and soon after, they asked me to come to a meeting to discuss designing a catalogue for an African art exhibition. Right from the start, however, things went wrong.

The exhibition's curator phoned me and announced that the meeting had been scheduled for 10 p.m. at the Frum residence.

'Why the Frum house?'

'The Frum residence? To let you see some of the collection, of course. The African art exhibition is based on their collection. Oh, and please use the tradesmen's entrance.'

When I rang the 'TE' bell, I was (prophetically) greeted by furious barking and sound of some huge, hostile animal throwing itself against the door. I stepped well away from the entrance. Then a man's shrill voice ordered the thing to 'Get down, get down, get down, get the … down!' And shouted, 'Will somebody please take this stupid dog out of here, and lock her up somewhere!'

Finally the door was opened, by a man I took to be Dr Frum. He greeted me with, 'You must be the designer of my catalogue!' Thereupon he held out a sample setting of Optima. 'This is my favourite typeface. I hope we'll be able to use it.' He smiled.

'I'm sure that Herman would be both delighted and surprised to have one of his typefaces selected for a catalogue on African art.'

'Herman?'

'Herman Zapf, the designer of Optima.'

Dr Frum ushered me into a sunken living room, which was more than three times the size of my studio. Waiting for us was the young curator from the AGO. He looked much as I had imagined: tall, and very Upper-Canada-College, complete with a navy blazer boasting a boating club crest and an impressive old boys' tie. 'This meeting was called for ten o'clock sharp,' he said. 'We've been waiting for you. I think we should get started.'

I had arrived at the Frum residence at a quarter past ten; still, I was a bit surprised by this greeting. 'You're absolutely right. Let's blame the dog. She won't care.'

A number of superb works from the Frums' African art collection were displayed around the raised level surrounding the sunken living room. I was given a tour of these pieces, and some others, as well: over twenty wood carvings, each as outstanding as the last. It put me in mind of *Masks: the many faces of man.* The prospect of working with this material made my mouth water.

We chatted for almost half an hour. I was given precise information as to the number of works to be exhibited. But when I asked about the direction the text would likely take – to get an idea about the young curator's interaction with the works (I assumed that he would write the thing) – both he and Dr Frum sidestepped the issue. Either it had not yet been decided who would provide the text, or it was not yet any of my business.

Dr Frum now took over. What he said ran something like this: 'We have a fairly clear idea of what we want the catalogue to look like. And of course we have certain preferences regarding typeface and size of catalogue. We haven't yet decided which image to put on the cover, but I know you'll be of great help in making that decision. Now, let me show you two catalogues from New York which I particularly like, and which I hope you will seriously consider as a jumping-off point.'

In the meantime, Barbara Frum had appeared, and discreetly

taken a seat at the dining-room table, which overlooked the living room. I hadn't noticed her arrival. A meal had been brought for her. We were introduced, and she indicated that she would join us as soon as she had finished eating.

But by now, I was having serious doubts about the job.

'Are you familiar with any of the catalogues I've designed?'

'Oh, several. And we thought they were all excellent. Offhand I don't remember them all. But the Picasso was the one we liked the most.'

'Then you have some idea of my style of work. To be perfectly honest, I'm not sure that you really need me. You seem to know exactly what you want. And I am certain that it will prove to be a winning catalogue. What you really need is a good layout man, rather than a designer.'

The young curator entered the fray. 'What makes you say that?'

'Well, a number of things. You already know the size of catalogue you want. You know the format. You even know the typeface: and without a manuscript, that *fact* is really impressive. Designers are quite expensive. The main reason for this is that the client is paying not only for layout and paste-up, but – more importantly – for personal style and visual philosophy. I haven't done layout or paste-up for someone else's design for years. I honestly doubt I could do a decent job.' In case they were unpersuaded, I added, 'Besides, I really don't think the job is my cup of tea. Nor do I think that you would find me your cup of tea.'

Dr Frum and the young curator argued with me for a good twenty minutes, without making any headway. I fear they found me rather pigheaded. Finally, the good doctor put forward what he surely expected to be the ultimate argument. He named a well-known Toronto architect. 'Are you familiar with his work?'

'Yes. We sit on the RCA council together.'

'Well, he is the architect who designed our house. And he certainly did not mind us outlining what we wanted. The number of bedrooms the house should have. What space we required for our African pieces. The sunken living room was one of our own notions. The size of pool we wanted. And so on! I suggested the two driveways, one for tradespeople and one for us. We did not want a Georgian mansion. We definitely wanted contemporary architecture. He encouraged us to put forward all our visual ideas. In fact, you might say that we collaborated on the design of this house. And at no time did the architect feel that he was being treated as a "layout man". Why should you?' (I am paraphrasing, but this was the tenor of the argument.)

'I'm not sure that's an apt analogy,' I said. 'What you commissioned your architect to do was to design a catalogue that you yourself were going to live in. A catalogue that mainly only you would use – that had to fulfil your personal and psychological needs twenty-four hours of the day, seven days of the week. I assume, for instance, that both of you swim; why else would you own a pool?

'But the house you ask me to design, is one that you will neither have to buy nor live in. You are going to get at least six copies free. You will certainly never need to use it as a reference source. At best, you might visit it and show it off to some of your friends.' I pontificated, 'The house I have to build is one that must play a number of different roles. It has to entertain. It has to guide. It has to teach. It has to comfort. It will be at once memento and proof of a unique cultural encounter. Finally, it must sell to a wide spectrum of visitors: appealing to the pundit without inhibiting the casual gallery-goer.'

The young curator made a final, irritated protest. 'Well, *I* didn't hear anything that should prevent you from taking the commission.'

'Let me give you a final reason: I am an SOB to work with.'

At this point, Barbara Frum interjected, 'He obviously doesn't want to do the job. I think we've all wasted enough of our time. I suggest we call it a day!'

And we did.

And so did the AGO – for some fourteen months!

Finally, Dennis Reid got in touch with me, to ask if I wanted to design both catalogue and poster for the A.Y. Jackson show *Alberta Rhythm.* Which I was more than happy to do!

* * *

There is a wonderful Japanese word, 'kimouchi'. A rough translation would be 'empathy plus'. I suppose that the definitive designer should be able to get the most out of challenging material even without kimouchi. I have to conclude that I never was the definitive designer.

Some people, invariably essential to the project – whether in a motivating role, such as author, or in an auxiliary role, such as editor – immediately evoked totally negative feelings in me, usually to a point of creative antagonism, even when the work was a designer's dream.

Then, there were certain other people – authors, editors, publishers – who would inspire me to approach a project with total enthusiasm. Even if the job was less than a designer's dream. (Many of the catalogues were well over 300 pages long – weighty art books, more than exhibition guides. This made design decisions complex, due to the dual role these volumes needed to play.)

With one or two exceptions, my gallery catalogues (and I can remember seventy-one of them) had all the ingredients of 'ideal' commissions, regardless of the time or budgetary constraints that were imposed. I found the curators with whom I worked to be eminently possessed of kimouchi: no doubt due to their experience in dealing with creative matters on the one hand – and capricious designers, on the other.

In addition to various AGO projects, two catalogues for other institutions stand out among my favourites.

In 1976, I was working as a publishing consultant to the National Gallery. For reasons of objectivity, I had decided not to do design work for the gallery during my tenure there – but a chance came up to design a Charles Nègre catalogue, and I could not resist. Nègre was a superb nineteenth-century French photographer. James Borcoman, the Gallery's curator of photography, had started collecting Nègre in 1967, and now had the world's best collection of his work.

This was probably my cleanest and most disciplined catalogue. Most of the images called for full-page treatment. In a very few instances the images had to be so small (it is a no-no for a gallery to reproduce a complete art object in a bigger size than the original) as to force two photographs onto a single page; but this was done only when the pair was obviously related. I was really lucky with the facing pages, too. Only once did I have to abuse the page – putting two plates the size of postage stamps on a spread, each on a page of its own, in order to achieve a logical pairing.

I devised a thin-line frame, printed in a deep-ochre colour, to house the plates. Beneath the constant frame, I left a standard space to accommodate the bilingual text. I chose Bodoni as my text type. The fact that both typeface and photographs were French was a happy justification. Bodoni went well with Nègre's chiaroscuro, too. For the titles, I chose a delicate script. And it worked!

My other standout catalogue, for an institution other than the AGO, was commissioned in 1983 by the National Museum of Man, for an exhibition of Canadian folk art. The catalogue was to be entitled *From the Heart/Du fond du coeur*. The subject-matter was delightful; the pieces ranged from the sublime to the ridiculous. Best of all, the museum decided to involve me from the very beginning of the catalogue's evolution.

At the preliminary meeting it became obvious that the museum would be mounting a really big show (279 pieces). When I remarked that this was a heck of a lot to expect a reader/viewer to absorb, the French editor of the catalogue suggested that the volume could be logically divided into a number of parts: 'Reflets'; 'Allégeances'; 'Fantaisies'; 'Quatre artistes populaires' ...

With just about every catalogue I'd worked on, the photography had been pre-commissioned by the gallery or museum. When the exhibition featured paintings, this seemed logical. But in the few cases where three-dimensional objects were involved (the Calder mobiles and the silver of the Covenant Chain show), I would have preferred to have been involved from the start. To my happy surprise, this is what happened with *From the Heart:* when I innocently inquired when I might have the photographs, I was asked when I would like to art-direct the photography shoot. They were actually going to pay me to attend the photography sessions!

The museum photographer knew exactly what he was doing. At the end of the shoot, he told me that he had enjoyed the sessions – which he had initially dreaded, thinking that I would art-direct like mad. This had never occurred to me. All I really wanted was an opportunity to suggest some logical relationships between images as far as backgrounds, pairings and colour selections were concerned. As I have said, almost every gallery/museum commission I've worked on has been a joy, both in terms of my compatibility with the client and in terms of my interest in the work. But this was the only catalogue where I laughed lovingly and appreciatively all the time I was designing it.

17. ALLIGATOR PIE

y 1969, McClelland & Stewart had become unrecognizable. David McGill and I were the last two left of the original directors' group. Mark Savage, vice-president of sales, was gone. Sam Totten, director of education, was gone. Owen Wilson, secretary-treasurer, was gone. Even my old friend and ally Hugh Kane was gone.

Larry Ritchie, the company's new wunderkind, and now senior vice-president, had come to M&S looking very Bay Streetish. By the summer of 1969, however, he had grown and permed his hair; he sported an artsy wardrobe, and had transformed Hugh Kane's old office, where he presided, into Scarborough's version of Kew Gardens. He obviously had decided to play the part of kulturnik/publisher to the extreme.

Larry had been a rather likable chap, when he originally came onto the scene as head of the Woods, Gordon team sent to put M&S straight. His conservative style had made eminent sense, and he was respected by all. But where his views on McClelland & Stewart's fiscal policies made sense, his excursion into publishing turned our operations from a Kew Gardens into an Amazon jungle. Worst of all, his new preoccupation with the editorial end of M&S led to a measure of neglect, on his part, of the company's financial handling. Frankly, I was dismayed. But Jack did not seem to mind. Possibly because Larry's neglect of finances gave Jack free rein over that aspect of *his* publishing company, too.

At our last few board meetings, Jack and I had been in disagreement on two points: Jack's decision to eliminate M&S's educational publishing program, and his curtailing of the non-Berton Canadiana on our nonfiction list. He would not publish, he said, in areas that he did not fully understand; nor did he wish to compete in these areas, 'when we could be building the best and most exclusive list of fiction, poetry, and art books in the country'. With the occasional (money-making) exception thrown in. Jack was surprised, he said, that I didn't endorse the same publishing direction, since his vision would surely garner me a few more design awards than would my own concept for *his* house.

At the time of Larry Ritchie's transformation, we had just finished printing Sandra Kolber's second book. Since I had a Montreal meeting, I decided to deliver her author's copies personally. When I asked her where and when I should bring the books, she invited me to dinner. There was one other guest at the dinner, a former Israeli general. The Kolbers were surprised when the two of us held a brief conversation in Hebrew. It had never occurred to me to tell them that I was an ex-kibbutznik.

During supper, we chatted about a number of different things: from Israel as I had known it, compared to Israel seventeen years later, to publishing in Canada and how it had changed during that same time. I mentioned that, in one way or another, I had been part of M&S for thirteen years.

Leo Kolber (now Senator Kolber), asked me if I was superstitious.

'Not really. But thirteen years is longer than I have stayed anywhere else. It may be time to move.'

To my surprise, both Kolbers readily concurred; in fact, Leo mentioned that, as a CEMP (Seagram) executive, he could get me a job as an art director in Hollywood. I assured him that that would be a mistake: I was an entirely different kind of 'art director', and would probably be a disaster in the movie business.

'Why do you say that?'

'I started out studying stage design, before the Macphersons and I came to Canada in 1947. Believe me, I was even a better soldier than I was a theatre student.'

The name Macpherson rang a bell for Leo. Since moving to Canada, my mother had gone into the *schmatte* business. Leo had heard of her shops. He mentioned that CEMP was going into the shopping mall business, and asked if she might be interested in having a ladies-wear store in the new Fairview Mall in Don Mills, which would be completed in August of the following year.

I consulted my mother upon my return to Toronto. She was interested; I duly contacted Mr Kolber.

When the lease arrived, there was one little surprise: I was named as the guarantor. My mother and I formed Macpherson-Newfeld

Fashions Limited, called the store Rose Macpherson, and returned the signed lease.

At the end of May, I handed Jack my resignation. In it, I proposed a three-month notice period, which would allow me to safely bring in the 1969 fall list. Jack scanned my letter. His only comment was that he probably needed more than three months' notice. Then he ended the meeting, saying that we were both too busy to take up any more time on the matter, at that moment.

I figured I must have just beaten Jack to the punch. I decided I would let him make the next move; there was no way I was going to creep back to him saying, 'Please, sir, when may I go home?'

A week later, I received a small printed folder from my insurance broker, with the heading, CONGRATULATIONS! WE HAVE BEEN READING ABOUT YOU! Inside was a newspaper clipping announcing that I had been appointed vice-president, publishing, of McClelland & Stewart.

The next day, an announcement to the same effect appeared on the staff notice board. 'You might have told me,' said Lorene.

'I would have, had I known, myself.'

I phoned Jack's office, only to be told that he would be out of town for a few days.

When Jack reappeared, he called me in for a meeting. I reiterated that I was leaving, and added that I was starting my own company (*not* a publishing house!)

Jack said that, given the added responsibilities I'd shouldered in the last few years, he had decided I needed to be a vice-president. Wasn't that what my notice was all about? He added that he had no intention of asking me to reconsider, but that I was now responsible for M&S's 1970 season. I could leave in June 1970.

I said that at least one member of editorial had bristled at the appointment – and that I, too, would have bristled, had he announced *her* appointment as, say, creative director.

Jack replied that Anna had indeed expressed some qualms.

'Well, I don't blame her. I am certainly no editor – and we don't even have a senior editor to represent our most important branch.'

'We will have, as of today. I am appointing a new editor-in-chief,' replied Jack, 'which should calm the situation.'

'May I ask who?'

'Me.'

Probably more out of perversity than accord, I agreed to retain my appointment.

As the year went along, Larry Ritchie took to coming to my office at least once a week, chatting about what a good job I was doing. At each visit, he hinted at my 'unfortunate' decision to leave. I stubbornly changed the subject each time. Larry would return to his office, saying something like, 'Well, we both must carry on.'

Then, one day, Larry found a new toy. This was a black cylindrical plastic ball, which had hundreds of slips of paper in it. Larry would ask it a question, turn a handle, and it would spit out a slip of paper. Printed on the slip, there would a pithy piece of advice, usually ambiguous enough that it could be interpreted in any number of ways.

On one of his weekly visits, Larry brought in his black box. 'Why don't you ask my magic box about leaving M&S? It really is most accurate in its prophecy and counsel.'

After declining several times, I gave in. I asked the box 'the question'. Larry twirled the handle, and out popped the slip of paper. On it was written: 'Your first decisions are usually correct!'

'It really is just a toy,' Larry protested. 'Don't take it too seriously.'

Still, changes had been in the wind for some time.

Simcoe Street had closed. A new M&S sister company was set up, with its offices around the corner from Hollinger House. Its publishing program was to be similar to that of the Canadian Centennial Library. The initial project was to be a series of popular Canadiana/science books.

One week after Jack's decision to 'promote' me, he insisted that I appoint an art director. He pointed out that our sister company had 'people to spare in the art department'. He suggested we bring one of the senior designers over to M&S, to fill my former role. There were two potential ex-Simcoe-Street candidates: Don Fernley and Peter Moulding. Of the two, I thought that Moulding, the more mature and classical designer, would better fill the role of art director at M&S. He had a good eye, and could visualize final results just from specifications. And Fernley, I thought, should become art director of the Canadiana books, under Pierre Berton.

When Jack inquired after my rationale, I told him that, since Don had spent all his career working on the sort of books the new division would be publishing, he seemed the logical man for Berton. What I didn't tell him was that I feared Fernley's more popular visual language might be scorned by the editors at M&S.

Jack asked me to hold off on making the announcement until after he had told Pierre. The next afternoon, he told me that Pierre preferred Peter, and that the offer had been made and accepted.

Where, at one time, I might have fought Jack, I simply shrugged my shoulders, and accepted things.

The design department had some pretty talented people in it. Probably the best of them was a young David Shaw. He and I worked successfully together on a number of coffee-table books, ranging from one on the Group of Seven to another on Canadian children's art. (Looking at them more than thirty years later, I still feel they pass muster.)

Bringing in the 1970 list took a great deal of effort. The editorial group – especially people like Claire Pratt, Pamela Fry, Jennifer Glossop and Linda McKnight, who had worked with me for quite some time – took my new status in good-humoured stride. But there was a marked reluctance to accept the reality of my appointment on the part of certain editorial and design supervisors. What was much more troubling, I began to feel a straining of relationships between editorial and design, which grew as my departure drew closer.

One new designer, hired by Fernley, asked me, 'Excuse my asking, but did you have to invest a lot of money into M&S?'

'What do you mean?' I asked, taken aback by his question.

'Why else would they have made you a vice-president?'

Late one evening, some three weeks before my scheduled date of departure, Jack came to my house unannounced. He asked if he could speak to both me and Joan, about this business of my threatening to leave M&S.

Joan told him it wasn't a threat. It was a fact.

Whereupon Jack asked me, 'Well, what exactly do you want? I made you a vice-president. What else am I supposed to do?'

I told him that my leaving really was a fait accompli; it wasn't some sinister manoeuvre to gain power. I was leaving.

Jack still did not believe me. He said that if I wanted shares in M&S, that possibility could be considered.

By this point, I was getting embarrassed.

I told him that Joan and I were going to open a boutique in Fairview Mall. In fact, I had not only formed a new company, the store was designed and would be opening in August.

'You are ruining McClelland & Stewart,' said Jack. Whereupon he left.

Neither of us believed this for one moment!

'Rose Macpherson' opened as scheduled. My mother spent three weeks in the store, and then declared that she couldn't work with the mall's clientele. She left the boutique in Joan's and my hands, and never returned. And that is how, for ten long years, I became Rose Macpherson.

* * *

In the winter of 1973, I was at the store, when the phone rang.

'There's a call for you, Mr Newfeld.'

The call happened to be from Hugh Kane.

'I suppose you were busy pinning a skirt!'

'As a matter of fact, no. I was pinning a pair of hot pants. Much more fun. It's good to hear your voice. My God, it's been ages. How are things at Macmillan?'

'Pretty good. It's great to be back in the saddle again. I was wondering if you could tear yourself away from your hot pants and evening gowns for a few hours, and have lunch? My treat.'

Lunch with Hugh precipitated a wild chain of events, some wonderful and some dreadful. It would lead to the most lucrative and successful commission I would ever be involved with, and would give me a chance to work with some of the nicest and most talented people in the business: Bob Wilkie, Shirley Knight Morris, Charlotte Weiss, George Gilmour and, of course, Hugh Kane. It would afford me the opportunity to give fun performances for kids at libraries and schools from Ontario to Manitoba. It would also mean struggling with one of the most talented, yet most opinionated authors I ever worked with. By the end, there was so much pejorative innuendo, I grew to hate the whole relationship. And when Hugh Kane left Macmillan, I lost my main and most indomitable support there. All of this was unimagined, however, when we met for lunch in the winter of 1973.

'I've got a manuscript by a young poet named Dennis Lee,' said Hugh. 'You probably know his *Civil Elegies*, which won a Governor

General's Award. Well, now he's turned out some children's poetry, which we think is pretty good. I wonder if you'd give us a reader's report? Of course, we would pay you for any time you have to spend away from pinning hot pants, or whatever else you do at that salon of yours. The only thing is, I need the report within a couple of weeks. Would you be interested?'

The manuscript turned out to contain some of the best kids' verse that had ever come my way. But the manuscript was far too long, especially for a kids' book. On top of this, the poems appeared to be aimed at a variety of different age groups.

I wrote out a report, advising that the property looked viable, but seemed long. Also, that that the poems could easily be divided into two groups for two distinct age groups – and that they might well fit into two separate books. The 'younger' book, I felt, would need to be liberally illustrated; and while it seemed obvious that the 'older' book should be illustrated as well, how lavishly was something best decided by Macmillan's editorial department.

I sent off the report and went back to my pinning. Ten days later, a messenger brought an envelope marked *Urgent*. In it, I found a surprisingly generous cheque, and a brief note thanking me for an excellent report. A postscript asked me for a shortlist of illustrators who might fit the bill (there was an added, handwritten note, which stated that Macmillan had no intention of paying any more money for '*that* particular bit of information'). I sent the names of three or four illustrators to Hugh, who promptly phoned me at Rose Macpherson.

'I received your recommendations for possible illustrators of the Lee book this morning. They look good; but I'm not sure that you haven't left at least one name out. Namely yourself! Can you come to my place, sometime this week, between whatever you do at Rose Macpherson? Meet Dennis, and let's talk about it.'

I brought a few of my books along, including *The Princess of Tomboso:* books that I had both designed and illustrated. I had seen Lee's *Wiggle to the Laundromat* and had not liked Charlie Pachter's art work all that much. But I figured that even if Lee was wedded to that kind of visual philosophy and the meeting came to naught, I would at least have met Lee and have seen Lorna Kane after much too long a time, which in itself would make the trip worthwhile.

The meeting, at Hugh Kane's place on Summerhill, went well. I quite liked Dennis. He said most of the right things, and wasn't gushy about poetry or illustration. Still, he had very definite opinions about the way that children's books should look. Some of these opinions started alarm bells ringing, all of which I blithely ignored.

In retrospect, I wish he had said, 'I know nothing about illustration. But I know what I like and I know exactly what my books need in the way of illustration.' Then I would have known where we stood!

To be honest, I really wanted to do the books. I was beginning to find the schmatte business less than totally stimulating, and missed the publishing world. Also, as I've said, Dennis's manuscript contained some of the best kidlit poetry I had read in manuscript form. It was head and shoulders above anything of that ilk published in Canada. And it promised to be an illustrator's dream – particularly the 'second' book, what would later come to be called *Nicholas Knock and Other People*. So I took the job.

Dennis left shortly thereafter. I made ready to depart at the same time, but Hugh asked me to stay, as he had 'some other matters' to discuss with me.

'Well,' he said, 'what do you think?'

'I'm sure it'll work out. But Lee has some definite ideas about book illustration. I just hope that he can be objective about it, and doesn't expect me to put portraits of his five-year-old son in the book. When do you want to bring the book out?'

'We want to publish two books, just like you suggested in your report. The younger one will be titled *Alligator Pie*. Dennis hasn't, as yet, come up with a title for the second one. And, hold on to your hat, I want to publish both books for the fall. We need them for our Christmas season. I have absolutely no doubt in my mind that if anyone can do it within that time schedule, you can.'

'I imagine that I can manage one title. Two books could be tough. But there's a chance it can be done. Mind you, I've thought of them as sixty-four-page books. Perhaps you're thinking of a smaller number of pages for the younger book?'

'No, sixty-four pages each is exactly our thinking. We've talked to Guy Upjohn about it, and Hunter Rose are pretty sure they are able to do it, as long as they can have everything by the end of July. Of course, you'd be designing the books under a separate contract. There's one other minor point. You once showed me a book called *Pageant of B.C.*

where you had prepared pre-separated four-colour artwork. It looks as though our budget will require that you turn out the four-colour illustrations for the Lee books as pre-separated art, as well.'

'You realize that *Alligator Pie* should require a minimum of thirty-five illustrations? I haven't any idea about the other book. I can't even get started until the poems, and their exact sequence, are finalized.'

'Yes.'

'Lee is going to be a hands-on author. I can just smell it. I can already see his vetoes and suggestions flying all over the place.'

'So can I. That will all be taken care of in the contract, I promise!'

'What about Rose Macpherson? I can't leave Joan to the tender mercies of my mother, or our staff. Not for that length of time.'

'What is your approximate design charge for a job like this?'

'God, I don't know. Somewhere around $1,250, plus the jacket. Say about $2,000.'

'I'll pay that for each of the two books, even though they should have a similar look. And, of course, we'll pay extra for camera-ready paste-up.'

The manufacturing budget for the book was 85 cents per case-bound, jacketed copy, with all plant costs amortized over 7,500 copies. That included typesetting, camera-strip and plates, vandykes, camera-ready paste-up, case stamps and proofs. No wonder Macmillan could not afford to have huge separation costs.

The first draft of the contract arrived two days later. I was astonished and delighted to find in it a clause – Clause 23, to be precise – that I had never seen before. It is most certainly worth immortalizing at this time:

It is understood that in commissioning the Illustrator to prepare the necessary Illustrations for the Work, the Publisher with the Author's Agreement was Seeking a new dimension for the Work and was looking to the Illustrator to Supply his originality, drawing skill and wit. While the Illustrator will welcome Suggestions and comments from either the Author or the Publisher, he will Not be bound to accept such suggestions nor to incorporate any of them in his drawings.

In the margin, Kane had jotted, 'That should give you the peace and quiet you'll need to finish the work in time.'

By coincidence, later that same day, I received a telephone call from Dennis. We chatted for a few minutes about some household names in Canadian publishing. Then he told me how happy he was that we would be working together, and that he now had only good vibes about the books. Also, that Hugh had not only shown him a number of my books done at McClelland & Stewart, but had told him that I was an ex-director of that company. He now felt that he really was in safe hands.

I was just trying to think up some reciprocal platitudes, when Dennis said, 'There is the small matter of royalty apportionment.'

'I haven't even looked at that, as yet. What have Macmillan proposed?' (I could smell that something irksome was coming.)

'A seventy/thirty split.'

'That seems okay. I realize that I'll be taking up more space than that in the book, but the motivating flight of fancy is yours.'

'No, no. You misunderstand! I really feel that the poetry is worth eighty per cent.'

'I'm sure you're right. I think you should call Hugh.'

'You mean you are willing to accept an eighty/twenty split?'

'Actually, no. I just thought that you might be able to talk Hugh into a higher royalty rate than they normally consider. Look, Dennis, the royalty rate is Macmillan's idea, and I'm quite happy with the thirty per cent that you say they're offering me. What you arrange with Macmillan, for yourself, is your business.'

Dennis made some remark to the effect that he had heard I could be 'difficult', and hung up, after a very curt goodbye. I told Joan that I had probably scuttled a lucrative commission before it had even gotten going, and that we might get a goodbye phone call from Hugh.

The phone call came two days later.

'Dennis is being a little bit difficult. He wants a greater share of the royalties. We've talked about this, and the opinion here is that we may have a most promising property.' With typical wry Irish wit, Hugh continued, 'We are also certain that you play a necessary part in the success of this project. Not that anyone likes your work, but you draw faster than anybody else I know. I think I also have the solution to Dennis's wishes regarding your royalties. I intend to propose that we hold on to the seventy/thirty split for the first printing of 7,500 copies, and thereafter go to a seventy-five/twenty-five split. Hold on.

At the same time we intend to amend your design fee to double the agreed sum. That should more than compensate you, even *when* the books become bestsellers. How does that sound?'

'Okay.'

In spite of all the haggling and the hassles, the two books – *Alligator Pie* and *Nicholas Knock and Other People* – remain two of my favourite keepsakes. They also turned out to be trailblazers in Canadian kidlit publishing, proving to both publishers and 'name' authors that they could profitably participate in this hitherto marginal area of our publishing world.

When Keith Scott and I had opened our shop on Grenville Street back in 1961, Keith had made me a present of a coffee mug with a drawing on it: a man, being shot out of a cannon. There was a brief caption under the drawing, which read 'I work best under pressure!'

I signed the contract to do both children's books with Macmillan and Dennis Lee in February 1974. I undertook to design the two books, provide camera-ready paste-up, and finish a total of 34 full-colour and 45 single or two-colour illustrations for the two texts, plus full colour artwork for the jackets. All the artwork to be pre-separated. And all to be ready by July of 1974. 'After all,' said Hugh, 'you have all of six months.'

What normally happens to full-colour illustrations is as follows: the artwork is photographed using a series of filters, which allow: 1) the blue colour image only to come through; then, 2) the yellow colour image only; then, 3) the red colour image only. In each case, the denser the colour, the deeper the tone – and, of course, the paler the colour, the lighter the tone – in the resulting image. Then, using a screen process, these 'continuous tone' images are translated into 'dot' images (in 1974, they ranged from 64 to 150 dots to the inch), which then became the basis for three of the four plates generally specified, in four-colour printing. Finally, a special process provided a continuous-tone image for the fourth plate – the black plate – which would provide greater definition and accenting.

What Hugh Kane wanted me to do was to provide pre-separated art. This meant that I would provide, for each illustration, four overlays – one for black, one for blue, one for yellow and one for red. Each overlay to be drawn in black and greys. This would save the photographic step described above – and, with it, some $8,500 to $9,000 on the preparatory part of the job.

As it turned out, after the first two or three illustrations – which Guy Upjohn offered, on the QT, to test – I realized that this was not only easier than I had hoped, it gave a rather pleasing result, quite different from any previous illustrations that I had done. I liked it.

I met privately with Hugh Kane, at his house, and showed him the test proofing. He liked what he saw, and gave me the green light to proceed. Then he asked why I'd insisted on the 'private meeting'; he suspected some 'nefarious' motive.

'Actually, I came here to get one of your nefarious Bloody Marys.

But I'd be happy if the existence of the test proof was kept just between us, since Guy printed the proof on the QT, and I don't want to set some kind of precedent for him.'

'God, you kibbutzniks can be devious. I don't even want to guess at your real reason for not wanting to show the darn proofs. Did you say "Bloody Mary"?'

About three weeks after 'the signing', Dennis phoned me and asked how things were getting along. I told him that I had just about plotted the books and more or less decided on the typeface I wanted to use – namely, Melior. Dennis allowed that he wasn't familiar with the face, but would trust me as long as it wasn't some sort of Gothic. I told him that I even had two pieces of finished art. He asked if I would mind if he spoke to Hugh, to set up a meeting.

At the meeting, Dennis was amazingly amenable, however. He led off with a learned explanation of the difference between 'soft' and 'hard' poems. But Dennis had some valid points regarding the relationships amongst poems on a number of my proposed spreads. This required some simple juggling on my part to rectify. He was absolutely on the mark in asking for the changes.

Finally, he asked if he could see the finished art. I pulled out the two pieces of pre-separated artwork and laid them on the boardroom table. Hugh took a long look at them, and said, 'I see that you've marked them for colour. I can just see them finished in the book, and I think they are great! Don't you agree, Dennis?'

'Ye-es,' said Dennis, very quietly. And the meeting broke up. But it occurred to both of us that Dennis seemed a bit unhappy and confused.

Both books were finished in time, and were launched as scheduled at the Children's Book Store, owned by Judy and Hy Sarick. (At that time, the Saricks were recognized as being the country's most knowledgeable couple in the area of kidlit, as well as having the best children's bookstore in all of Canada.) Both books received excellent reviews, and had only a few detractors. *Alligator Pie*, in particular, received a goodly number of raves; and to the surprise of all concerned it sold more than 20,000 copies in the first seven weeks.

Macmillan then initiated an even more aggressive promotion campaign, which included an endless number of poetry readings, with Dennis taking the brunt of them. He covered all the Toronto one-man appearances and also went 'East of Eden'. I was sent to points west, from Brantford to Regina – though not to Vancouver or Victoria, which were considered to have sufficient 'sales potential' to warrant Dennis's presence.

We also did a number of 'Abbot and Costello' gigs, with Dennis in the role of Costello and me playing straight man and fourth fiddle. First Dennis would read his poems – to a rapt audience, I have to admit. Then I would do a couple of turns at producing 'instant drawings' – to a slightly less rapt audience, I also have to admit.

When Dennis first suggested this format, I concurred, but said that I'd like to pick the subjects that I would draw 'off the top of my head', since I didn't want to make too much of a fool of myself.

Naturally, at the first performance, Dennis announced, 'And now Frank will draw a *such-and-such.*' By now, I've forgotten what it was: probably a monkey in a zoo. But I do recall that I managed to make a fool of myself. In fact, I remember it well!

After the show was over, I pulled Dennis aside. 'For Christ's sake, please don't do that to me. This may come as a surprise to you, but drawing doesn't come easily to me. And I'm not a performing seal – or a performing Czech, for that matter.'

Although Dennis apologized, pleading poetic passion, he did precisely the same thing at the next show, and the next show.

I let it go. I really loved getting together with the kids. Especially when I was on my own. Looking through some press clippings from those times, I found one from Brantford, which said that I asked my audience questions to do with the plot lines of some of the poems. And that these were all enthusiastically answered – a couple even by (blushing) parents.

Near the end of the publicity blitz, we appeared at the 'Boys and Girls House' in Toronto; lo and behold, Dennis announced, 'And now, Frank will produce one of his marvellous instant drawings.' Then he asked the audience, 'What would you like him to draw?'

Before anyone had a chance to demand an impossible masterpiece, I jumped in. 'I have a better idea! Why don't we ask Dennis for a new, instant poem. Then I'll do an instant illustration for it. What should this poem be about?'

Suggestions came from all parts of the audience. Finally a subject found favour with everyone, except for Dennis. After five minutes of false starts, Dennis demurred, pleading that it really wasn't such a good idea – and that it would be much better if I drew *my* favourite character out of *Alligator Pie*. That was the end of instant drawings specified by Mr Lee.

At the conclusion of the Boys-and-Girls-House performance, a Mr Kelly from *Books in Canada* asked to interview me. The next day, I received a phone call from him, saying that the magazine wanted to do a lead article on me, and put me on the cover (this would be their first full-colour cover). Could he come to my studio to fill out the interview a bit more and also bring a photographer (professional, yet) to take my picture? The article came out a number of weeks later, and looked pretty damned good to me.

Unfortunately, it wasn't received as enthusiastically by some of my partners, who felt that I should have cleared the whole idea with them, to make sure that the article would be considered 'beneficial to the sale of the book'.

Still, *Alligator Pie* succeeded in getting on the Hans Christian Andersen Awards Honour List. It set a new sales record for its category in Canada. And the book's succession of publishers – of which there were four (Macmillan, Maclean-Hunter, Canadian Publishing Co. and CDG) – faithfully kept on sending (gradually decreasing) royalty cheques until the year 2000, at which time the bounty ran aground.

But Dennis and I never did work well together! Meetings were tense for me. And, I suspect, just as unbearable for Dennis. In hindsight, I can understand how he felt. The poems were his. The invention was his. The magic was his. And he felt he knew better than anyone else what was best for the poems, as far as visuals were concerned.

Our philosophies regarding the role played by the illustration were miles apart. Dennis felt that the illustrator's only function was to *describe* the poet's invention – to translate it, exactly, into the visual realm. Whereas I argued that the role of the illustration (in kidlit, for the age group we were intent on addressing) was to challenge the child to take the poet's flight of fancy and use it as a springboard for his/her own invention.

Dennis would probably have loved the Norman Rockwell cover of 'The First Haircut', with the kid sitting in the barber's chair being sheared. But I would simply have drawn barber and lad by an empty chair, and left it for the young reader to 'finish the picture' as he/she personally needed. I would have stayed clear of ultra-realism for so young an age group.

As time went by, the success of *Alligator Pie* grew. A competition for young people was set up in partnership with *Weekend Magazine*. Where we had hoped for as many as one thousand entries, to everybody's surprise we hit close to ten thousand. Dennis fared well in other ways: a play was put on by the (English) Theatre Passe-Muraille in Toronto; a record and tape appeared in the U.S.A.

The continuing strained relations between Dennis and me, weighed against the Brobdingnagian profits, made for a rather bothersome dilemma for Macmillan.

And things got worse!

Bob Fulford apparently refused to serialize *Alligator Pie* (according to a letter from Dennis – I had forgotten this bit) on the grounds that the only good things in the book were my drawings. On the other hand, there were insinuations by Dennis that my artwork might hamper spinoffs.

Where reproductions from the book were concerned, I lived with a vexing disparity in the shared royalties: where I got 10 percent of the fee for a poem used without illustration, Dennis got 33 percent of the fee for an illustration used without poem. Neither Dennis nor I was happy about this: I, because I felt it was inequitable; Dennis, because he felt he'd been bushwhacked into sharing royalties in the first place. Certainly, he let it be known that with future books he 'would know what he was going to insist on'!

Then, along came *Garbage Delight*. A letter that I wrote to Bob Stuart, vice-president at Macmillan, gives a sense of the 'peculiar frame of mind' with which I entered into this new 'collaboration'. I listed my concerns:

1. ALLIGATOR PIE/NICHOLAS KNOCK: His [Dennis's] complaints about the size of my royalty share (suggested by Macmillan, incidentally); and attitudes which motivated the inclusion by Macmillan (without my collusion, or even knowledge) of the protective (23, I believe) clause.

2. GARBAGE DELIGHT: Demands to further reduce my share of royalties; and his questioning (in documented form) my ability to properly illustrate his poems.

3. CALENDAR 1979: Dennis' threat – in face of what opposition? – to withdraw, if the Manitoba artwork was not redone; yet, the refusal to allow me potent voice in the matter of the date quiz, even though there now appears [to be] some justification to my protest.

4. This new clause, the substance of which is traditionally the Publisher's responsibility; and [which] could be interpreted as a lack of faith in your ability as much as mine.

'What is Dennis after?' I asked. 'Why this constant stream of (psychological) demands?'

The 'new clause' referred to in No. 4 was a proposed clause giving Dennis Lee veto power over all artwork appearing in his book(s).

My letter provoked another, from George Gilmour, publisher at Macmillan, asserting that my work played a vital part in the success of the Lee/Newfeld books. And things quieted down somewhat.

But not for long.

Garbage Delight was the 1978 recipient of the Ruth Schwartz Award. The Award dinner was to be held in Quebec City, and both Dennis and I were invited to sit at the head table. Then I was informed that I would also have to say a few words. At the last minute, Dennis remembered a previous engagement, so my wife Joan took his seat. I probably read too much into this sudden change of plans – but by then I was pretty sensitive about anything untoward from Dennis.

Then, in November of 1979, *Jelly Belly* reared its ugly paunch. Douglas Gibson had by now arrived at Macmillan (replacing the gentlemanly George Gilmour) and wrote an impassioned memorandum titled 'A Response and a Promise', which showed why Macmillan 'would be the best possible publisher for *Jelly Belly* and [its planned sequel] *Dinosaur Dinner*'. He went on to say:

First, without having read a word of the manuscript or seen a single flourish of illustration, I can state that we wish to publish *Jelly Belly* and *The Dinosaur Dinner*. I make this normally imprudent statement with full confidence, ... because I know the talents of the two creators involved.... So I take it for granted that, once Dennis and Frank have worried their way through their roles, we shall be dealing with two superb children's books.

The memo went on for five pages, heaping puffery upon cajolery, until

I felt like God's gift to Canada's kids. Still, I wasn't sure that I could survive not just one, but two new projects permeated by Dennis's inquisitorial touch.

By coincidence, in the middle of all this, I was invited to give one of the key addresses, and also to run a workshop on book design, at the Pacific Rim Conference, which was going to be held in Vancouver. On the plane, I was seated next to Jack Stoddart (senior), whom I had met once or twice at different publishing functions. Of course, he had no idea who on earth I was. But after I had introduced myself, he said, 'Of course. I'm sorry, I should have recognized you.'

We gossiped for a while, and then he said, 'You know, I almost became your publisher.'

'How is that? Not that I would have minded, you have a most successful house, and I am sure that the change would have been refreshing. But how did I miss out?'

'Well, you knew that Macmillan is for sale.'

'Actually, I don't believe I knew that.'

'Well, you should have been told. *Alligator Pie* and *Garbage Delight* have made Lee and you quite valuable properties. In fact, we thought about it for quite a while; but there wasn't too much else that Maclean-Hunter were offering.' And though, as he went on to say, he would have loved to publish Dennis and me, he finally decided to pass. He thought that Ron Besse was a likely candidate, and hoped that this information would be of some use to me.

When I returned to Toronto, I found a draft contract waiting for me at the studio. The terms were the same as they had been for *Garbage Delight*, and though Dennis's 'veto clause' was nowhere to be seen (amen), there were mentions of allowing the author critical access to the art.

But I had already decided that neither of us really enjoyed our marriage of inconvenience. And Jack Stoddart's mid-flight revelation had made me suspicious of the *kashrut* of Douglas Gibson's promises. I began to imagine all sorts of Machiavellian Macmillan motives. It didn't help that Gibson's enthusiasm just didn't ring true to me. I felt sure that he was 'an author's man'; and doubted that he did anything but tolerate designers and illustrators.

I decided to simply ask him straight out whether Macmillan was for sale.

(Perhaps my direct approach was undiplomatic. I guess my Czech heritage hadn't prepared me for that sort of thing. If only I could have handled intrigue in the tradition of the Austro-Hungarians!)

He denied it absolutely. 'As publisher, I should know!' He assured me that I was totally misinformed. In fact, he proclaimed the statement to be libellous.

I retorted that I didn't feel at all happy about going into a partnership with one party that didn't want me, and another that might change at a moment's notice – since this would likely turn out to be too much of a risk to my pocketbook, my reputation and my health.

Gibson countered that he was prepared to sign an illustration and design contract. He asked what I would charge for such a commission. I threw out a figure of $17,500, plus 25 percent additional for pre-separated art (and a special fee for 'author-initiated changes'). I would also need $5,000 for design. Twenty-five percent to be paid on signing.

I was certain he would balk at my extortionate demands.

To my surprise, he phoned me that same afternoon and said that he had discussed the fee with Bob Wilkie, and they had decided the figure was most fair. I told him that I had decided against accepting the offer.

This initiated a string of phone calls, along with visits by divers Macmillan people, offers of more money.... All culminating in veiled accusations of breach of contract.

The week following all this nonsense, Joan and I had supper with Alec Epstein and his wife. Alec had been in Ben Dunkelman's 7th Brigade in Israel. His brother Morris (Eppy) had been a member of Kissufim, and our number one *nahag* (driver).

Alec was the senior partner of Barkin & Epstein, a law firm on Bloor Street. After supper I regaled the Epsteins with an embroidered version of my *Jelly Belly* travails. Alec asked me if I was absolutely serious about killing such a cash cow.

I said, 'You have no idea! I know that I'm probably whistling some thirty thousand bucks goodbye, but I'd sooner spend another month in Beit Hakerem than suffer this bloody job.'

'Leave it with me. It'll be my pleasure to handle. I won't charge you a cent. They sound like real shmocks!'

Alec wrote one of those 'without prejudice' letters, which I thought would be the end of that part of my life.

Well, almost, but not quite!

Jelly Belly came out, illustrated by an English literalist; and Messrs Gibson and Lee gave an interview to Robert Fulford, which appeared in *Saturday Night*, where it was duly reported that both Macmillan (Gibson) and Lee had felt for some time that Newfeld's illustrations were wrong for the Dennis Lee book(s), and that they had finally found an illustrator whose work and visual philosophy were much more sympathetic to the essence of the new Lee opus.

To my (blush) relief, their new star did not draw all that well.

★ ★ ★

In early 1980, Hunter Rose closed shop. The Lee-Newfeld books were now at another printer's. To my horror, the four-colour work was awful. The two-colour work was even worse. Somebody, somewhere, had decided that my two-colour pages – designed in a soft green as the second colour – needed jazzing up. All kinds of strange colours suddenly appeared. By the time *Alligator Pie* reached its third printer, the book looked disgusting.

I phoned Linda McKnight, the new publisher at Macmillan (and, later, Dennis's agent) to complain. What had happened was that the first new printer, working on a large four-colour press, was unaware – as apparently was the next new printer, who had made things even worse – that Guy Upjohn and I had decided not to use the conventional process colours. Instead, we had fabricated special colours for the two first titles.

After many months of my complaints, I was invited to meet with Anna Kress, the new production manager at Canada Publishing Corporation, which now owned Macmillan. Our meeting turned macabre, with her telling me that in fact the editors preferred the way the books looked now.

By this time, I had been appointed head of the illustration program at Sheridan College, and I neither had the time nor the strength to argue with Ms Kress, who didn't seem to understand what I meant when I told her that the books were never intended to be printed in process colours.

In the '90s, with the 'new colours' reigning supreme, our royalties dropped by over 75 percent – this in spite of Ms Kress's theory that the book would sell to an unwavering *Alligator Pie* market, regardless of its appearance.

By 1992, Dennis had decided that he needed a new illustrator once again – and a new publisher, to boot. *The Ice Cream Store* came out, published by HarperCollins, and decorated by David McPhail, a well-known American children's illustrator. A full-page review in the *Globe and Mail,* written by Elizabeth MacCallum, appeared that year and had this to say:

If *Alligator Pie*'s arrival in 1974 was startling and liberating, today its vocabulary – ookpiks and silver dollars – is suspended in amber. So also are Frank Newfeld's original quirky illustrations. It's not just because my copy is covered with the heritage of sticky fingers that the pages look old, even old fashioned. It's the basic colour reproduction, the layout, the linear detail that carries the spirit of another era before computer chips and Bart Simpson. Newfeld's engaging illustrations are full of allusions and illusions, and not the least apologetic about the visual puns on offer.

The Lee-Newfeld marriage continued for two more volumes, *Garbage Delight* and *Nicholas Knock and Other People....*

Eight years later, Lee has left Macmillan for HarperCollins to publish another poetry book, *The Ice Cream Store.... If The Ice Cream Store* is indicative, don't hold your breath waiting for the innovation, the distinctive individualism, and the vital regionalism sparkling over borders that has distinguished the best in Canadian children's publishing in the last few years.

Rather than risking a good Canadian illustrator, probably relatively unknown in the international market, HarperCollins has chosen the American David McPhail to portray a universe appropriate to the children of sensitive, aware yuppies.... True to the words, the children illustrated are white, black, yellow and beige. So that's all clear and settled. School librarians can relax. This is a politically correct work.

... McPhail faithfully paints the animals to accommodate the various verses. They are cute and furry and fun in a predictable way, but they are not a patch on....

In 2000, *Alligator Pie* came back again. I seemed to be the phoenix in the story, this time, though I was not at all sure I wanted to be reborn – even in a blaze that gory!

But that's another tale.

PIERRE BERTON

THE
KLONDIKE
QUEST

A PHOTOGRAPHIC ESSAY/1897 – 1899

The Klondike Quest, M&S, 1983.
The last book I designed for Jack McClelland.

18. THE JAGUAR MESSENGER SYSTEM

After four years dedicated exclusively to Rose Macpherson Limited, Hugh Kane's awakening kiss (*Alligator Pie*) led to a whole series of calls asking if the Frank Newfeld Studio was back. I said no to several requests asking me to design forthcoming books.

But when Dr Jean Sutherland Boggs – with whom I'd worked at the AGO – telephoned one day, her invitation was too enticing to turn down. She asked if I would give a one-day seminar on publishing to precede the establishing of a National Gallery of Canada publishing division. I reiterated that I was 'out of the book-design business' – but, as I have said, my love affair with the schmatte business was waxing decidedly cooler.

And so, when the National Gallery followed up the seminar by offering me a six-month consultancy, on a one-day-a-week basis, I accepted with alacrity.

During my second six-month contract, Peter Smith took over as head of the publications division. This made the department almost feel like old home week at M&S! Peter had been one of McClelland's untouchable editors. Not only was he one of the best editors in the business, he was also totally obscure in his presentations, or in any commentary solicited from him at an editorial meeting. Both Jack McClelland and Hugh Kane would listen attentively and concur gravely. Once Peter had left the meeting, Jack or Hugh, whoever was running the meeting, would admit that he had not understood a word that Peter had said!

The other M&S alumnus at the National Gallery was the very English Pamela Fry: 'veddy English' in accent, taste and editorial zeal! She regularly fell in love with her young male authors. And suffered unrequited affection most stoically, on the grounds that the 'dear man' was the epitome of decorum.

All the people at the publications division were a pleasure to work with – the French editors, in particular. Without being obvious, they switched over to English as soon as I appeared. And where the English editors, all of whom spoke French, usually continued *en français*, the French editors – Hélène, Jean-Claude and Serge – never did.

Also, of course, we had Arnold Witty, the production manager. I was used to production managers assuming that designers were an unnecessary burden. Arnold was confident enough to accept proven scholarship without feeling threatened by it. And I had sense enough to leave him to his own devices on matters of printing. We worked well together.

My friendship with Dennis Reid – with whom I'd also worked at the AGO – continued. He was a frequent visitor to the division that he had headed pro tem prior to Peter's enlistment. He was one of Jean Boggs's own, and was trusted by most of the National Gallery's hierarchy – the more avidly ambitious excepted. But he obviously had the department's best interests at heart. Art historian, curator, author and aesthete, he encouraged exploration and opportune experimentation. Dennis and Peter got on well together. It was obvious that Reid had no personal ambitions as far as the publication department was concerned.

I looked forward to my Tuesday trips to Ottawa. Not only were we producing cutting-edge editions; the process was as enjoyable as the printed result. My consultancy contract was renewed for a third term. (Unfortunately, not all was well in Camelot. Power struggles had become the vogue around Ottawa. The Museum Corporation was not exempt. Eventually, Jean Boggs would resign – and shortly after her resignation, I was told that I had fulfilled my contract two months early. I was paid for the remainder of the contract, and was told that the National Gallery of Canada could find no occasion for me to take any more Tuesday trips to Ottawa!)

* * *

The mid-seventies saw the seeds of the great changes that Canada's publishing industry would have to endure. Although the decline of the fortunes of many houses was not yet in sight, warning signals were becoming evident on the design end of things. Emphasis on the book jacket, to the exclusion of all else, was back. The inside look of the 'ordinary' book was shrugged off, once again – whether the title was prose, poetry, politics, even philosophy.

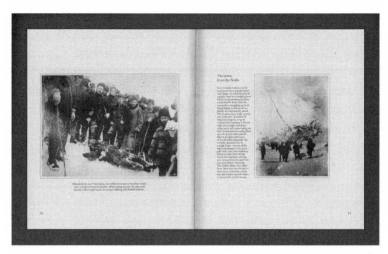

Page spread from *The Klondike Quest*. McClelland & Stewart, 1983.

Soon, only coffee-table books – in which the publisher had a large investment to protect – and the more complex textbooks were seen as requiring the services of a name designer. (The kidlit book would not be taken seriously by publishers as a financial investment deserving careful visual treatment, until the late eighties.) There were, of course, a few exceptions, such as Groundwood Books, Tundra and KidsCan Press: publishers who never forgot or gave up on book design.

I worked on many coffee-table books over the course of my career. Pierre Berton's *The Klondike Quest* was easily my favourite, typographically speaking. I was no longer part of the editorial group at M&S when I designed it. One advantage of this was that I was not so conscience-ridden about costs as I might once have been. That was now somebody else's responsibility. So I quietly specified hanging punctuation. And finally got the look that I had wanted for a long time, and that, whilst an officer of M&S, I had thought too much of an indulgence.

As I have said, Pierre Berton and I worked really well together. As a result, designing another Berton book was never drudgery. He would philosophize about the intent. We would go over the visual material I had selected. And once any gaps had been filled, the book was 'mine' – not because of any question of proprietorship, but because we were both secure in what we were doing.

Little, Brown, the American co-publishers, went with my jacket design. Jack, naturally, insisted on a revision of the photographic image. Boston happily approved the dummy of the inside of the book. I suspect that Jack had never really looked at it. And never knew that my typographic acrobatics cost him quite a bit extra.

Another coffee-table book that stands out for me is *Celebrate the Sun*. This was a delightful book of children's art. I had, thank heavens, the common sense to handle it as simply as possible. I took my cue from the title, and decided to celebrate each piece of art by giving it its own spread. The accompanying text, in double column, was placed on the verso; the artwork appeared on the facing recto. Though I did go a bit berserk with the title page, the design worked out well. And it allowed the children to be the stars of the 'performance'. The jacket of this book was beautifully designed by Don Fernley. Its style was vaguely reminiscent of a nice little book about the National Ballet that I had designed years before, and which, at one point, I had thought of using as a visual jumping-off point for *Celebrate the Sun*. Where the ballet jacket boasted a beautiful illustration by Carlos Marchiori, the *Celebrate the Sun* jacket countered with a charming painting by one of the young artists.

* * *

By 1975, Joan had more or less taken over the running of Rose Macpherson. And was doing a far better job of it than I had ever done. The National Gallery had extended my tour of duty for a third term. I was spending less and less time at Fairview Mall. One day, toward the end of the year, Guy Upjohn at Hunter Rose phoned, and asked if I would be interested in packaging an Olympics project.

For Edgar Spallek, the president of proSport, publishing was new territory. Even for a seasoned publisher, his idea was audaciously ambitious. ProSport wanted to sell a 'two-book-package' to 'a Canadian conglomerate'. To succeed, they would need an impressive brief, boosted by a persuasive publishing plan complete with convincing visuals: in other words, a sales package, for a piece of prospective vanity publishing.

I submitted an outrageous figure for my estimate; proSport's speedy acceptance made me all the more certain that Guy's hopes were just pie in the sky.

Surprisingly, the idea was sold! The conglomerate turned out to be CEMP Investments (where Leo Kolber was an executive).

But there were a couple of 'minor' complications. The first wasn't too bad: Leo wanted a general book for the run-of-the-mill international recipients, and a special edition for a 'select few'. I proposed a Montreal/Innsbruck condensed version in a simple slipcase for the 'common herd', and a lavish, extended, two-volume boxed set for the select group. I felt that, with proper planning, this could be achieved in an expeditious and economical manner.

The second 'complication', which had Spallek wringing his hands and Upjohn wanting to back out, saying it was impossible, was CEMP's required delivery date. Mr Kolber wanted the 'select' copies by the middle of October. This was not a simple problem. The Montreal Olympics were scheduled to finish on August 1st. This gave us just about ten weeks to write and edit, picture-edit, design, set, copyedit, print, bind and ship the books.

For me, the project was an irresistible challenge. I proposed that: 1) the book be published without folios (page numbers); 2) all spaces for both packages be pre-allocated; 3) four-colour printing be designed to fit printing formes (this would necessitate absolutely minimal plate changes); 4) black-white-printed text sections be designed to fit either before or after the four-colour work (the text sections, too, would be designed to fit formes).

'Are you sure you can do this? Have you designed anything like this before?' Fair questions from Michael Pitman, since Pitmans owned Hunter Rose.

'No, to both of your questions.'

Guy Upjohn, who was at the meeting, shrugged his shoulders, 'Well, it should be interesting.'

'And fun,' Pitman added.

Hunter Rose scheduled the printing on a two-colour Rolland press. It accommodated an 8/8 page sheet. I felt sure that this would give us all the flexibility we needed to increase or decrease the number colour pages in each edition. But how was one to explain the lack of folios? I suggested that the Olympics be presented day-to-day, which should justify the exclusion of either dates or folios..

The sample pages that we'd used in our sales presentation had been done with pics from proSport's selection from the extensive and first-rate file of its own Innsbruck photo shoot. The sample pages had turned out well, and I based my 'final' grid on these same spreads. Hunter Rose promptly printed up some three hundred blue double spreads of my grid.

The Innsbruck pictorial page design was finished in good time. Captions were written to my autocratic stipulations – without anybody on the editorial side complaining. The schedule might even be described as leisurely. The 'paring down' of text and pictorial elements to fit the formes was less of a problem than any of us had predicted. Guy proceeded with printing the colour work. The presswork was so good, no one could believe it had been done on a two-colour press.

Early on, Edgar Spallek had let drop promises of bonuses, if the design could be accomplished within the (impossible) schedule the October delivery date demanded. I had mentally dismissed these promises as stratagems. To my surprise, I suddenly received a fair-sized cheque, which was accompanied by a note saying that this was an advance on my bonus, and not my fee.

Looking towards the Montreal sections, two things became clear to me. First, I would need to design whilst the Games were still in progress. This meant that the accepted order of the three major courses in the art of 'book-cookery' – 1) editorial; 2) design; 3) manufacture – would have to be junked. The Olympics timetable gave us a pretty good idea of which days would provide the best visual spectacle, and also of when the major events were taking place. Armed with this information, we established space allocations, and it became possible to predict where we should be able to remove pages (in formes) from the printing of the 'run-of-the-mill' edition.

The second thing that became clear to me, looking towards Montreal, was that I would have to hire an assistant. The Innsbruck book had already showed that the sorting and bookkeeping of the material itself was going to be pretty nerve-racking. I mentioned this to Guy Upjohn, who concurred.

I hired Wendy Brown for the duration of the proSports commission. Though she had no 'book' experience per se, she had worked for a time in the art department of a 'little magazine' for children. The magazine was so 'little' that she had had to be a Jacqueline-of-all-trades. The magazine had folded, however, and she was between jobs.

Wendy was attractive, talented and efficient, and had super people skills. I accordingly made her our contact with Edgar's editorial and production. After one week at the studio, it was obvious that she had taken to the work like a swan to water.

Edgar established 'the Jaguar messenger system', by which slides arrived at the studio, which was at my home, every second morning. 'Jaguar' meant Edgar's personal car; 'messenger' meant Afzal Rahman, a VP at proSport. 'Every second morning' meant, at the latest, eight o'clock! Wendy and I would immediately select all suitable and appealing slides, which she then catalogued and filed into three slide categories: 1) Must use; 2) Should use; 3) Could use.

With the Innsbruck design, I had had to work with a finite group of very good photographs. Just two photographers were involved, David Patterson and Robert Warren. Luckily, their takes included some marvellous pre-game and local shots. I settled on a strategy which would eat up the pages and at the same time make it look as though the design had dictated the direction of the oversize – often double-spread – bold illustration style: I used the pre-game shots as a mood-setting section preceding the prelims of the book.

The Montreal design had no such problem. We worked with the talents of a dozen photographers. And had such a visual cornucopia from which to choose that many excellent works sadly never did make it into the book. This embarrassment of riches made our job easier – but it did, I admit, result in some visual inconsistency as far as the treatment of the two venues was concerned.

We met the deadline, however. And, true to his word, Edgar sent along another generous bonus.

The 'charioteer' logo I redesigned
for McClelland & Stewart in 1961.

Garbage Delight. Poems by Dennis Lee.
Pictures by Frank Newfeld. Macmillan, 1977.

19. AUTHORS, ILLUSTRATORS, ART DIRECTORS

nce upon a time, long, long ago, McMaster University invited me to appear on a panel on the topic of 'Kidlit and Book Illustration.' The obligatory question period followed the panellists' divers presentations. A number of the 'usual questions' followed.

Q: Should an author include some drawings when bringing the manuscript to the publisher?

A: Only in those cases where the author is also the illustrator. And then, no more than one or two finished pieces, and a number of roughs.

Q: Why do publishers ask unsolicited manuscripts not be sent?

A: Without that stipulation, they would receive hundreds of manuscripts. Not all of which would fit their particular editorial direction. They need to pre-vet them.

Q: Should an author get an illustrator to do drawings to accompany the manuscript, in those cases where the author isn't an artist?

A: In most cases, no. In fact, only if the project started as a team effort; and then just some samples of the illustrator's suggested work.

At this point, a rather imperious lady stood up and said, 'My question is for Mr Newfeld! When you illustrate a book, do you work closely with the author?'

'Occasionally. Most of the time I prefer to work just with the editor, or the art director, if the house has one. In some cases (mostly when the author is a "golden cow") there are – quite valid – reasons why the publisher might need to bring author and illustrator together.'

'But wouldn't it be advantageous for the author to direct the illustrator?'

'Well, there are a number of publishing contingencies which suggest that the publisher/illustrator contact is the more objective and efficient one.'

'Such as?'

'The mathematics of the project, which affects a variety of

decisions: for instance, the total number of illustrations needed, including the quantity and size of colour illustrations. The "house look" is also important. As is the analysis of market expectation. And then there are editorial and design factors, in the most objective sense.'

The imperious lady glowered. 'I am told, Mr Newfeld, that you personally don't like working with authors.'

'I don't think that is true. It all depends on the complexity of the work and on the geniality of the author.' *One should never joke!*

'*I* am an author. I am pretty sure that I know my books better than most. And I know my characters better than anyone. I know intimately the kind of portrayal my characters need.'

'I am sure you do. But a publisher seldom engages an illustrator just because the author needs one. Rather, a publisher engages an illustrator because the *package* needs one. The editor represents the publisher, and has the objectivity needed to successfully meld the two types of communication – the visual and the verbal.'

'Why should I entrust my creations to just you and an editor? These are *my* babies. I know exactly what they look like.'

It was becoming obvious that the discussion was going to go on forever, and achieve little. Also, I was starting to become rancorous. Turning to the audience of some two hundred folk (who were beginning to enjoy these Roman games) I wondered aloud if I could ask them some rather personal questions.

'How many of you are married?'

Well over a hundred raised their hands.

'How many of you have children?'

Well over half raised their hands.

'How many of you have ugly children?'

Not one hand was raised.

'Come now, at least one of you must have an ugly child!'

* * *

Essentially, there are three main categories of book illustration:

1) *The diagrammatic illustration.* Its function is purely to produce a visual clarification of a specific reference in the text. That function is wholly one of impassive explanation.

2) *The interpretive illustration.* Though the function is mainly descriptive, this type of illustration may also seek to offer interpretive response to the text: explanation, artistic complement, or juxtaposition.

3) *The decorative illustration.* Its primary function is to embellish, though it too may introduce appropriate interpretation, at times.

Different books will require of the illustrator one or another of these types, or sometimes a combination.

Books requiring diagrammatic illustration include technical textbooks and science books. These, at first glance, appear pretty clear-cut in their requiring of a realistic approach. But then I remember *The Giant Golden Book of Biology* published by the Golden Press of New York in the 1960s, which was handsomely illustrated by Charles Harper, in quite a stylized manner. And was meant for quite a young reader. And was quite successful.

The category of books requiring interpretive illustration is large. These books range from fiction to nonfiction, via adventure, saga, fantasy, history – any work that requires visual interpretation to augment or simply describe the verbal. Here, the visual convention may vary from the determinedly realistic to the forcefully stylized. The latter seems seldom to have problems communicating with the reader. I remember books beautifully illustrated by Maurice Sendak and Edward Ardizonne, and in Canada by Michele Lemieux, Ken Nutt, Theo Dimson, Lazlo Gal and so many others, each artist having a distinctive voice – and not one of them distracting the reader from the author's account.

The category of works requiring decorative illustration comprises a very special group of books: poetry, folk and fairy tales, proverbs and the like – works where the illustrator assumes the responsibility of providing the text with rich yet unassuming decoration. I fondly remember Carlos Marchiori's magical and challenging artwork for Edith Fowke's *Sally Go Round the Sun,* and Jimmy Hill's magic-realist illuminations for *The Pied Piper and Other Fairy Tales.*

While the diagrammatic and the decorative illustration seldom present too many emotional problems for author and illustrator, the interpretive illustration can become a veritable minefield, which the hapless publisher must then negotiate with great care. This is particularly the case when an illustrator is thrust upon an unwilling author, who may take the proffered illustration as an assault either on the quality of his writing or on his command over his creations. Sometimes, the illustrator's visual response to the text does not correspond to the image conjured up by the author, and vociferous protests ensue.

Some have argued that the author might be compared to a composer, the illustrator to a soloist: the composer's intent establishes specific auditory 'rules', which the musician-soloist has to follow. The problem is that *there* the interpretive translation is between two versions of the same art form: music written becomes music played, but in both cases we are dealing with music. In our case, two very different forms of artistic communication are involved.

Imagine a curator leading a discussion on a work of art, and simply presenting a factual description of the marks the painter had made on the surface of the canvas, without any reference to the unseen. This would likely just constitute a belabouring of something already imparted visually. It might even suggest that the artwork itself lacked force. Yet it is exactly this sort of un-interpretive 'description' that some authors seem to want from their illustrators.

Others see the illustrator as, essentially, a pair of talented hands: provided by the publisher for the sole purpose of executing the author's own visual concept.

Still others fear that the illustration, in the hands of a greedy craftsman, might compete with the written word and the author's creative concept; any sidestepping of direct 'description' on the part of the illustrator – as a device to prod readers to conjure their own imagery – is especially spurned.

Authors certainly must realize that, with a newly acquired book, the drawings are scrutinized well before the text. What they may not grasp is that this first contact does establish an immediate relationship. Furthermore, the picture is not the text, any more than the title is the story. As with a good title, at no time is a good text ever compromised by a good illustration. No honest illustration will take away the author's rightful claim to make intimate contact with the reader in the written medium.

There are obvious occasions where it is essential for the picture to hold close to the word. Long John Silver's wooden leg, for instance. Depriving him of his stump would make the illustration very confusing. (Who is this two-legged pirate?) But in *Garbage Delight* I purposely 'forgot' Bloody Bill's hook, with the intent of leaving the poem to the reader's own imagination.

Earlier, I poked fun at Dennis Lee's lecture about 'hard' and 'soft' poems. But I admit that the distinction can be helpful. The 'hard poem', he said, is essentially descriptive and quite direct; the 'soft poem', on the other hand, is introspective, and meant to establish a very personal and private relationship with the reader.

With the 'hard' poem, the illustration's main function is to set the scene – please note, I did not say 'describe the scene' – hopefully without misrepresenting it, or predetermining the outcome. The 'soft' poem presents a more delicate problem. If a visual portrayal is sought, then at most it should only be a decoration, or an image that accommodates the poem's *mood*.

Validly, authors are vitally concerned about the visual manipulations foisted upon them by the publisher. What they need to bear in mind, however, is that just as there are professional authors, so there also are professional illustrators. True, there are lousy practitioners in both vocations. Luckily, most every book has a publisher, who hopefully employs capable editors and art directors with the expertise and objectivity to fairly (and passionately) do only what is best for *both* reader and author.

* * *

For me, illustrating for children has always been much more of a challenge than illustrating for adults. And much more complex! But there seem to be some logical tenets for the illustrator to respect.

First, don't deprive the reader of his/her own flight of fancy. In other words, don't present him or her with visual dogma.

Second, don't steal the climax. In other words, where possible, establish a 'before' or an 'after'. Let the reader's imagination assume responsibility for illustrating the actual 'deed', spurred by the author's account. Kids can be much more bloodthirsty than publishers would ever let an illustrator be.

Third, don't make visual evasions: don't insult the reader by using sweet, endearing substitutes for the real thing. An insidious practice is the portrayal of people as cute beasties! Or beasties as cute people! It is logical in a Burgess Book type of publication, where the author's characters are Mr Mole and Mrs Hedgehog, to begin with. But where the author describes an array of vibrant human individuals, to depict them in fallow formulae only confuses; it hardly gives the author room to stimulate the young reader's imagination.

Fourth, don't underestimate the younger readers' ability – especially the very young readers' ability – to come to quite comfortable terms with abstraction or stylization. Children are abstractionists by nature, until we mould them into visual conformists. For just two examples of work that has recognized this, take the extremely challenging (and successful) work of England's Brian Wildsmith and of Canada's Marchiori. Marchiori's stylized illustrations for *Sally Go Round the Sun* brought a new boldness to Canadian kidlit. (I still believe that the key to Carlos's success with this commission was his fierce determination to avoid as many meetings with the art director – me – as possible. As I remember it, he turned up for two only. Which, luckily for the book, gave me little or no opportunity to help him 'improve' his illustrations.)

It is now over forty-six years since the first of my children's books, *The Princess of Tomboso*, was published. A lot has changed in our world, both socially and technologically. Certainly, the Canadian publishing scene of today in no way – at first I wrote in *few* ways – resembles that of 1960. A large number of familiar publishing names, such as Stoddart, and booksellers, such as Britnell's, have disappeared, once declared victims of our technological 'new order'. By now, their demise is so long a fait accompli that we neither blame the new technology, nor even identify it as a cause. Though we do wistfully lament other effects of technology on our society – especially in areas concerning our young. Some years ago, for instance, I was told at KidsCan Press that the fairy tale or folk tale book had become an impossible sell in our new, technological world. 'Unfortunately, we can no longer find a market for folklore such as Ti-Jean.'

This is both sad and strange. It seems that, while the fantastical picture book has been designated as beyond the pale, new movies abound in magical motifs, from epic fantasies like *Harry Potter* and *The Lord of the Rings*, to science fictions like *The Matrix*, to 'children's movies' like *Shrek* or *Pirates of the Caribbean*. Movie-going audiences seem to be quite comfortable with the 'adult' topics these fantasies involve. (Of course, such movies have been excoriated by fringe ecclesiastics or over-zealous 'educators'. But this hue and cry has not proved much of a deterrent.) Yet in the book-world, fantasy and fairy tale seem to have become subject matter unfit for little people's diets.

For a time, the advent first of television, and then of the computer sent me in a scrambled perambulation to decipher their effect on the reading habits of 'man'. How should designers respond to these new conditions? What should I do to proselytize our soon-to-be-lost readers to return to the fold?

After quite a few years, I have decided that looking for *the* answer was simply an exercise in futility. Those who want to read books, still do. Those who never aspired to read, still only peruse a book when forced to. But now, I have discovered, the computer forces them to *read* more than they ever did before. And read without complaint.

So much for that!

Admittedly, awful visual travesties are found, especially on the Internet. There is no logical reason to expect the look of the text to outshine the lexicon of the laic. Still, it is a pity that, more often than not, the skilled computer typographer seems to be missing.

While head of the Illustration Program at Sheridan College, I became quite disturbed by the artificial isolation of the divers arts programs in the School of Visual Arts, particularly where logically allied programs, like graphic design, computer graphics, illustration and, to a lesser degree, animation were concerned. It was obvious that these programs advocated isolation not for reasons of pedagogical philosophy, but rather for reasons of administrative autonomy - or departmental xenophobia!

Several years ago, well into my retirement, I proposed to Mike Collins, the new dean of Visual Arts, a possibly worthwhile session, to be held between the departments of illustration, design and computer graphics, in order to examine the obvious links between their spheres - certainly, for instance, in the field of the picture book. Mr Collins was going to get back to me. Not surprisingly, both of us forgot about the conversation.

That is, until today. I happened to come across my late mother's copy of *The Princess of Tomboso*. Looking through, I found myself pondering how easily it could be 'translated' - with the help of some minor, deft animation - into a more 'technological' form. I went through the book page by page, and imagined a number of simple animation embellishments, surely easily achieved with the new technology. And I tried to avoid any undue infringement on the reader's flight of fancy.

The Princess of Tomboso seemed to offer opportunity upon opportunity for interactive fun. Starting immediately with the second spread, where each of the three brothers in his turn tries out his magical inheritance.

The eldest brother receives a purse with the message 'Every time I open wide, a hundred florins are inside!' Though I handled it in a fairly decent graphic manner, how much more fun could have been had with animated florins (still graphic!) flying all over the place.

The second brother got a bugle. 'Blow one end your troops appear – the other and the field is clear!' Again, the message spells out the chain of events. Simple animation would easily serve to enhance the fantasy.

Finally, Jacques (our hero) tries out his gift, a belt. 'Put me on, tell me where; quick as lightning you'll be there!' In the 1960 version, Jacques buckles up in a two-tree apple orchard, near a horse and two grazing sheep. In the book, I composed a sort of a three-stage Muybridge for Jacques's flight back to the castle. Imagine what magic moves could be made, digitally!

In fact, the idea of the computer book was raised by Jack McClelland way back in 1969. At that time, he asked me to investigate the possibility of a computer-based 'paperback' which, most particularly, might be sold at airports, et cetera. Trying to take this further – or even have it taken seriously by local technologues – proved impossible. After many weeks of getting nowhere, we gave up on Jack's brainwave.

Now, the same idea is getting a fair bit of press. But redundantly, I suspect. The computer airport book is just doing what the paperback already does efficiently and cheaply.

Still, I suspect that *The Princess of Tomboso* would be quite acceptable in this 'New Technology Picture Book' format. And then, with the precedent set, perhaps we might once again entertain the publishing of the traditional folktale.

Even as the traditional book?

★ ★ ★

After the first of my book designs reached the warehouse, Mr McClelland Sr appeared at my studio. He had two of my books in hand.

'Are you the designer chappie Jack hired?'

'Yes, sir.'

'Did you design these two books?'

'Yes, sir.'

'Type's much too small! I can't read either of the damn things!' With this he heaved both books into the wastepaper basket.

Forty-five years later, I find that Jack's father was right. I can only read the damn things now with a great deal of difficulty. But then, I suffer from macular puckering. (After looking at some of my current artsy output, my ophthalmologist decided not to do anything about it.)

But the vast majority of young readers have good eyesight. Where most of our better book designers have long been well aware of this – Solomon, Shaw, Toye, Rueter – there are still an awful lot of early-reader books evidently designed for children with advanced cases of macular degeneration. We see far too many Golden-Book style publications that are set in

20-point type;
some play it even safer
and use 24-point type,
as though using 18 point isn't enough.
In fact, most times, 14 point will do admirably.

Once the younger reader gets to, say, grade three textbooks,

12 point is almost always adequate.

(Of course, the selection of the typeface has a great impact on one's decision. Twelve-point Bembo barely measures up to ten-point Times.)

I am equally puzzled by some unwritten rules regarding style of letterform in children's books, still followed by a number of our publishing houses.

For instance, it still is widely assumed that beginners had best master the sans serif letterform, before moving on to the serif. This in spite of the fact that we live in a world of letters, filled with Roman typefaces. We are somehow taught that these are for adults, and happily look forward to children's 'Roman initiation' as soon as they've rid themselves of diapers.

Sans serif type is often seen – predominantly by educators, but also by some authors and a few editors – as simpler and more effective. It isn't, really; at least, not enough to account for a meaningful stage in learning to read. That is like claiming that mastering a child's scooter is a prerequisite to driving a car. The serif is not a huge distraction; it really is quite small compared to the rest of the letter. Also, word recognition is established far more easily with a Roman typeface than with a sans-serif typeface, because the weight differential found in the letterforms of a Roman typeface affords a more natural flow amongst letters in a word.

* * *

Children's books are of course not the only ones that require – or may be enhanced by – illustration. But there is one unfortunate reality that publishers must confront vis-à-vis the illustrated adult book. Just as the transformation from individualist to conformist manifests itself conspicuously and predictably in the maturing of our younger readers, so also does the switch from abstract cognizance to acceptance (and expectation) of the safer and more prosaic image. With a larger market, publishers can allow themselves to occasionally experiment; in our small market, this can become a money-losing indulgence. Fortunately, Canada still seems to have a small group of daring publishing idealists.

Amongst illustrated adult books, there is the odd volume of poetry; mostly, however, this category is confined to the 'non-book', such as *The Joy of Sex* or *The Joy of Cooking*. But then, once in a blue moon, along comes a vehicle that is every illustrator's dream.

I have been lucky enough to complete two such commissions. Both were brought my way via the University of Toronto Press. And both titles, in addition to giving me the chance to work with an empathic publishing group, brought out some of my best work. The U. of T. group consisted of Laurie Lewis, Will Rueter and Ian Montagnes. The books were Bernard Suits' *The Grasshopper* and Shirley Kumove's *Words like Arrows*.

The Grasshopper was the last vehicle one would think of as a logical candidate for illustration. It consisted of a curious set of psychological paradoxes, and carried a wonderful subtitle: 'Games, Life and Utopia'. There were wonderful chapter titles, ranging from 'Construction of a Definition' to 'Resurrection', via 'Triflers, Cheats, and Spoilsports'. Suits' language, for me, was pure calligraphy.

It seemed logical to incorporate Suits' words into my drawings. The danger was of using an apparent comic-strip convention. I wanted to do the word-incorporating drawings in Suits' own tongue, without pre-empting his message, distorting his use of metaphor, or trivializing his thesis. Rueter had asked for illustrated chapter openers with room for titles and long descriptive blurbs. I struggled unsuccessfully with this for a long while.

Finally, I came to the conclusion that I had no idea how to get all this in. Also, I greedily wanted lots of space for the illustration plus calligraphic treatment. Nor was I all that keen on separating Suits' text from his titles. This, I felt, any pen scratching around and on his chapter titles would succeed in doing; typesetting the titles would avoid the problem. I decided to propose a format of preliminary double spreads with illustrations and chapter numbers – on the verso of which would be found the conventional (typeset) chapter title and subtitle.

I took a chance, and prepared finished art for one of the double spreads, complete with calligraphic phrase and stylized Roman numeral. I then called Laurie Lewis and set up a meeting. I described to her how I hoped to handle the commission, and showed her the illustration. Laurie mentioned that Bernard Suits happened to be at U. of T., and would I mind showing him my proposal.

To my surprise, both Suits and Ian Montagnes were not only immediately available but immediately receptive to my idea. Diplomatically, I suggested that Suits select the extracts for calligraphic treatment (I remembered the fuss that Lee had made, because I had used text in one of my drawings, putting the word *toester* on a bowl.) Suits decided it would be better if I chose the extracts with which I felt most comfortable (with the proviso that, should he hate any of them, I would look for a substitute). This, for me, established *The Grasshopper* as being as much mine as his, and turned it into my favourite illustration commission.

Words like Arrows was quite a different sort of publication. I have no idea why U. of T. decided to publish a book of Yiddish sayings; still, it turned out to be fun to illustrate. I knew very little about Eastern Europe's Jewry, and next to nothing about life in Europe's ghettos. And I knew just two words of Yiddish. I had, however, lived for almost six months not far from the Mea Shearim district in Jerusalem, so I knew what the Hasidim looked and acted like. And I still retained vivid visual images, from my visits as a young child to my grandparents' farm in Czechoslovakia, of the whimsy and regalia of the Slavic peasantry.

I was not sure, however, who would buy the book. Certainly not the Jewish Orthodox community – just because of the illustrations. Then I remembered Arthur Czyk's *Hagaddah,* and the success his illustrated version had enjoyed. So I decided I had to draw for a progressive audience, not even exclusively Jewish. I decided on a liberal yet, at times, acidic approach.

By chance, I had just bought a large quantity of English scraperboard. I decided to simulate a woodcut look. I got rather carried away by the spirit of the work, and turned out well over fifty 'woodcuts'. The work went quickly. Not all of my illustrations were used. Some because of space problems. Some, the author labelled derogatory: 'At times, your drawings seem derisive of the religious Jew. And some readers might even take certain ones as being anti-Semitic.'

'I guess one just can't trust an ex-kibbutznik,' I replied.

Years later, I have looked at the drawings again. And I still do not wince one bit, either as an illustrator or as an ex-kibbutznik.

I have been involved in a number of textbook illustration projects over the years, as well. For junior grades, I have mostly drawn for poetry. Only once did I illustrate a story within a pre-designed English anthology text. But I learnt an invaluable lesson, which became my mantra as an art director: *Never lay out a book before commissioning the artwork, and then give the illustrator an impossible shape to fill!*

The odd other textbook has come my way. Usually, I made designing the book a condition of accepting the commission. Invariably, the textbooks were anthologies. Which only too often seemed to require a variety of styles to suit the variety of both subjects and authors. Luckily, I was generally able to draw on a fair list of good young illustrators who were willing to participate, and who also needed some decent portfolio pieces.

Textbooks get lugged around by two student groups: a) juniors, who are happy to show that they are the official, legitimate owners of this badge of erudition, and b) seniors, who are unwilling to broadcast that they are actually high-school-book bearers. There is really no reason why a designer (or illustrator) should not cater to both these groups individually. And, unless the artwork is for a medical or scientific text, there is no reason to be so literal as to draw down to the students, in either case. Certainly, the senior students must resent any suggestion that the printed word alone is too obscure for them. Better then, that the illustration be viewed as an (interpretive) decoration, bringing the look of the book closer to that of a belle livre.

As an example: one publisher who, in the early days, understood this approach was Ron Besse's W.J. Gage. Irene de Clute, their visually sensitive production manager, commissioned me to design several textbooks, including two series for English language studies. The first series, a poetry series of three books, was for juniors; the second series, also of three books, and titled *CONNECTIONS*, was aimed at reluctant or slow high-school readers. The original commission was to design one title. The Frank Newfeld Studio finally designed the whole series.

It was an interesting problem, and became a reference point.

First of all, what format to use? Second, what style of illustration? Third, what sort of cover would be effective, without seeming to 'label' the student?

When I looked for a common denominator for the *CONNECTIONS* student group, somebody or other was always excluded. The only shared trait seemingly applicable was some affinity to music. I finally hit upon the idea of an extremely abstract representation of a jukebox, in vivid colours, floating on a glossy black background. I did not want the carried-about image to signal any direct link to 'the Textbook'.

The budget, as was often the case with senior language textbooks, only allowed for one-colour printing of the text. Which turned out to be a blessing. Full-colour illustrations would just have branded the books as kiddish. The black and white seemed to keep things on a more adult keel. Of course, once the books were opened, it would be clear that they were textbooks. Each book was divided into four to five sections. I proposed a book-section/illustrator format, rather than the accepted author/illustrator format. The illustrations had only one common denominator: they were drawn to the author's message, not the student's 'level'.

Illustrated cookbooks are projects of a different – and much easier – sort. All you need is an enlightened publisher, and a talented illustrator. Even prosaic subjects like weights and measures need not be rendered prosaically: there need be nothing prosaic about drawing spoonfuls of sugar and honey! Invariably, decorative art is the solution. You can have the 'single-illustrator book'. You can have the 'multi-illustrator book'. It doesn't seem to matter, as long as the artwork is properly ambitious and engaging.

I have had a number of cookbooks to design, or illustrate, or art-direct – or all three. Two stick out in my memory: *The Laura Secord Cookbook* and *Picnics for Lovers*.

The Laura Secord Cookbook was richly illustrated with still-life photographs by Dennis Colwell, and decorated with colourful spots by the illustrators at the Canadian Illustrated Library on Simcoe Street. Sally Henry, of Laura Secord, taught me a most important point about the designing of a cookbook. Cooking being a messy job, it's best to design in such a way that a recipe starts and finishes on a page or spread. Spot illustrations help by serving as both ornaments and space eaters. The book sold well!

Picnics for Lovers, a freelance commission from Van Nostrand Reinhold, Ltd., was an artsy cookbook, with flowery section-titles like 'A Midsummer Night's Dream', 'Autumn Leaves', 'Chestnuts Roasting on an Open Fire', and 'Cherry Blossoms'. Each recipe was presented as a tour de force, with a Kirschbaum (the author) homily. We were commissioned late in the schedule. The manuscript came with some sample couplets or sonnets – section epigraphs – which the author was still in the process of assembling, 'but of which we would, most definitely, get a large number within two or three weeks'. I worked around the missing epigraphs by allowing for large fore-edge margins. The design was approved, and, the schedule being tight, we were forced to start immediately.

I shared the illustration work with Dianne Richardson, who was then at the studio. She had a most sensitive and delicate style of illustration, which contrasted tellingly with my own pencil-shovelling way of drawing. Again, we each had our own sections. Dianne opted for recipes such as 'For Summertime Lovers', 'A Hammock for Two',

'A Picnic on the Danube'. I chose less sensitive subjects: 'For Those Who are Game', 'Rasputin's Retreat'.

As it happens, the epigraphs never materialized. The author searched and searched, and finally gave up. But the design could not be changed, at this point. We had to do twenty-four more drawings, to fill the space. Van Nostrand's Canadian manager offered to put the design and illustration copyright in my name, as protection, were the property sold to another publisher. Which he thought was not unlikely.

Both books met sorry ends. *The Laura Secord* recently appeared as a paperback, with the colour work now in black and white. The book looks awful. *Picnics for Lovers* was sold to Key Porter. Sadly, Dianne and I are still listed! The publisher not only allowed the work to be reprinted using horrible colours, but also ignored the fact that the copyright for the illustrations was in my name (and ignored, as well, the remuneration for subsequent publication that we had agreed to!)

Today, the adult book designed with newly commissioned art seems to be a thing of the past. Certainly in Canada. Certainly in the category of 'literature'. When art *is* sought, it is invariably commissioned for the non-book. A pity.

★ ★ ★

The greatest bonus of Canadian publishing's love affair with book design back in the fifties and sixties was the non-discriminatory nature of commissions available. All manner of books – prose and poetry alike – were allowed to undergo designers' beauty treatments, at least where our enlightened publishers were involved.

Then Expo 67 came along, and brought with it more and more ambitious publishing projects. Too often, the ambition was out of proportion to the market – for with increased ambition came increased expense. Everybody wanted to get in on the windfall of the moment. The public sector – jumping in with both feet – opened suppliers' eyes and its own purse. Even on the design end, costs took on a new and more exorbitant face. The titanic coffee-table book and art catalogue monopolized all our available design talents, new and old. Slowly but surely, the simple, common book sank back into passive disregard, where design was concerned. The days of even the *presque* belle livre were numbered, if not gone altogether. Recent visits to bookstores indicate that our publishers' interest in the look (and, unfortunately, sometimes even the readability) of the common book is once again confined to the jacket.

Looking back on those earlier days, I find myself regretting the chain of events. At McClelland & Stewart, each promotion took me further and further from personally dealing with the design of our everyday books. Post-M&S, just about every one of my commissions was a Big, Big Book. These publications were well endowed and major in scope. Many of the gallery catalogues turned into case-bound tomes, which at times ran well over three hundred pages. The coffee-table books entrusted to me boasted neither budget restrictions nor design preconceptions. And the variety of subject matter – from *The Olympic Games* to *Trésors des Archives nationales du Canada* to *Dinosaurs of North America* – was mouthwatering. But the intimacy of personal dialogue that one could achieve when working on the design of, for instance, a poetry book could rarely be established with them.

The blanket label 'poetry book' is a bit of a red herring. It is obvious that an epic poem like *The Song of Hiawatha* demands a distinctly different vehicle than a collection of poetic personal definitions, like Irving Layton's *Balls for a One-armed Juggler.* What is less obvious, at first glance – though no less important – is the difference in appropriate translation into type and into physical form between Ralph Gustafson's *Rivers among Rocks* and Roy Daniels' *The Chequered Shade.* What is permissible with a collection like Phyllis Gotlieb's *Within the Zodiac* could well become peacockish when imposed on David Weisstub's *Heaven Take My Hand.* Even two books by one author might beg different treatments: *The Spice-Box of Earth,* as compared to *Flowers for Hitler.*

The 'epic poem', like a Charles Dickens classic, is meant to be savoured leisurely, yet religiously, page by page, from start to finish. Which necessitates either a bookmark or a folded-over corner, unless the reader has a wonderful memory or lots of uninterrupted time. The 'collection of poems', on the other hand, resembles more a book of Aesop fables, each fable complete unto itself, yet all the fables conjoined. This is easily recognized by the reader when the poems have titles; it is less clear in a collection of untitled poems or 'nuggets'.

Even with the 'epic poem', in those cases where there are no pre-established sections, it helps if some logical breaks are conjured up by editor or author. Whether the breaks are to be subliminal or conscious must be an editorial decision – but the visible, easily grasped break helps establish a reader's empathy for the book at first encounter.

In the standard 'collection of poems', one breathes a sigh of relief whenever the poet has specific sections pre-established in the manuscript. Although not indispensable, the breaks do give added opportunities for the desired relationships between book and reader to be established, on both the visual and the editorial front. Parts or sections seem to provide comfortable boundaries that readers willingly accede to.

Every poetry book with which I have worked came to me with a pre-determined sequence, which was *not* to be violated. Some of these poems logically had to face each other; others could *not* appear on the same page or spread, under any circumstance. Most of the editors and/or authors were prepared to make minor changes of sequence, but one – at least – was not prepared to make any compromise. Not even when asked what was to prevent a reader from flicking through the book and selecting a poem with a tempting title. The first time I asked the question, I foolishly compared the book at hand to an anthology of stories by O. Henry – only to be chided that there was no comparison between O. Henry's 'lightweight prose' and the poetry entrusted to me. From then on, I was careful to throw the problem to the editor, where it had properly belonged in the first place.

Just as the poet is concerned with the relationships between theme and sound, the designer must be concerned with the relationships between typographic shape and conveying paper, on the one hand, and theme and sound, on the other. Whether the poem is given room to breathe (and if so how much) affects the empathy between poet and reader as markedly as does the sequence of poems – at times, more so. Placing an (occidental) haiku at the foot of a page because there is space there may not always be salubrious; at times, it may be hurtful to the health of adjoining pages. By the same token, it helps if the designer knows the difference between a haiku and a limerick.

The poetry book – of every stripe – establishes quite a different relationship with the reader than do other types of (printed) communication. It begs a certain quietude – whether that quietude bespeaks tranquility or tumult. Letterform becomes far more suggestive and persuasive in books of poetry than it is in books of prose. Even colour (of typeface or of paper) takes on meaning in a poetry book – or precipitates a search for reason – while it is simply accepted by just about all readers of prose. White paper may not always make for a happy union with a manuscript of poems; nor, for that matter, may black ink.

Illustration, the terror of many poets, is happily accepted by readers when used as decoration, and savoured when used as interpretation. And few if any readers are likely to look for some hidden code in the illustrations – as they might when reading a plot-driven novel – whether the art is germane or abstract. It is much harder to waylay a poem than it is to give a plot away. I have seen several productions of *King Lear*, with divers (period-specific) costumes and make-up designs. The play always stayed Shakespeare's. Just as good costume design – regardless of style or period – leaves the playwright alone, so good illustration will leave the poet alone. Having said that, it must be up to the poet to decide whether the work can bear illustration. In fact, it is really preferable for the poet to preclude any inclusion of artwork, than for him or her to want sole control over its style and over its interpretations of the poems.

The poet's concurrence that illustrations are to be a vital part of the total message may culminate in different ways. If the poet comes to the publisher with an illustrator-confrere, then the 'package' is pre-ordained. If the poet proposes an illustrator – one with whom previous rapport has been established – then editorial might have to allot the poet some art-directional leeway. Should the total commissioning of the artwork be achieved by the publisher, then editorial must bear the responsibility for (and sway over) its particulars.

Once committed to publication, the collection of poems suddenly becomes a package. This is the first change of ownership that a 'poet's poetry' undergoes. That package includes the poet's text, in his or her unique voice: the product of selective use of an established vocabulary. It may also include, however, pictorial elements – and these, too, are drawn from a private vocabulary, unique to the artisan. Other package components – such as cover, cloth, paper, typeface, design and decoration – are necessary augmentations requiring professional treatment, just as the writing of the poetry did originally. Though made in cognizance of the poems' creator, the choice of these components must be made for the welfare of the package as a whole. As the poet-creator initiates the rendezvous, so the packager-publisher must ensure its fruitful consummation.

Why this colloquy, you might ask, since the publishing of the poetry book is afforded so little attention. I can only protest that all things are cyclic – perhaps even the popular resurgence of the poetry book. And it seems to be one of the very few opportunities we might have to pursue again a version of the belle livre.

* * *

I am now conveniently quite old. This gives me the advantage of being able to speak my mind about one rather grating circumstance, without being accused of wanting to be self-justifying with an eye towards my next commission. This circumstance is the peculiar disparity in the credence afforded by certain book-professionals (and book-amateurs) to writers, on the one hand, and designers/illustrators, on the other.

It seems that writers are credited most every time with profound insight into both visual and verbal matters related to book production, while, often, designers – and, just about always, illustrators – are engaged merely to follow the concepts of author and editor, regardless of the designer's or illustrator's experience in the book world. As an art director, I never could bring myself to use a respected and accomplished professional simply as a pair of hands. Especially if his English was better than the author's ability to draw.

On the whole, I was lucky. As a freelancer, I can only remember the odd time when I felt the common complaint – 'They see me as an illiterate, mad artist' – of many itinerant illustrators and designers. But then, I worked for a most enlightened publisher.

At M&S, Jack would tell an author with art-directional ambition, 'You really must talk to Newfeld, our vice-president, publishing.'

Which none of these ambitious authors ever did.

Had they, I might have told them that it wasn't what the *author wanted*. It was what the *book needed*, that it was all about.

* * *

I have few regrets from my long career in publishing. Admittedly, I have been most lucky, inasmuch as I have scarcely ever had to take on commissions that went against my 'grain'. I was usually able to withdraw from a project rather than acquiesce when I felt that my concept was jeopardized.

One episode stands out, however, as in need of explanation.

Toward the end of my career as vice-president, publishing, at M&S, one of the titles on our upcoming list was a book on a famous Toronto artist. Jack McClelland was handling the project himself, and he and the artist were 'bosom buddies'. The artist had a well-known columnist in mind to write the book; a meeting was duly set up at M&S.

The day before the meeting, Jack told me that his friend had suddenly decided that he wanted a *different* author to write the book – but had not as yet informed his original choice of this change of mind. The meeting would have to proceed, since Jack had not yet figured out how to break the news to the jettisoned writer – a man whom I knew and respected. I wanted neither to go to the meeting, nor to aid in the subterfuge, but could not avoid it.

After a few minutes of chitchat, the meeting got under way. The unsuspecting author mentioned that he had put some ideas together, and wanted to sound me out regarding the visual end of the project. I interrupted him, a bit abruptly, saying that this would be premature and a waste of time – as no budget had as yet been set, nor the extent and direction of the visual determined. With this, I excused myself and left the room. Soon after the meeting, the author refused the commission – mainly because of my negative attitude toward the establishment of a harmonious visual/verbal dialogue.

In hindsight, I should have piped up at the meeting, and said: 'Charlie [not his name], you aren't never gonna get this book!'

* * *

I have had the opportunity to work with some very fine authors, editors, and art directors over the course of my career. A shortlist of my favourites would of course include Pierre Berton. Despite his frustrating habit of having an infallible memory, Pierre was the most tolerant and generous of authors. His main concern was the book; he was not concerned with from whom the appropriate interpretation of *his* concept emanated.

My favourite art directors are without a doubt Laurie Lewis and Will Rueter of U. of T. Press: the most caring and empathetic of the

An illustration for Bernard Suits' *The Grasshopper*, University of Toronto Press, 1978. My favourite commission.

many good art directors who have 'babied' me. Somehow, they managed to get my best work without apparent flattery or discipline.

I remember only one time that Laurie threw her weight around.

I was working on the illustrations for *The Grasshopper*. In order to keep the drawings as spontaneous as possible, I wanted to go straight from thumbnails to finished art. I asked if I could therefore just show the thumbnails, rather than the usual roughs. To which UTP agreed.

One illustration gave me no end of problems. After much unproductive doodling, I did an angry, savage doodle of the hero, with all his glory hanging out.

And it really looked good!

It was already Friday, and I was behind schedule. But frontal male nudity? I decided I should really phone Laurie and let her know what I hoped to draw. Just in case. In spite of my reputation, even I was mindful of the limits of sexual provocation possible for Toronto's publishers at that time.

I was still explaining my plan when Laurie interrupted: 'I really don't have time for this. I'm too busy with other matters. Phone me on Tuesday, and tell me again what your problem is.'

I dutifully phoned on the Tuesday, and explained my dilemma all over again.

'Well, I can't see where there's any quandary. Of course you can have frontal nudity. We are so behind schedule, don't even bring in the thumbnail. Just bring in the final art as soon as possible.'

The problem turned out not to be so simple! No matter what I tried, my hero's thingamajig turned out looking like a comic piece of string.

Finally, I tried a rear view. The full-fleshed globes worked beautifully. In fact, the drawing was perfect! I waxed the patch onto the otherwise finished illustration, and called U. of T. Press.

At the presentation meeting, I was surprised to find a full assembly of the press's executive. I unveiled my latest illustration to thunderous silence. After what seemed like an eternity, Laurie asked, 'What happened with your famous frontal nudity?'

'I couldn't get the phallus to perform. So I've created two delectable buttocks instead. They not only work compositionally, they are yummy aesthetically. I'm sure they're much better.'

'They most certainly are NOT. You must bring back our penis.'

Apparently, editorial had discussed the matter with the board, which thought that discretion was the better part of valour. And raised the spectre of pornography allegations. Thereupon, both editorial and production threatened to resign. And U. of T. gave in.

I stitched back the phallus.

Finally, I should mention my favourite editor: William (Bill) Toye of Oxford University Press. I am certain that I share my favourite editor with most, if not all, of his authors. He was an excellent designer in his own right, and his visual acumen allowed him to achieve a unity and balance between our twin disciplines, the written illustration and the drawn word. I played author in just two Oxford books, *The Princess of Tomboso* and *Simon and the Golden Sword*, but worked with him on a number of design commissions, as well.

Toye, of all 'my' editors, had the knack of making me feel an integral part of the creation, rather than just an adjunct to the creative process. And, without condescension, he taught me more than I had ever guessed about the nature of an author's intent.

20. MANY TYPES

I n 1958, when Hugh Kane offered me the retainer, he stated, 'We want our reader to say: "I can always recognize an M&S book."' Then he added, 'And we want to commission you to achieve this.' Out of that came a trusting relationship, both combative and pleasurable, that lasted for over twenty years. At the start it was a bit embarrassing, since Hugh gave my 'expertise' more credence than even I did. (In fact, in 1958, I had problems remembering the difference between 'font' and 'fount'.) Any visual philosophy, personality or patois I brought to my work at McClelland & Stewart came from my absorption of new experiences there, rather than from any pre-stocked arsenal of conviction.

There were a fair number of factors that helped my learning process along. Not least was the eagerness for change on the part of a number of the important local publishing houses.

Canada's fledgling publishing industry existed in a state of visual poverty. Recognition of this fact had created a climate of eager encouragement of available talents. In particular, Hugh Kane and Bill Toye, along with Marsh Jeanneret (U of T Press), Bob Kilpatrick (Longmans), and Bernard Neary (Nelson), spawned a drive to improve the look of the Canadian book.

This coincided with the fortuitous and timely arrival, from both England and Germany, of a small contingent of typographers in the early 1950s. Those émigrés most attracted to book design – besides myself – were Sam Smart and Frank Davies from England and Antje Lingner from Germany. There were a number of passionate and talented Canadian typographic designers, as well – spearheaded by Jack Birdsall, Carl Dair, Allan Fleming and Harold Kurschenska, in Toronto. But of these, only Kurschenska had much, if anything, to do with books. Paul Arthur, the only well-known local book designer at that time, was away, working for Graphis in Switzerland. (Also to be counted amongst the designers, fortunately and felicitously, was Bill Toye: by profession an editor; by aptitude a most natural and skilled designer as well as art director; and also an esteemed author and connoisseur of the book.)

These few pioneers went largely unnoticed outside their own profession, however. The bulk of Toronto's publishing fraternity simply turned manuscripts over to their chosen printer to design. It took about two years for me to make any meaningful inroad as a designer.

But the publishers' apathy was compensated for by the remarkable enthusiasm for design on the part of a number of the Toronto book-printing houses: T.H. Best, Hunter Rose, Bryant Press. Bud Best and I became good friends. (Good enough that he let me talk him into stocking Pilgrim, a linotype face beautifully designed by Eric Gill.)

Over the course of my career – with just a few (idiosyncratic-title) exceptions – I used a fairly small group of fonts. Those were still mostly the days of hot metal. And though there were many – too many, in fact – typefaces available, for me the workable ones were the following:

1) Baskerville. Probably the most versatile face for books (with the possible exception of science texts, for which it was inappropriate).

2) Caledonia. Initially, this was the only American (Dwiggins) face that I used on a regular basis. An excellent workhorse for both fiction and nonfiction titles, as experience taught me. I used it mainly for 'non-flowery' titles.

3) Palatino. This was perhaps the closest to a 'flowery face' I would come. In my opinion, it was probably the best typeface designed by Herman Zapf. Eminently legible and warm, the face lent itself to children's books as aptly as it did to poetry, gentle trade books, and even educational publishing.

4) Pilgrim. The only face in my repertoire with an attitude. It was a gutsier version of Perpetua. Unlike its mannered cousin, however, it seemed able to preserve both its own character and an appropriate anonymity that didn't interfere with an author's text. I first used it for Farley Mowat's book *Coppermine Journey*, without any clash of temperament.

5) Times New Roman. About the best things about Times, for me, were its anonymity and its economy of fit. I really always thought of it as a lighter and less successful version of Plantin. It did its job, but there was nothing much to really like or dislike about it.

Years later, I added Dwiggins' Electra to my list. In the early days I wasn't quite sure how to use it.

Anyhow, those were, for me, the bearable linotype faces at that time. Publishers could rarely afford monotype in the early days. Canadian printings were seldom more than 3,000 copies. The amortization of an extra $300 would have played havoc with the well-established pricing formula, which our local publishing houses religiously obeyed.

But when the rare opportunity came along for me to use monotype, Bembo, Plantin, Bodoni and once even Polyphilus/Blado were spec'd with lightning speed.

I had a number of definite taboos. I could not bring myself to use local bad cuttings of faces like Garamond, Goudy and, unbelievably, Caslon. The cuttings available were too idiosyncratic, especially in the italic, which invariably had the worst possible fit. And when Toronto's printing plants switched away from letterpress, one major shop after the other, and embraced the offset world, these faces suffered markedly. Neither the kiss impression nor the harder offset papers provided enough cushion to ensure the intended weight of line. The result was often a spindly and nervous letter, which bore only a vague resemblance to the original.

The sans serif offered by the typesetting departments of the printing houses invariably was Futura, which I just could not bring myself to use. Until Helvetica (Universe) became available, I simply pretended that sans serif had never been invented.

The Chicago Manual of Style was the Bible of Toronto editorial departments (except *Oxford*). On top of that, the composing rooms of most book-printing houses were avidly dedicated to the wide spaceband. Many pages resembled the Snake River, and the reader had to come up for air repeatedly, in the pursuit of a misplaced line. Both composing rooms and editorial departments were, furthermore, dedicated to the em-dash. Though everybody allowed that too often a book's pages were pockmarked with these, no one had the courage of his or her convictions to change them. I had always maintained that the tradition was mainly recognized by editor, not reader. To show M&S a better course, I had specimen pages set, using an en-dash and close word spacing, and with a few other refinements. To my relief, there was almost total acceptance – or possibly lack of notice – when I showed editorial the 'new look'.

The editorial department did, however, dig its feet in on one issue. It adamantly rejected my proposal to go with the Cambridge convention of single quotation-marks (') out, double quotation-marks (") in.

I had long been bothered by the effect on a level indent of double quotation marks:

"Allow me to demonstrate!"

Do you see what I mean?

This seemed to me unnecessarily distracting. But editorial was right to protest. There had to be a way of solving my problem without turning established convention upside down. It took me over six months to come up with the solution, which now looks quite simple:

"Allow me to demonstrate!"

Do you see what I mean?

Unfortunately, I was too unfamiliar with the workings of the lino-type machine to know whether this nicety would be the cause of increased composition costs for M&S.

By happy coincidence, Ross Robinson, the plant foreman at T.H. Best, invited me to give a talk on book design to the members of the Printing House Craftsmen's Club of Toronto. When I mentioned my conundrum to him, he suggested that I pose it as a problem for the assembled craftsmen to solve. 'I'm not a compositor,' he said. 'But there will be lots of typesetters at the meeting; and you can pose a challenge. They'll be eager to pass the test. And then you'll know whether to propose your "hanging quotes" or not.'

As a result of all this, the convention of the hanging quote and the substitution of an en-dash for the conventional em-dash became the first two distinguishing marks of the new McClelland & Stewart house style. (I had initially proposed the substitution of a swung dash (~) for the em-dash, but Conway Turton, M&S's dean of Canadian editors, had promptly rejected this, on the grounds that the swung dash had its own meaning and purpose. When I suggested that very, very, very few readers would have any idea what a swung dash meant, she replied, 'Well, I would!' And that was that.)

The specification of a thin space band, where local composing rooms had traditionally used a mid-band, was not questioned by editorial. The printers sure questioned it, however!

A couple of the local printing houses warned that this would result in poor legibility and greatly increase the number of hyphenated lines. But after seeing the improvement in just a small number of galleys, they said nothing more. The tighter word space was really nothing new; it was visible practice in just about every imported book. The wider word space just made for a less demanding life for the compositor. And the owners of Toronto's printing houses immediately realized this, and made no further objection. (Years later, in *The Klondike Quest*, I got away not only with hanging quotes but with hanging minor punctuation at the end of a line, as well, as I have said. For me, *The Klondike Quest* still has the best-looking page of any of my books.)

One of the things I became known for, as a designer, was my extended treatment of the prelims. (Randall Speller called these sequential title pages a 'Newfeld trademark'.) It all came about almost by accident.

In 1955, I saw two movies which made a huge impression on me – not so much the movies themselves (though one of them, *The Man with the Golden Arm*, was a memorable piece of cinematography) but the novel treatment of the credits. (The other film was *Around the World in Eighty Days*.) The innovator was Saul Bass.

In both movies, the audience was brought into an immediate sensory relationship with the drama, by way of the credits-sequence, before the film even began. I borrowed the idea, and introduced M&S's extended prelims.

In that pre-computer age, the go-ahead to proceed with many of the different steps needed to publish a book – such as the establishing of design and production specifications, the securing of reliable estimates, the typesetting, the establishing of reliable catalogue data and selling price, et cetera – depended on accurate forecasts on the part of both designer and production manager. Predictions became commitments. In-house and/or computer setting facilities did not yet exist.

Once in a (rare) while, I would be out in my conceptual mathematics. Invariably, I established the book length with a cushion up my sleeve. One could usually effect minor remedies without any radical surgery.

However, with the book *Dynamic Decade*, I found myself with pages to spare. I liked the mise-en-page and did not want to mess with it. And I was still trying to fulfill Hugh's mandate of 'the recognizable M&S book'. So I ate up the leftover pages with extended, decorated preliminary pages, Saul-Bass style. But very few, and very tentatively.

This first experiment, done in 1958, was well received by both editorial and sales at M&S, and remarked upon by reviewers. Which surprised and pleased me, since I honestly did not think that anyone would notice. The only qualms came from Jack, who asked that this (self-indulgence) not be used indiscriminately.

Among the titles that followed, however, there were a number of books which not only were bold pieces of (1950s Canadian) publishing, but lent themselves perfectly to my 'indulgence'. M&S was both adventurous and supportive enough to foster these occasional experiments.

The titles included *Tête Blanche* and *The Double Hook*. In both cases, Jack gave me my head. Even the jacket designs bore little relation to what was the accepted norm. It wasn't until years later that Hugh told me Jack had stuck with my cover proposals over the advice of his sales group.

It was the poetry book that intrigued and puzzled me the most. The buyers of the poetry book fall into a number of disparate categories:

A. The dedicated lover and student of poetry.

B. The forced lover of poetry.

C. The neophyte lover of poetry.

D. The donor of a book of poetry to a lover of poetry.

E. The monogamous lover of just one writer of poetry.

Of these, group 'A' – a loyal though rather small bunch – does not have a history of providing a financially viable publishing rationale. Certainly not in Toronto in the late fifties. And though group 'E' once in a while produced unexpected gainful returns – with Leonard Cohen's books, for instance – these were the exception rather than the rule for the poetry-book venture.

For a designer, the poetry book is both visually challenging, and frustrating. Challenging, inasmuch as each spread truly requires special visual consideration. Frustrating, inasmuch as the standard small Canadian print run, for poetry, precluded any extravagance; no economies of scale were possible.

For me, the poetry book had to afford an atmosphere for intimacy between performer and audience. Not unlike the opera. Not unlike the ballet. Of all of the publishing categories, the poetry book was the logical candidate for any special design treatment. It would fit Kane's mandate, and accommodate McClelland's qualms.

One day, a manuscript of poems by Ralph Gustafson arrived at my studio.

The number of poems was modest, and the poems were brief. The imagery and melody were delectable. The next time I repaired to Hollinger House for my 'one day a week' retainer, I suggested to Hugh Kane that I would throw in some linocuts for free. Later that day, Jack asked me to come to a meeting with him and Hugh. Out of that grew a special poetry series, best explained by M&S's generous colophon (taken here from the second book in the series, Leonard Cohen's *The Spice Box of Earth*):

A NOTE ON PUBLICATION

This book is the result of a unique association dedicated to the improvement of the standards of design and manufacture in the making of Canadian books. It is the second of a group of selected works of poetry and belle lettres chosen both to inspire and to complement fine craftsmanship in the designing and manufacturing arts.

It has been published in a limited edition and will not be reprinted in this format. Its publication is experimental in the sense that the strict economic limitations that might normally prevail were waived to permit adequate attention to detail in the various stages of production.

It also was planned and illustrated by Frank Newfeld, the Canadian designer, typographer and art director, whose work has earned him an imposing series of awards in various fields of design.

It was produced under the joint auspices of the Rolland Paper Company Limited who supplied the stock, Rolland DeLuxe Book India and Ropace White; H&S Reliance Limited who supplied engravings for the illustrations, the jacket, and the case; T.H. Best Printing Company Limited, in whose plant the type was set and the books printed and bound; and McClelland and Stewart Limited.

M&S published four books in the series – Gustafson's *Rivers among Rocks*, Cohen's *The Spice Box of Earth*, Daniels' *The Chequered Shade* and Gotlieb's *Within the Zodiac* – before the associations were amicably terminated. But the books established a precedent, which I happily exploited whenever the vehicle was right and I found consenting collaborators.

THE
SPECTACULAR
2001

A Show for all Ages ✦ For Your Holiday Fun

Join us at the Oakville Centre for the Performing Arts

SATURDAY DECEMBER 29, 2001 AT 7:00 PM~AND~SUNDAY DECEMBER 30, 2001 AT 2:00 PM

TICKETS NOW ON SALE~$12.00 EACH~THE OAKVILLE CENTRE BOX OFFICE~(905)815-2021

Presented by the Seniors' Centres of Oakville

OAKVILLE

My last poster!

21. HOME IS WHERE?

Where are you from?'
'I'm from Oakville.'
'No. Originally.'
This morning, Joan and I were at a Royal Bank branch in order to open a new U.S. funds account, when this was asked. It's a question that I seem to have been answering just about all my life.

Let me see.

The first nine years of my life I spent in Brno, Czechoslovakia. Like most scions of wealthy Moravians, I attended a German school. It was the sensible thing to do, since very little international business was conducted in Czech. Thus my Czech was poor enough, that Czechs often asked me, 'Where are you from?'

The next ten years I spent in Hove and London, England. Over protests of family and friends, my mother had insisted on getting out of Europe eighteen months ahead of World War II. Naturally, I started off with quite an accent. (Curiously, I still seem to have much the same accent, though now somewhat bastardized.) To the end of my stay in England, I was – often suspiciously – asked, 'Where are you from?'

The next eight months I spent in Toronto, Canada. And here a slight twist was introduced into the question: 'What part of England are you from?'

The next (almost) five years I spent in Israel (with short essays at visits to Egypt and Lebanon). There I was repeatedly asked for my 'papers', which is really just another way of asking, 'Where are you from?'

The fifty-plus years of my life since then I have spent in Toronto and Oakville. And I am still asked, 'Where are you from?'

It's my accent!

I don't seem to be able to speak any language without an accent. What is even worse, it seems that I have several accents. And people are confused, insofar as they can't reliably place it. 'You [that's me] speak English with a German or Hungarian or Dutch or English accent' – depending on the climate or country I'm in. 'You speak German with a Polish or English or American accent.' 'You speak French (badly) with an English or Canadian accent.' 'You speak Hebrew with an English or Dutch or Austrian or American accent.' 'You speak Czech really badly' – so badly, that the question of accent luckily never comes up. (And I've forgotten what little Arabic I ever knew, much to everybody's relief.)

The predominant outcome of all this is the feeling I have that I've spent my whole life a visitor. Even when I was head of Sheridan's illustration program, a 'figure to be feared' by faculty and students alike, I was often politely asked by first year students what my nationality was. In the course of time, I became ready for the question, and had a silly response up my sleeve.

'Canadian,' I would say.

'Come on, Mr Newfeld!'

'What nationality are you?' I would then ask the inquisitor.

'Canadian, of course.'

'And how old are you?'

'Eighteen.'

'Well, I've been a Canadian for over forty-five years. So that must make me two and a half times the Canadian that you are.'

Of course, this is just a bit of flummery. By the second semester, nine out of ten of the remaining students would have shed any prejudices they might have brought with them. This seems to be the commendable norm in every art school I have known, as either student or teacher, whether in England or in Canada.

But I have been made well aware of the widespread existence of xenophobia, on a couple of levels. One, launched by my accent; and another, born of my profession. Let me qualify that. As a designer, mainly thanks to my wise boardroom-dress code, I was accepted as a sane and safe specialist. As an illustrator, however – regardless of my doing my best to project an image of prudent professionalism – I was regularly prejudged as yet another arrogant and addled artist.

Looking back on my career, I have come to the conclusion that, where I have a recognizable 'accent' as far as my design philosophy is concerned, I did not manage a consistent accent in my illustration. Years ago, one late evening in an Ottawa hotel room, Allan Fleming described me, as a designer, as 'practising experimental classicism with determination'. My illustration, on the other hand, he called 'international cookery'. I guess he was right.

By the time I set up design specifications for a book or catalogue, I generally knew exactly how I intended to handle the design. With illustration, I frequently had no idea how I was going to treat the visual until I was well into the job. Years later I can readily recognize my design work, and see my style quite clearly and consistently. My illustration, on the other hand, seems to have many faces. So many, that at times I have to check the credits to make sure the illustration is really mine.

Again, looking back at my huge amount of work, I regret that after a beginning filled with exploration and experimentation, I became entrusted with 'Important, Major Commissions'. This 'trust' engendered one level-headed solution after another – which too often bordered on design ennui. The fault wasn't my clients'; it was mine. In many of my later commissions, I not only affected a boardroom image, I allowed it to temper my flight of fancy!

Still, all in all, my career in Canada has more than come up to expectations. The opportunity to work almost exclusively in areas of my own choice has been a dream come true. The time-honoured plight of a designer's having to 'pay his dues' by money-grubbing in the fields of 'commercial art' never really befell me. Somehow, I was allowed to confine my craft to the book, museum and magazine worlds. Even my few, imprudent ventures into 'visual image design' were (for the most part) received with courtesy. And to be allowed to finish my career, still 'doing my own thing', in the field of education was a pure bonus! The few commissions that came my way during my later, Sheridan College years had practically no constraints. These commissions were either my own, such as my alphabet book, *Creatures*, or they were freelance jobs involving money-making mavens such as Pierre Berton or the National Archives of Canada. If these projects have any visual flaws, they must be laid at my feet, alone.

My only real regret, then, is that I never thanked the Macphersons for dragging me to Canada.

In 1999, Mr Randall Speller penned a far-too-laudatory article on my work. It was published by *DA, A Journal of the Printing Arts.* At one point during the interview, Speller asked me what I thought was the most important element of a career in my field. I have looked up my reply. It went like this: 'In my mature years I have always felt, and still do, that a full career should have three stages: 1) to try to learn responsibly; 2) to try to do responsibly; 3) to try to teach responsibly.'

That's really not bad. I hope I've done that!

In 1956, Keith Scott told me, 'You really must get to know more people in the field. There is a meeting of the Toronto Art Directors Club next week, and you will be my guest.'

At the meeting, an 'elderly' man got up, and lectured to the assembly for what seemed like ages.

'Who is that gentleman?' I asked Keith.

'His name is Eric Aldwinkle. He is one of Canada's top illustrators.'

'And he's still sermonizing? My God, he must be pushing sixty years of age!'

Now that I'm pushing *eighty* years of age, I think it's time for me to shut up!

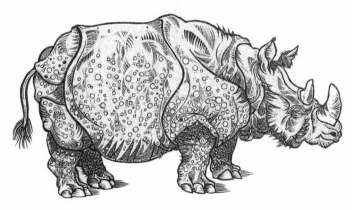

From *Creatures*, Douglas & McIntyre, 1998.

GLOSSARY

Chaver: Friend, comrade, partner [chavera(f), chaverim(p)] (Hebrew)

Galut: Countries outside of Israel (Hebrew & Yiddish)

Ganeff: Thief (Y)

Garin: Group in training to establish own kibbutz (H)

Gibor: Hero (H)

Goy: Non-Jew (H & Y)

Katzin: Officer (H)

Kashrut: Dietary law (H & Y)

Kimouchi: Empathy (Japanese)

Machal: Military overseas volunteer (H)

Madrich: Instructor (H)

Magen David Adom: Israeli ambulance (H)

Malon: Hotel (H)

Mazal Tov: Good luck (H)

Mensch: Human being, nice guy (Y)

Meshek: Farm (H)

Mishtara Tzwait: Military police (H)

Mumche: Expert, often used sardonically (H & Y)

Nackette Mädlach: Naked girl (Y)

Pachon: Corrugated metal hut or building (H)

Rittmeister: Master of horse / Colonel of horse (German)

Sabreh (m) Sabra (f): Born Israeli – actually prickly pear: thorny out,
    sweet in (H)

Shamir: Sentry (H)

Schmatte: Rag (Y)

Tembil: Idiot – can be used affectionately (H)

From the Menu for the first *Typo-graphic Designers of Canada* Awards dinner, 1958.

Educated in England, Frank Newfeld immigrated to Canada in 1954. He subsequently founded his own design company in Toronto. In 1956 Newfeld, along with Frank Davies, Leslie (Sam) Smart and John Gibson founded the Society of Typographic Designers of Canada (TDC). He was elected president of the Society in 1959, the year that it received its Ontario charter.

In 1963 Frank joined the firm of McClelland & Stewart as an art director, and within six years he was to become vice-president, publishing and a member of the board of directors.

Over his career Frank Newfeld has designed, illustrated or art directed well over 600 books for publishers in Canada, Israel, the United Kingdom and the United States. He has won over 170 awards including three medals from the prestigious Leipzig Book Show, two Hans Christian Andersen awards, and two from Typomundus 20, as well as awards from the AIGA, Art Directors and Type Directors Clubs of Chicago, New York, The Society of Illustrators USA, Montreal and Toronto. Other awards include the Canadian Centennial Medal and the Elizabeth II Jubilee Medal. Frank represented Canada at the 1976 Illustration Bienale in the Czech Republic, and his work was exhibited in Bologna in 1990. He has created three children's books, two of which were published by Oxford University Press, and the third published by Groundwood Books. He is a member of the Royal Canadian Academy.

For many years Frank Newfeld was associated with Sheridan College where he served first as an instructor of illustration, and later as Head, Illustration Program.